Namesake

by Isabelle Melançon and Megan Lavey-Heaton

Namesake vol. 1 by Isabelle Melançon and Megan Lavey-Heaton, colors by Pascal Michaud
148 pages

Copyright © 2010-2017

Printed in Canada

Third Printing, 2017

ISBN 978-0-9853095-4-1 (hardcover)
ISBN 978-0-9853095-0-3 (softcover)

10 9 8 7 6 5 4 3

Fairylogue Press
4173 Grouse Ct. #115
Mechanicsburg, PA 17050

www.fairyloguepress.com
www.thehiveworks.com

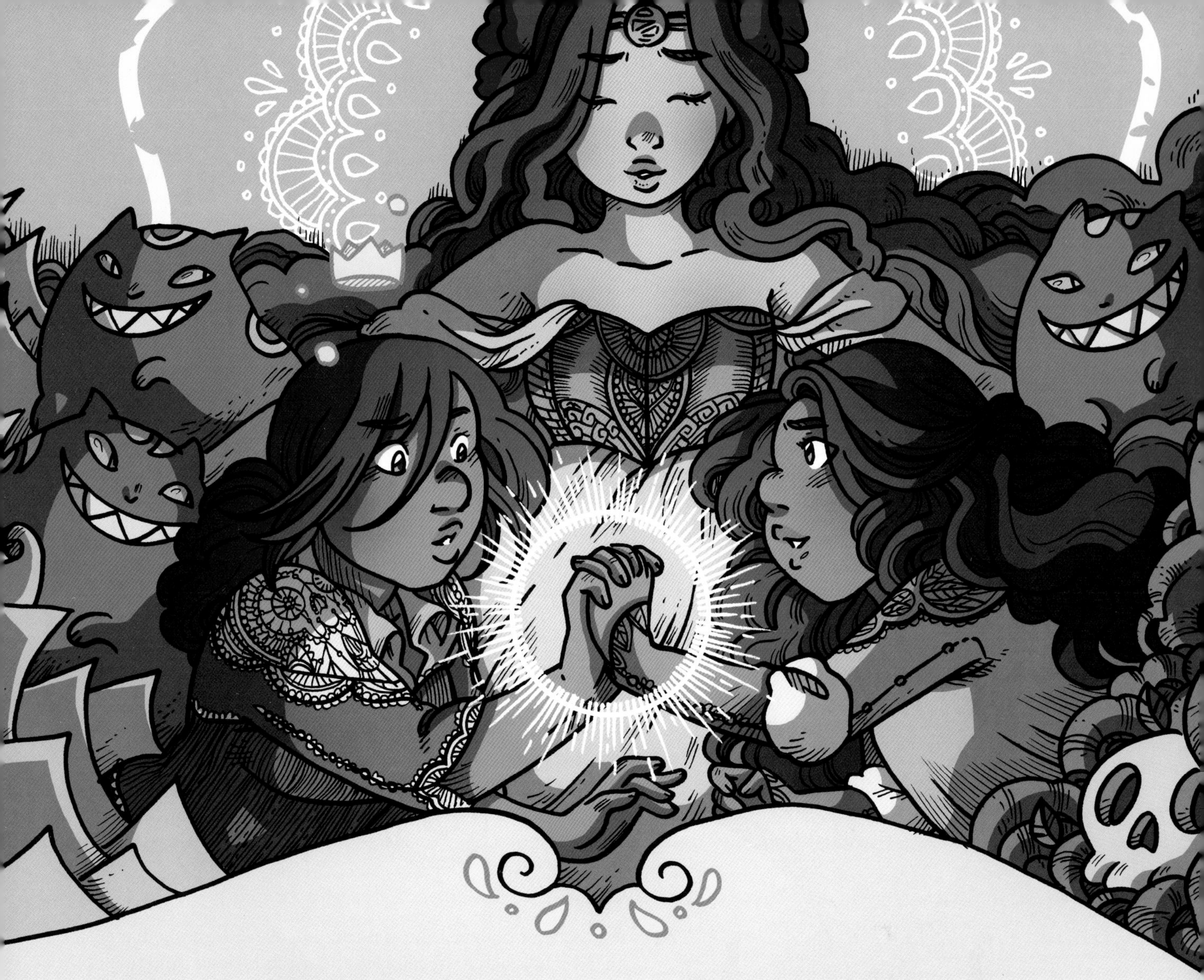

Namesake

by Isabelle Melançon and Megan Lavey-Heaton

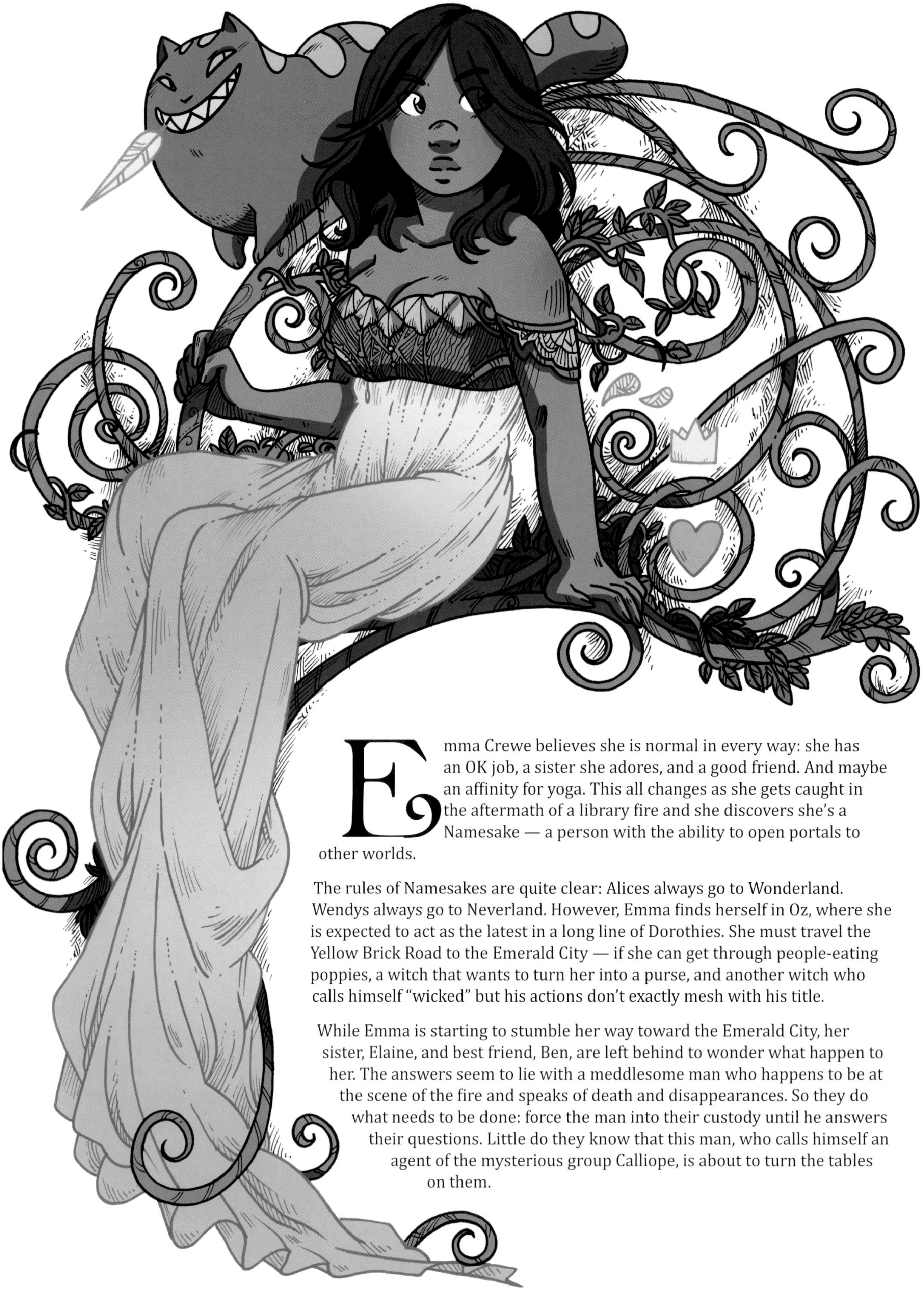

Emma Crewe believes she is normal in every way: she has an OK job, a sister she adores, and a good friend. And maybe an affinity for yoga. This all changes as she gets caught in the aftermath of a library fire and she discovers she's a Namesake — a person with the ability to open portals to other worlds.

The rules of Namesakes are quite clear: Alices always go to Wonderland. Wendys always go to Neverland. However, Emma finds herself in Oz, where she is expected to act as the latest in a long line of Dorothies. She must travel the Yellow Brick Road to the Emerald City — if she can get through people-eating poppies, a witch that wants to turn her into a purse, and another witch who calls himself "wicked" but his actions don't exactly mesh with his title.

While Emma is starting to stumble her way toward the Emerald City, her sister, Elaine, and best friend, Ben, are left behind to wonder what happen to her. The answers seem to lie with a meddlesome man who happens to be at the scene of the fire and speaks of death and disappearances. So they do what needs to be done: force the man into their custody until he answers their questions. Little do they know that this man, who calls himself an agent of the mysterious group Calliope, is about to turn the tables on them.

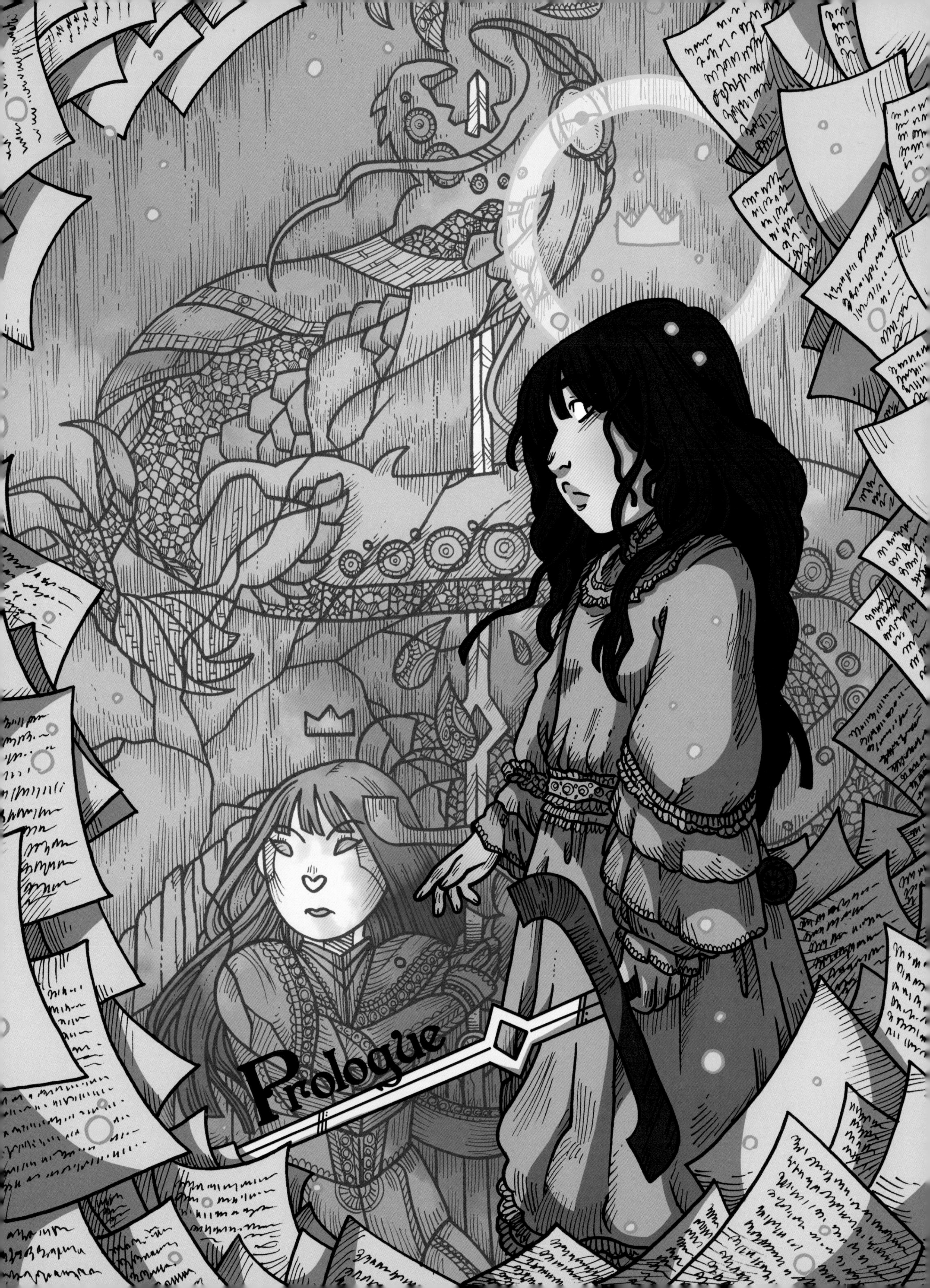
Prologue

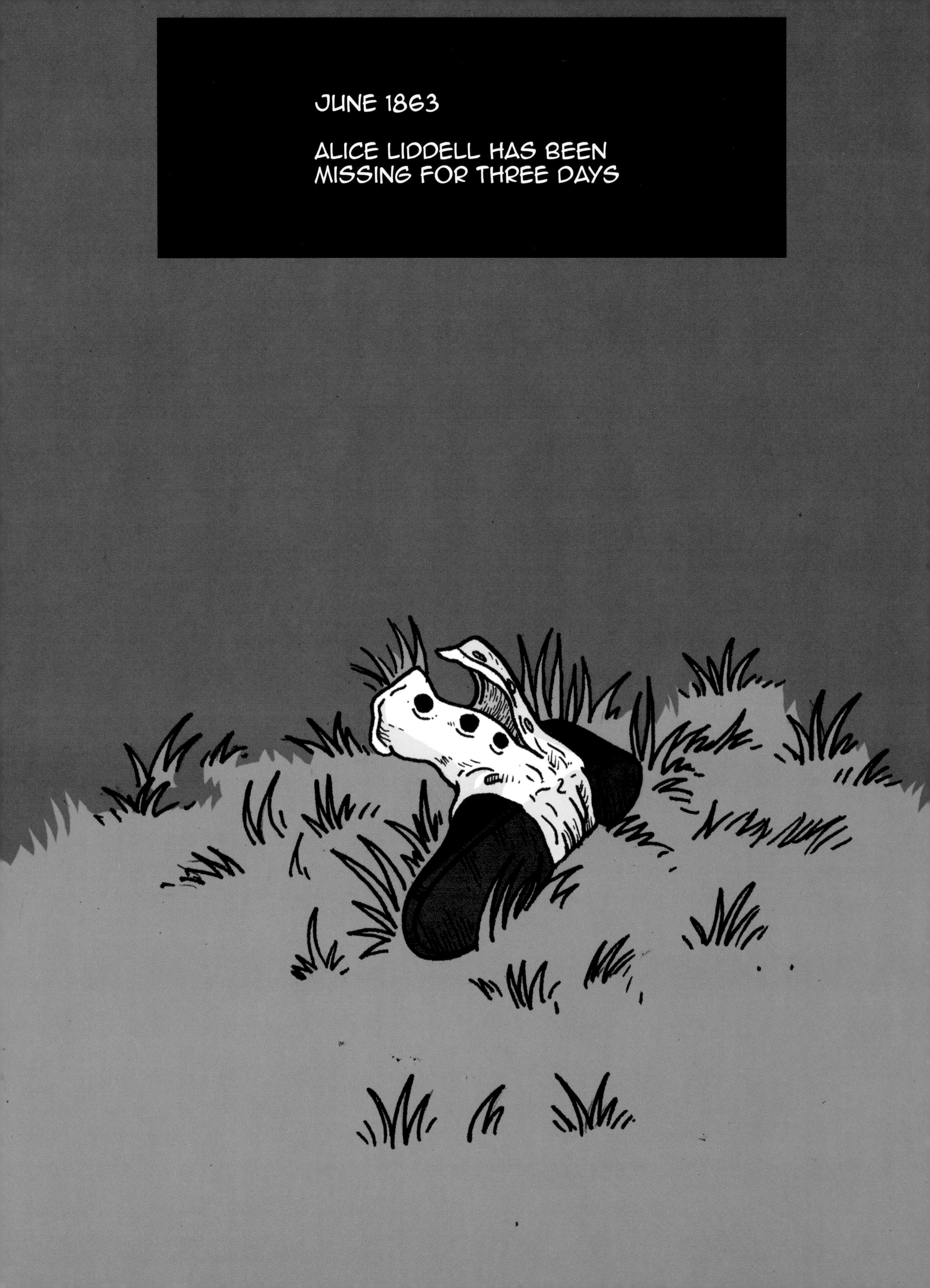
JUNE 1863
ALICE LIDDELL HAS BEEN MISSING FOR THREE DAYS

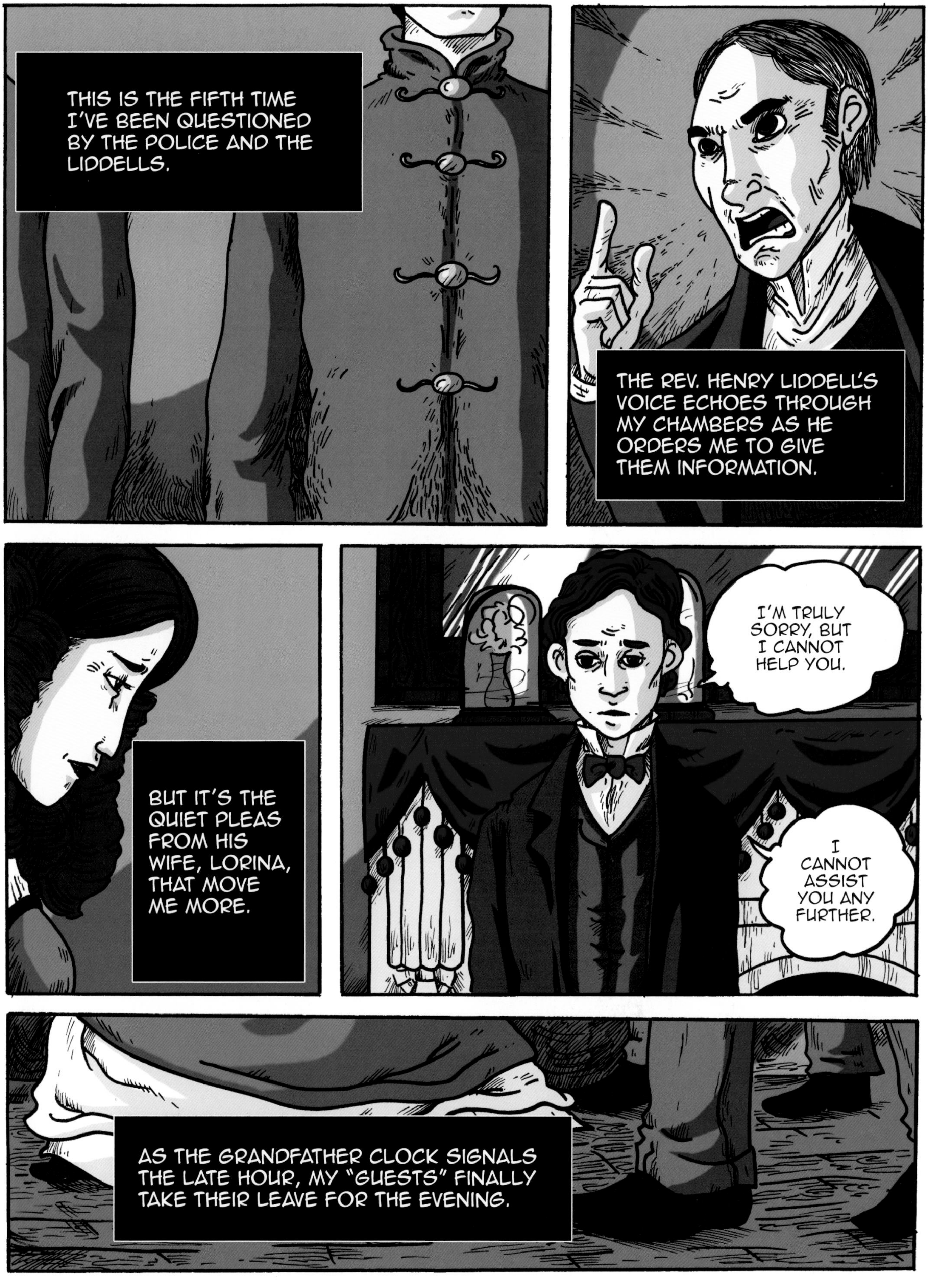
THIS IS THE FIFTH TIME I'VE BEEN QUESTIONED BY THE POLICE AND THE LIDDELLS.
THE REV. HENRY LIDDELL'S VOICE ECHOES THROUGH MY CHAMBERS AS HE ORDERS ME TO GIVE THEM INFORMATION.
BUT IT'S THE QUIET PLEAS FROM HIS WIFE, LORINA, THAT MOVE ME MORE.
I'M TRULY SORRY, BUT I CANNOT HELP YOU.
I CANNOT ASSIST YOU ANY FURTHER.
AS THE GRANDFATHER CLOCK SIGNALS THE LATE HOUR, MY "GUESTS" FINALLY TAKE THEIR LEAVE FOR THE EVENING.

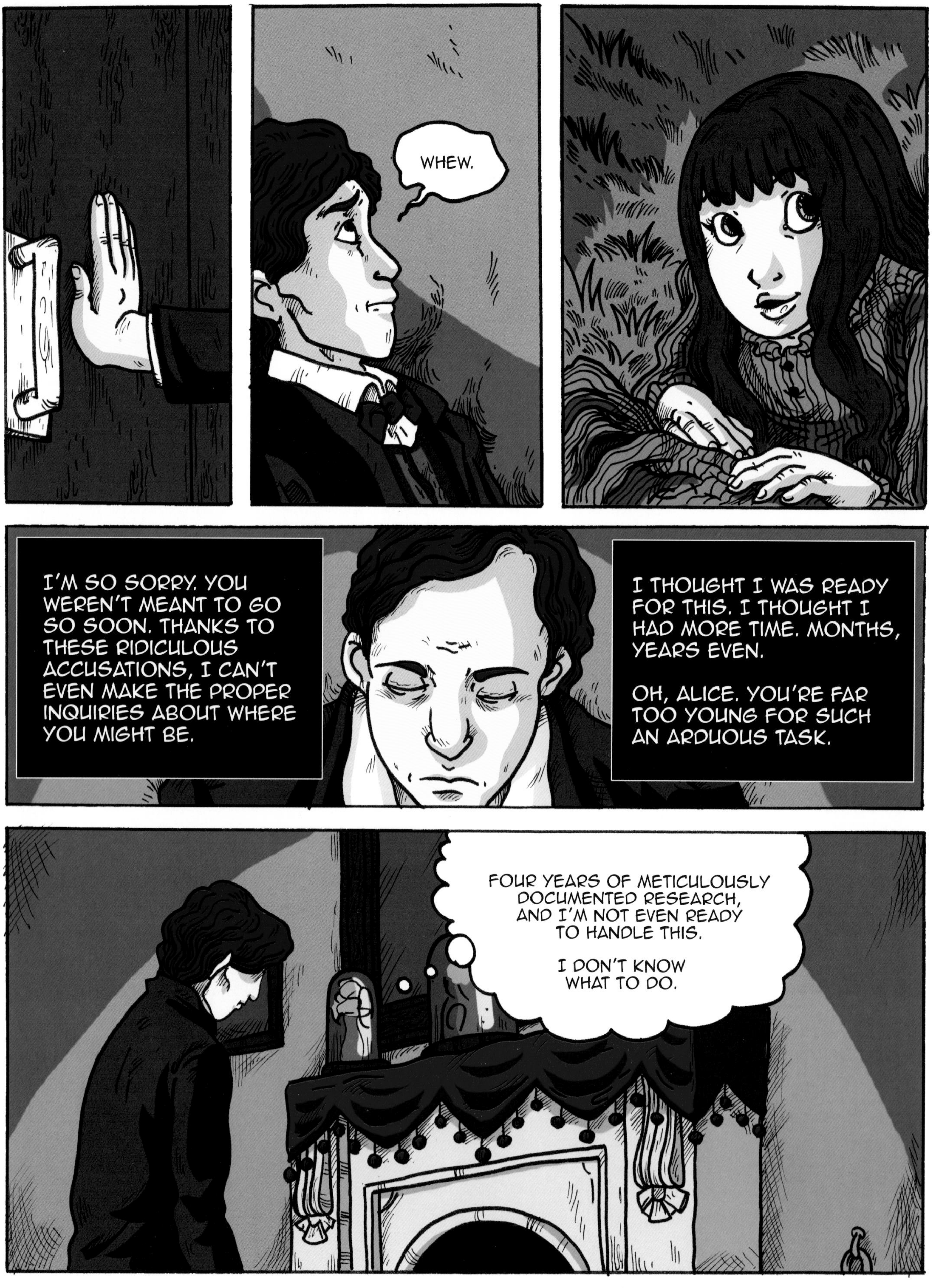
WHEW.
I'M SO SORRY. YOU WEREN'T MEANT TO GO SO SOON. THANKS TO THESE RIDICULOUS ACCUSATIONS, I CAN'T EVEN MAKE THE PROPER INQUIRIES ABOUT WHERE YOU MIGHT BE.
I THOUGHT I WAS READY FOR THIS. I THOUGHT I HAD MORE TIME. MONTHS, YEARS EVEN.
OH, ALICE. YOU'RE FAR TOO YOUNG FOR SUCH AN ARDUOUS TASK.
FOUR YEARS OF METICULOUSLY DOCUMENTED RESEARCH, AND I'M NOT EVEN READY TO HANDLE THIS.
I DON'T KNOW WHAT TO DO.

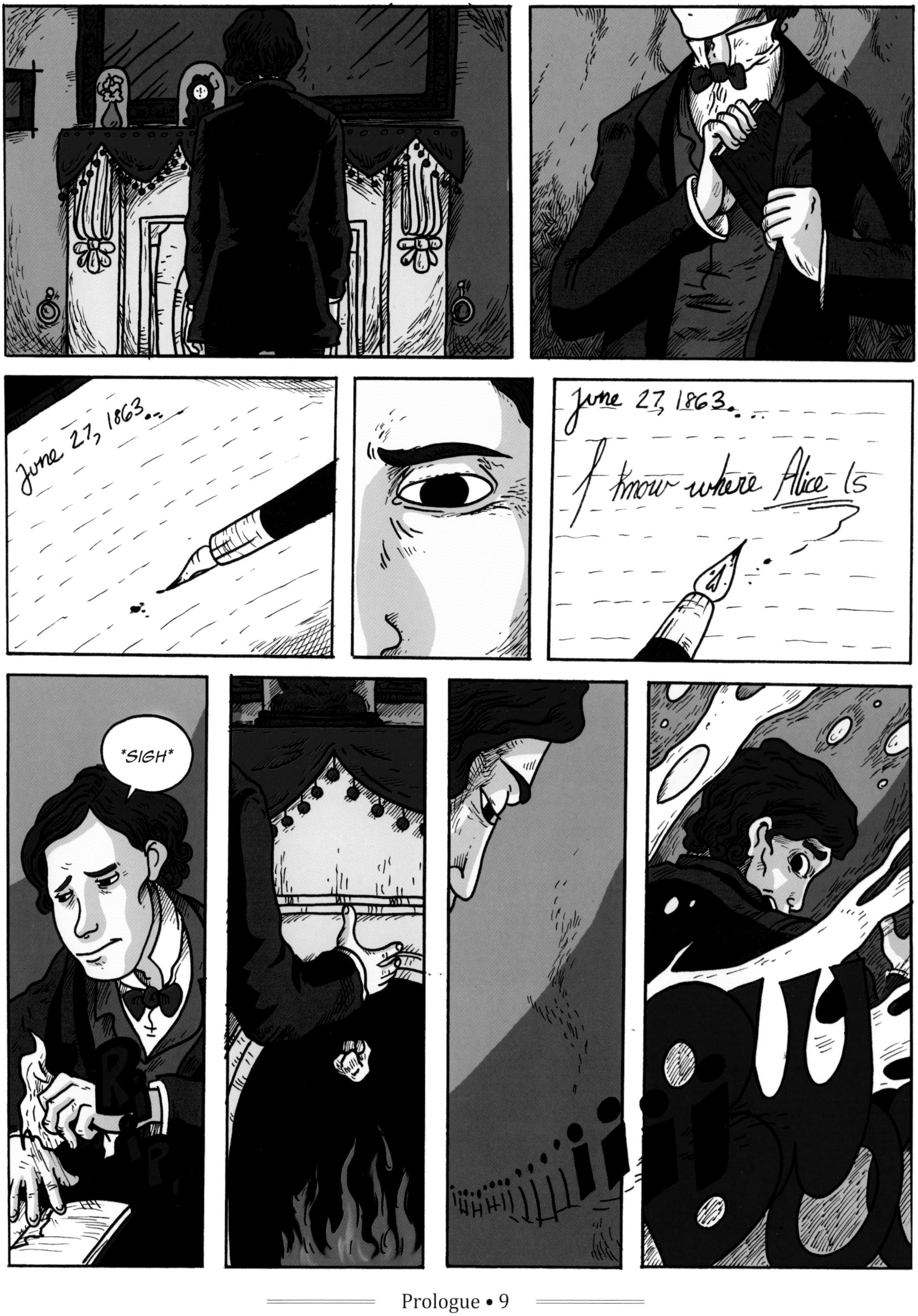
June 27, 1863...
June 27, 1863...
I know where Alice Is
SIGH
RiP

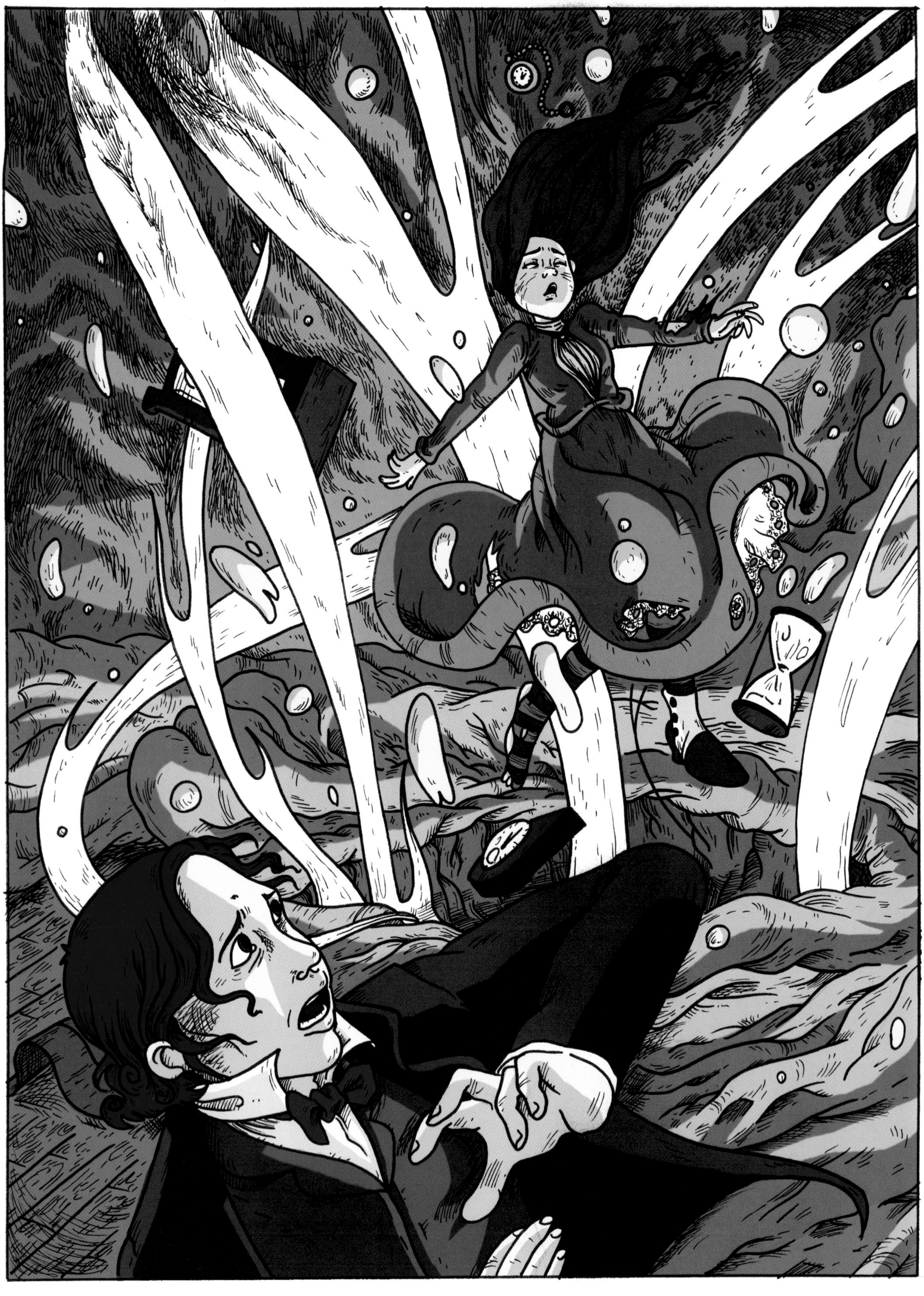

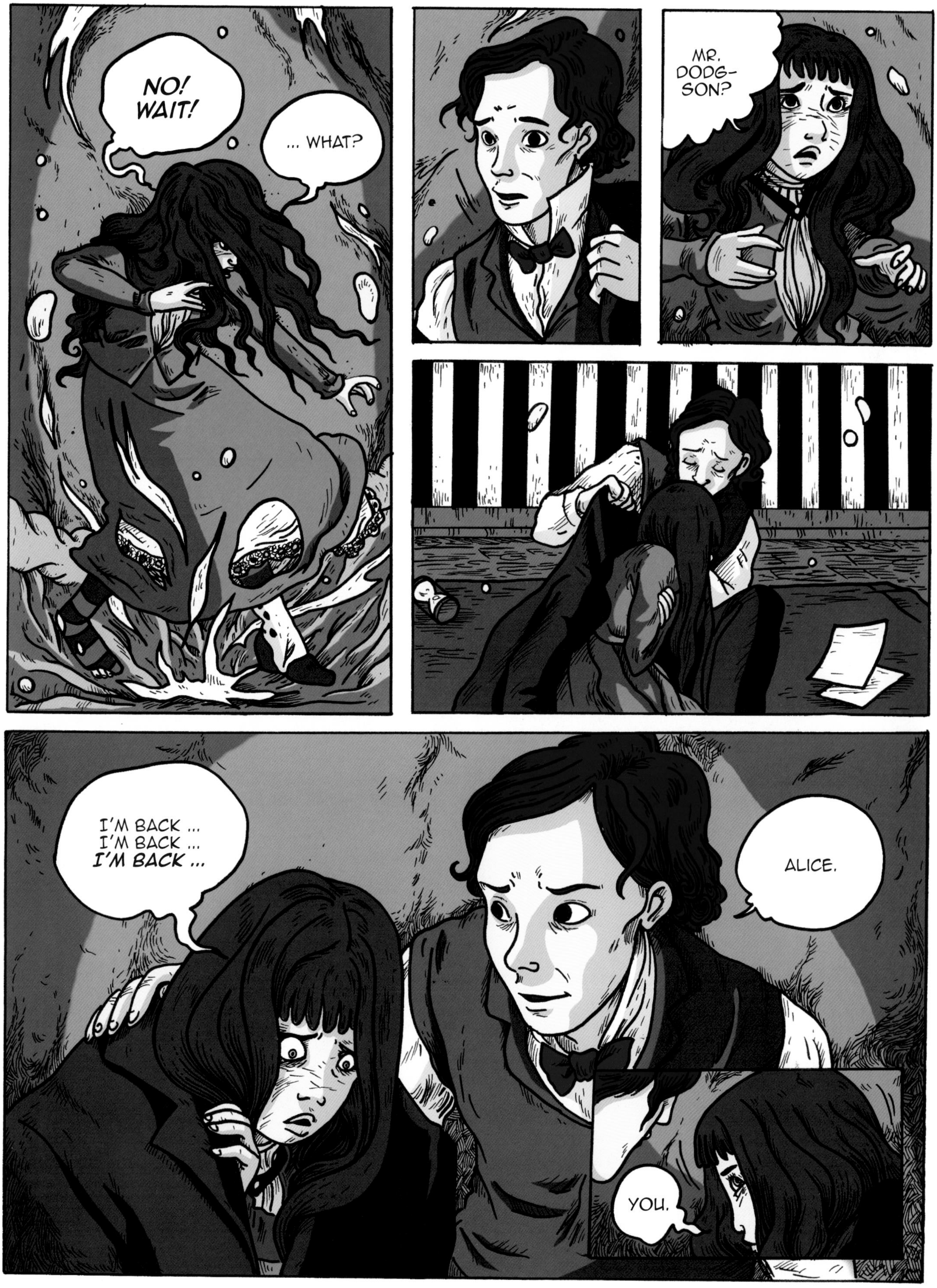
NO! WAIT!
... WHAT?
MR. DODG-SON?
I'M BACK ...
I'M BACK ...
I'M BACK ...
ALICE.
YOU.

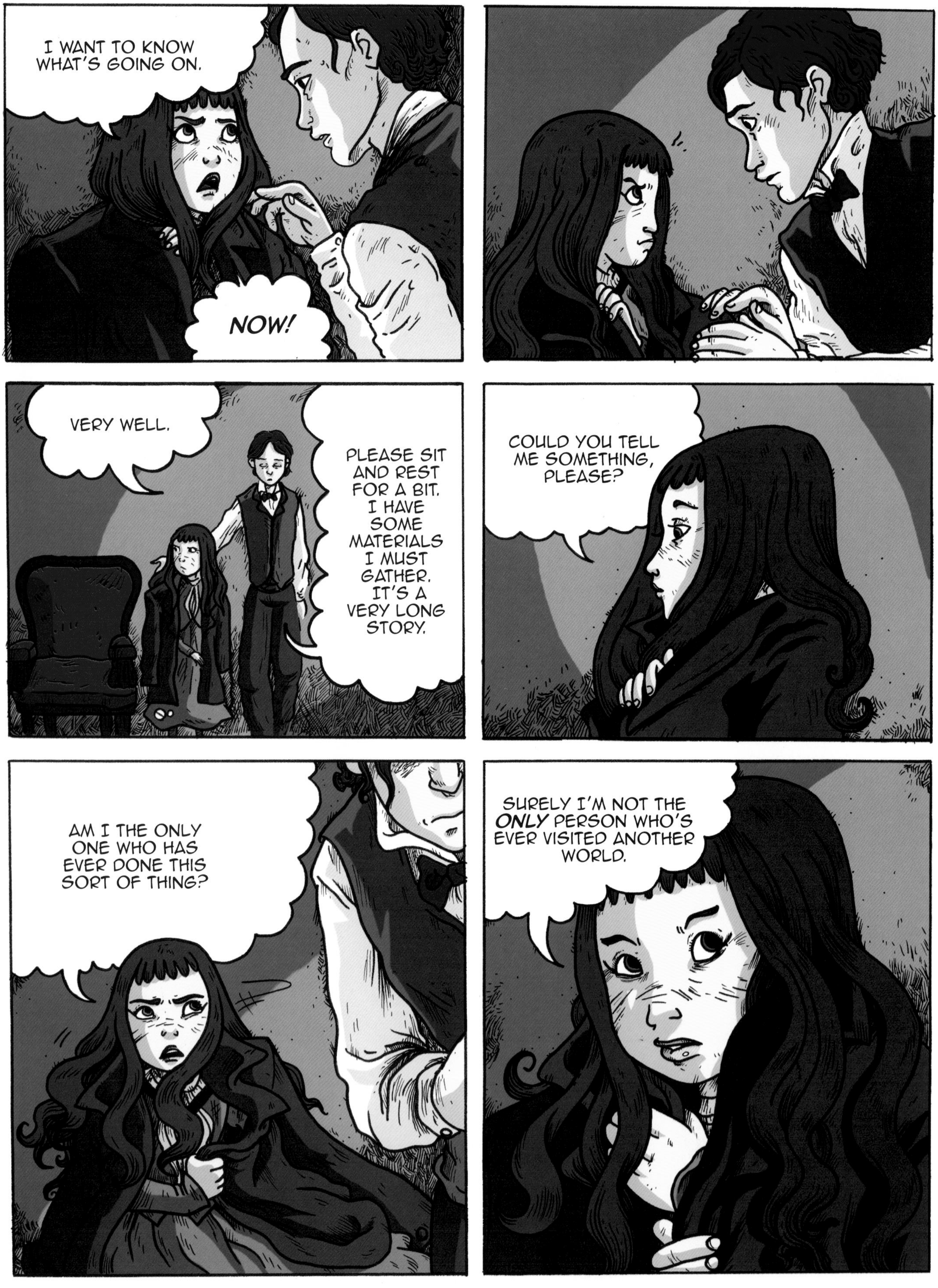
I WANT TO KNOW WHAT'S GOING ON.
NOW!
VERY WELL.
PLEASE SIT AND REST FOR A BIT. I HAVE SOME MATERIALS I MUST GATHER. IT'S A VERY LONG STORY.
COULD YOU TELL ME SOMETHING, PLEASE?
AM I THE ONLY ONE WHO HAS EVER DONE THIS SORT OF THING?
SURELY I'M NOT THE ONLY PERSON WHO'S EVER VISITED ANOTHER WORLD.

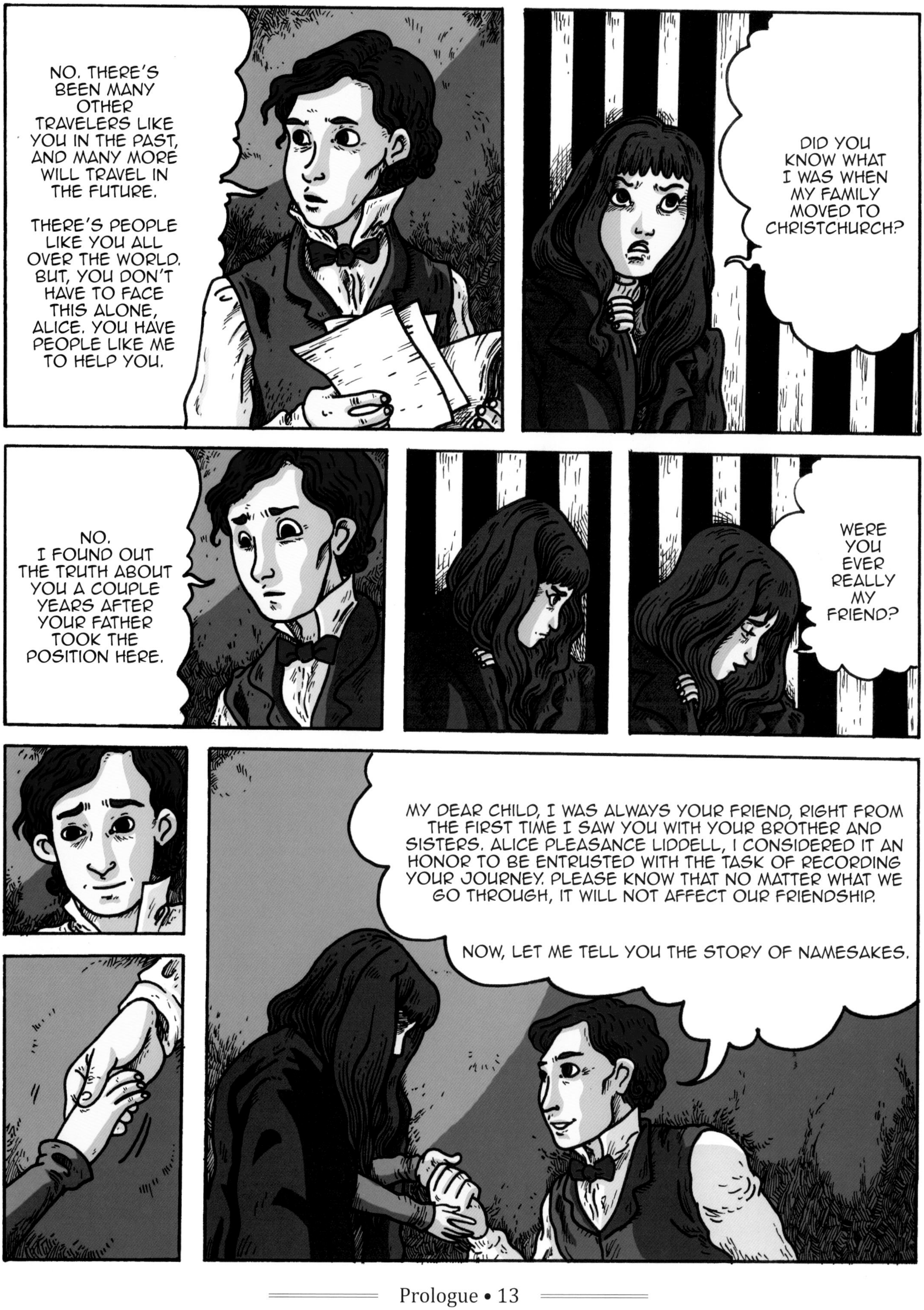
NO. THERE'S BEEN MANY OTHER TRAVELERS LIKE YOU IN THE PAST, AND MANY MORE WILL TRAVEL IN THE FUTURE.
THERE'S PEOPLE LIKE YOU ALL OVER THE WORLD. BUT, YOU DON'T HAVE TO FACE THIS ALONE, ALICE. YOU HAVE PEOPLE LIKE ME TO HELP YOU.
DID YOU KNOW WHAT I WAS WHEN MY FAMILY MOVED TO CHRISTCHURCH?
NO. I FOUND OUT THE TRUTH ABOUT YOU A COUPLE YEARS AFTER YOUR FATHER TOOK THE POSITION HERE.
WERE YOU EVER REALLY MY FRIEND?
MY DEAR CHILD, I WAS ALWAYS YOUR FRIEND, RIGHT FROM THE FIRST TIME I SAW YOU WITH YOUR BROTHER AND SISTERS. ALICE PLEASANCE LIDDELL, I CONSIDERED IT AN HONOR TO BE ENTRUSTED WITH THE TASK OF RECORDING YOUR JOURNEY. PLEASE KNOW THAT NO MATTER WHAT WE GO THROUGH, IT WILL NOT AFFECT OUR FRIENDSHIP.
NOW, LET ME TELL YOU THE STORY OF NAMESAKES.

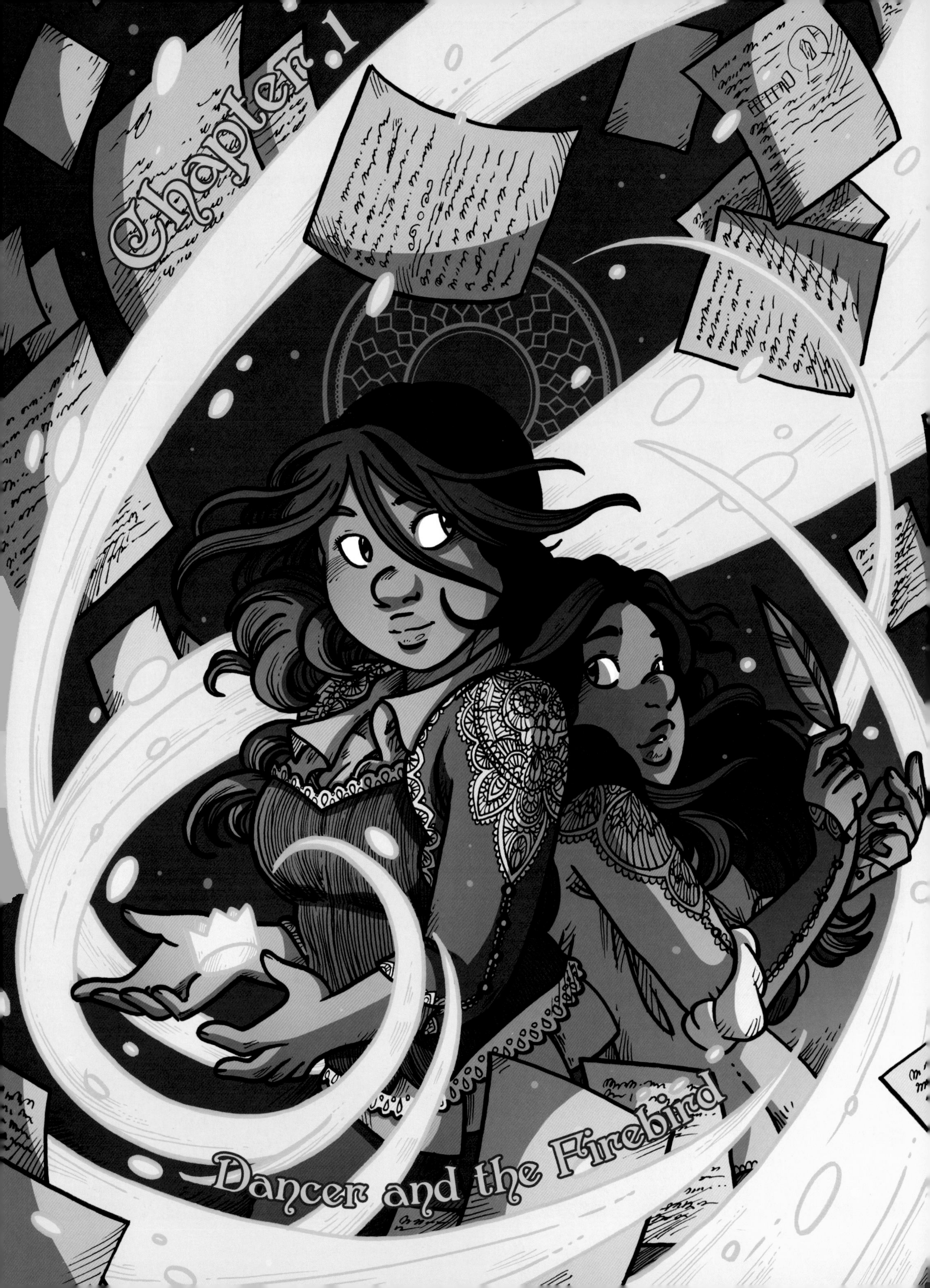
Chapter 1
Dancer and the Firebird

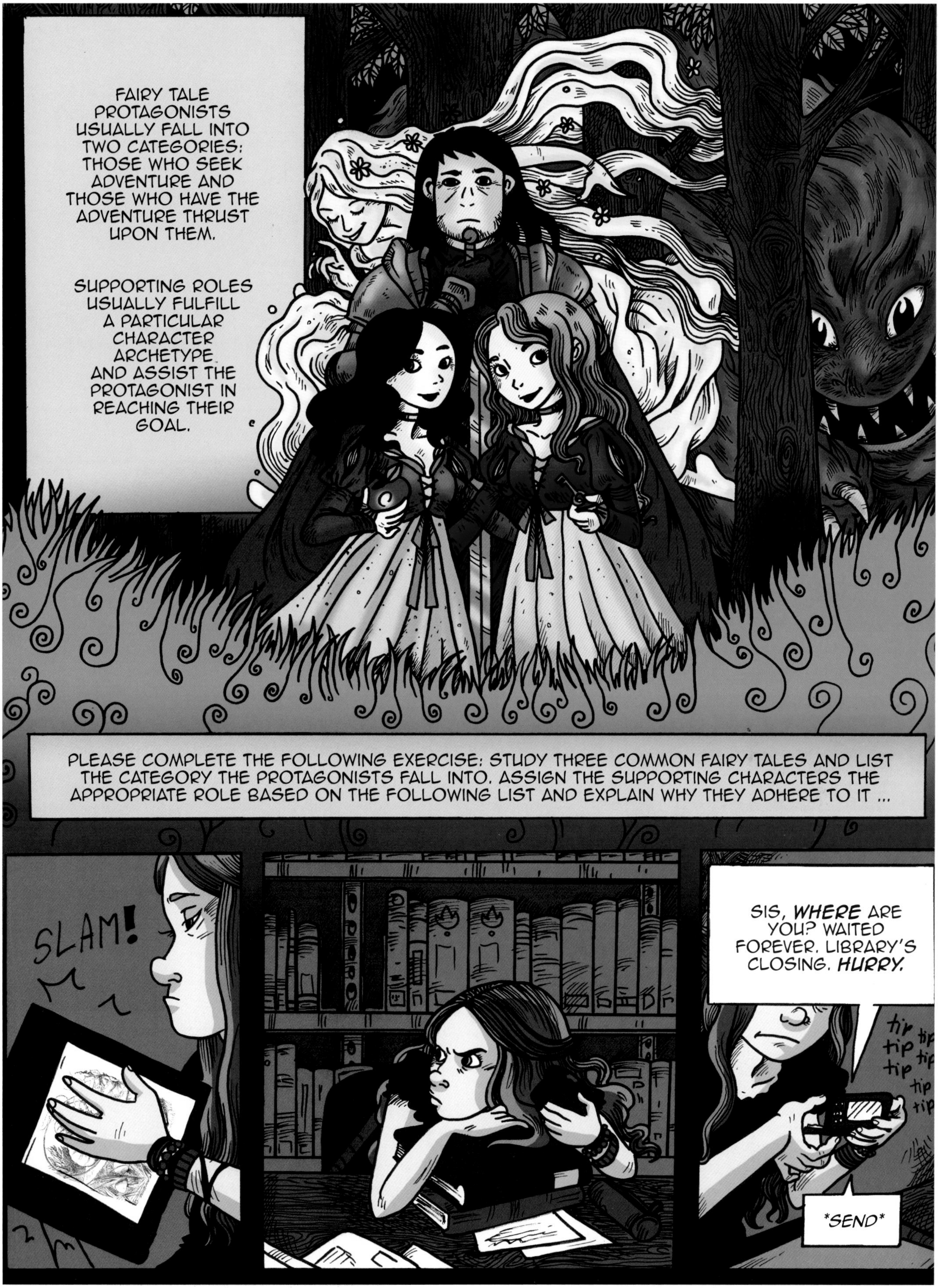
FAIRY TALE PROTAGONISTS USUALLY FALL INTO TWO CATEGORIES: THOSE WHO SEEK ADVENTURE AND THOSE WHO HAVE THE ADVENTURE THRUST UPON THEM.
SUPPORTING ROLES USUALLY FULFILL A PARTICULAR CHARACTER ARCHETYPE AND ASSIST THE PROTAGONIST IN REACHING THEIR GOAL.
PLEASE COMPLETE THE FOLLOWING EXERCISE: STUDY THREE COMMON FAIRY TALES AND LIST THE CATEGORY THE PROTAGONISTS FALL INTO. ASSIGN THE SUPPORTING CHARACTERS THE APPROPRIATE ROLE BASED ON THE FOLLOWING LIST AND EXPLAIN WHY THEY ADHERE TO IT ...
SLAM!
SIS, *WHERE* ARE YOU? WAITED FOREVER. LIBRARY'S CLOSING. *HURRY.*
tip tip tip tip tip tip tip tip
SEND

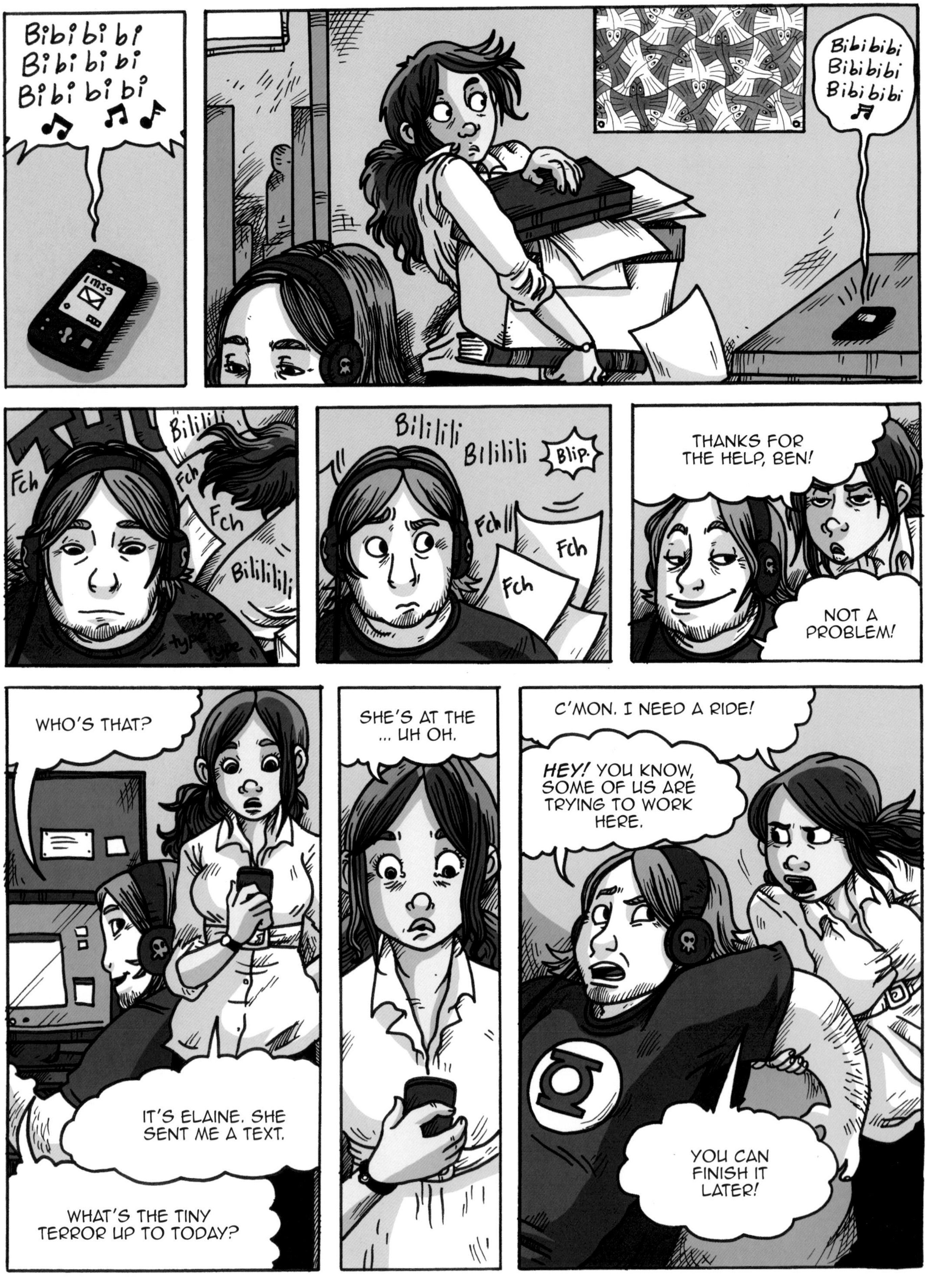

Bibibibi
Bibibibi
Bibibibi
1msg
Bibibibi
Bibibibi
Bibibibi
Bilili
Fch
Fch
Fch
Bililili
type
type
type
Bililili
Bililili
Blip.
Fch
Fch
Fch
THANKS FOR THE HELP, BEN!
NOT A PROBLEM!
WHO'S THAT?
IT'S ELAINE. SHE SENT ME A TEXT.
WHAT'S THE TINY TERROR UP TO TODAY?
SHE'S AT THE ... UH OH.
C'MON. I NEED A RIDE!
HEY! YOU KNOW, SOME OF US ARE TRYING TO WORK HERE.
YOU CAN FINISH IT LATER!

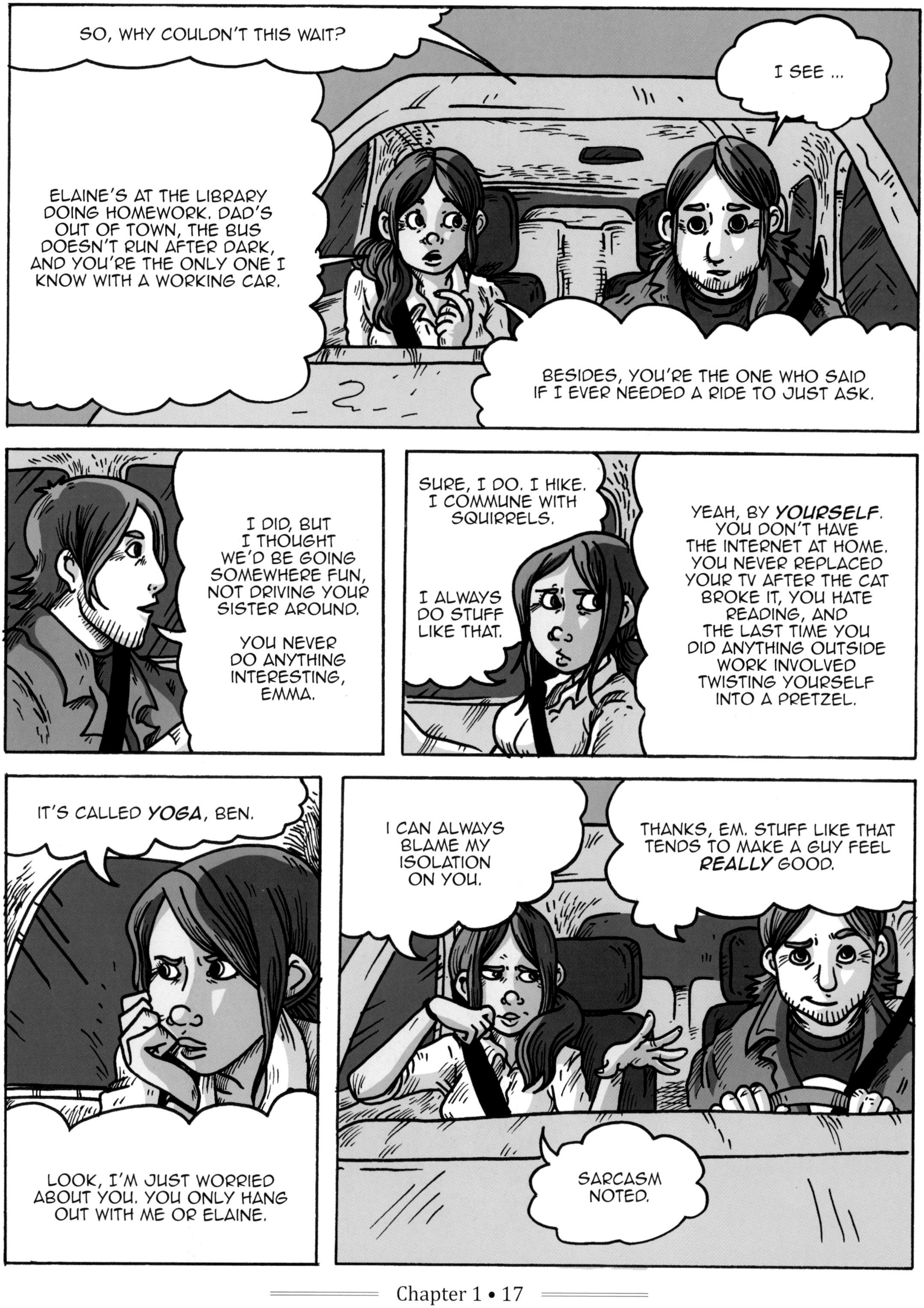
SO, WHY COULDN'T THIS WAIT?
ELAINE'S AT THE LIBRARY DOING HOMEWORK. DAD'S OUT OF TOWN, THE BUS DOESN'T RUN AFTER DARK, AND YOU'RE THE ONLY ONE I KNOW WITH A WORKING CAR.
I SEE ...
BESIDES, YOU'RE THE ONE WHO SAID IF I EVER NEEDED A RIDE TO JUST ASK.
I DID, BUT I THOUGHT WE'D BE GOING SOMEWHERE FUN, NOT DRIVING YOUR SISTER AROUND.
YOU NEVER DO ANYTHING INTERESTING, EMMA.
SURE, I DO. I HIKE. I COMMUNE WITH SQUIRRELS.
I ALWAYS DO STUFF LIKE THAT.
YEAH, BY ***YOURSELF***. YOU DON'T HAVE THE INTERNET AT HOME. YOU NEVER REPLACED YOUR TV AFTER THE CAT BROKE IT, YOU HATE READING, AND THE LAST TIME YOU DID ANYTHING OUTSIDE WORK INVOLVED TWISTING YOURSELF INTO A PRETZEL.
IT'S CALLED ***YOGA***, BEN.
LOOK, I'M JUST WORRIED ABOUT YOU. YOU ONLY HANG OUT WITH ME OR ELAINE.
I CAN ALWAYS BLAME MY ISOLATION ON YOU.
THANKS, EM. STUFF LIKE THAT TENDS TO MAKE A GUY FEEL ***REALLY*** GOOD.
SARCASM NOTED.

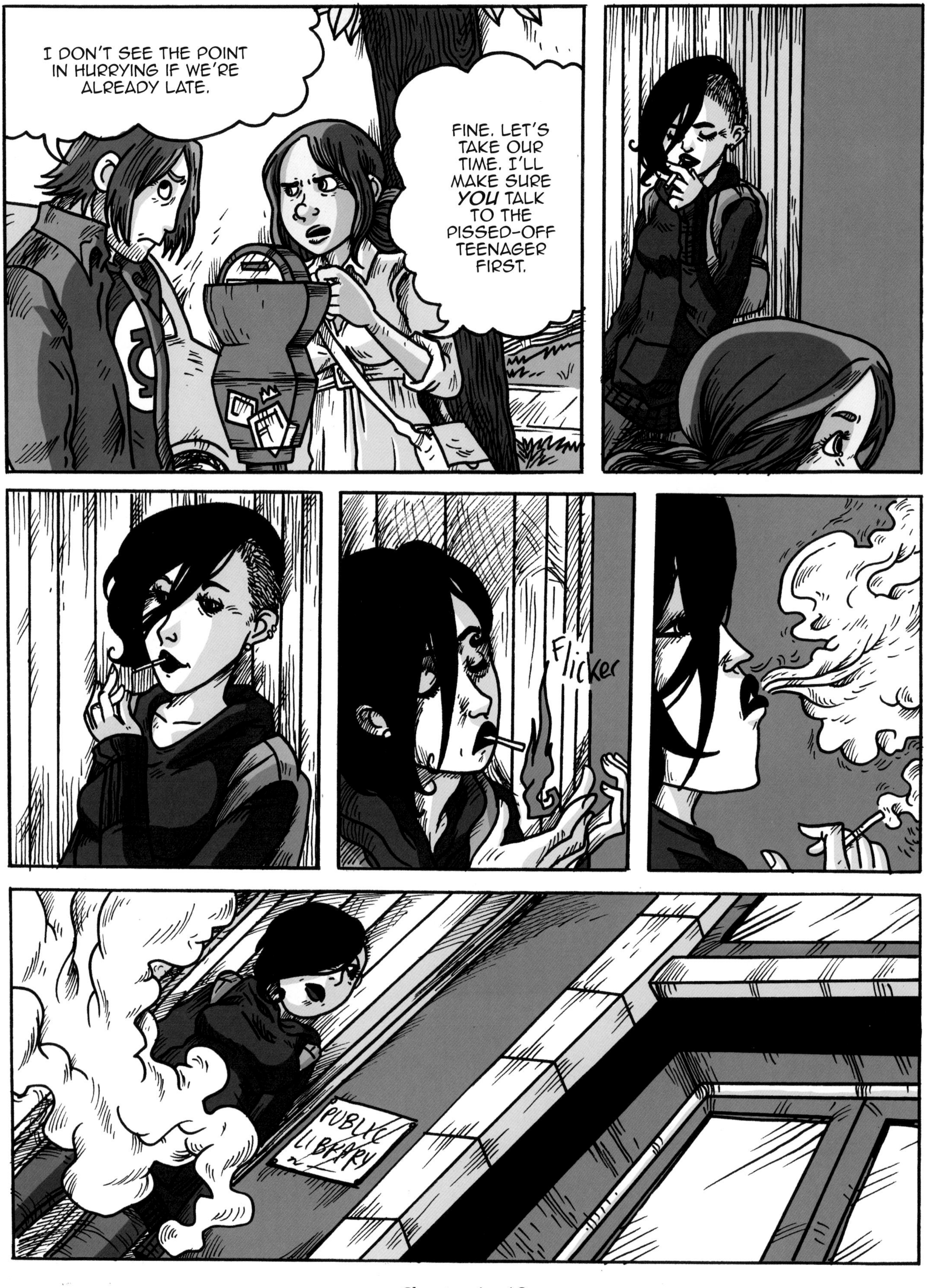
I DON'T SEE THE POINT IN HURRYING IF WE'RE ALREADY LATE.
FINE. LET'S TAKE OUR TIME. I'LL MAKE SURE ***YOU*** TALK TO THE PISSED-OFF TEENAGER FIRST.
Flicker
PUBLIC LIBRARY

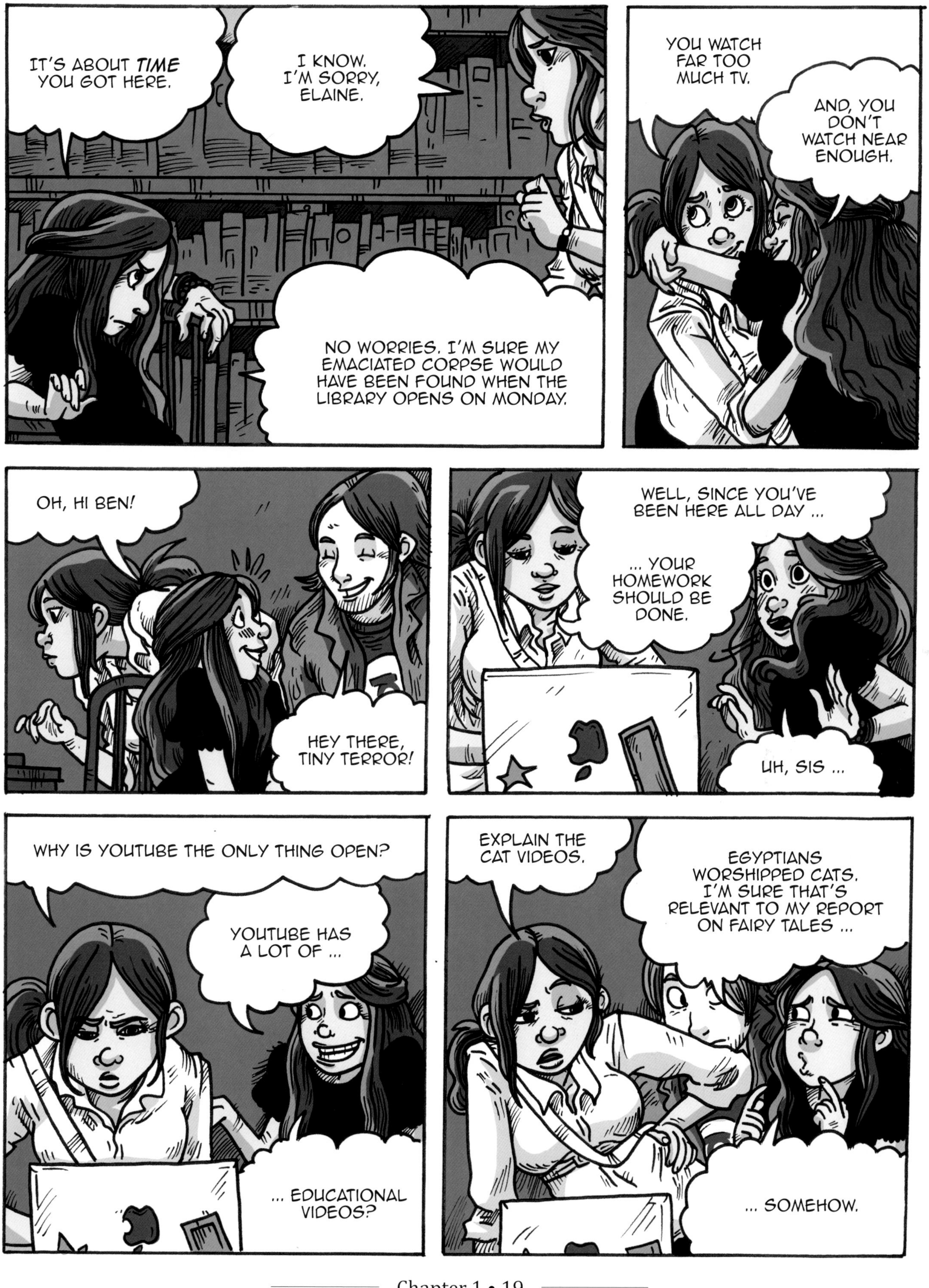
IT'S ABOUT *TIME* YOU GOT HERE.
I KNOW. I'M SORRY, ELAINE.
NO WORRIES. I'M SURE MY EMACIATED CORPSE WOULD HAVE BEEN FOUND WHEN THE LIBRARY OPENS ON MONDAY.
YOU WATCH FAR TOO MUCH TV.
AND, YOU DON'T WATCH NEAR ENOUGH.
OH, HI BEN!
HEY THERE, TINY TERROR!
WELL, SINCE YOU'VE BEEN HERE ALL DAY ...
... YOUR HOMEWORK SHOULD BE DONE.
UH, SIS ...
WHY IS YOUTUBE THE ONLY THING OPEN?
YOUTUBE HAS A LOT OF ...
... EDUCATIONAL VIDEOS?
EXPLAIN THE CAT VIDEOS.
EGYPTIANS WORSHIPPED CATS. I'M SURE THAT'S RELEVANT TO MY REPORT ON FAIRY TALES ...
... SOMEHOW.

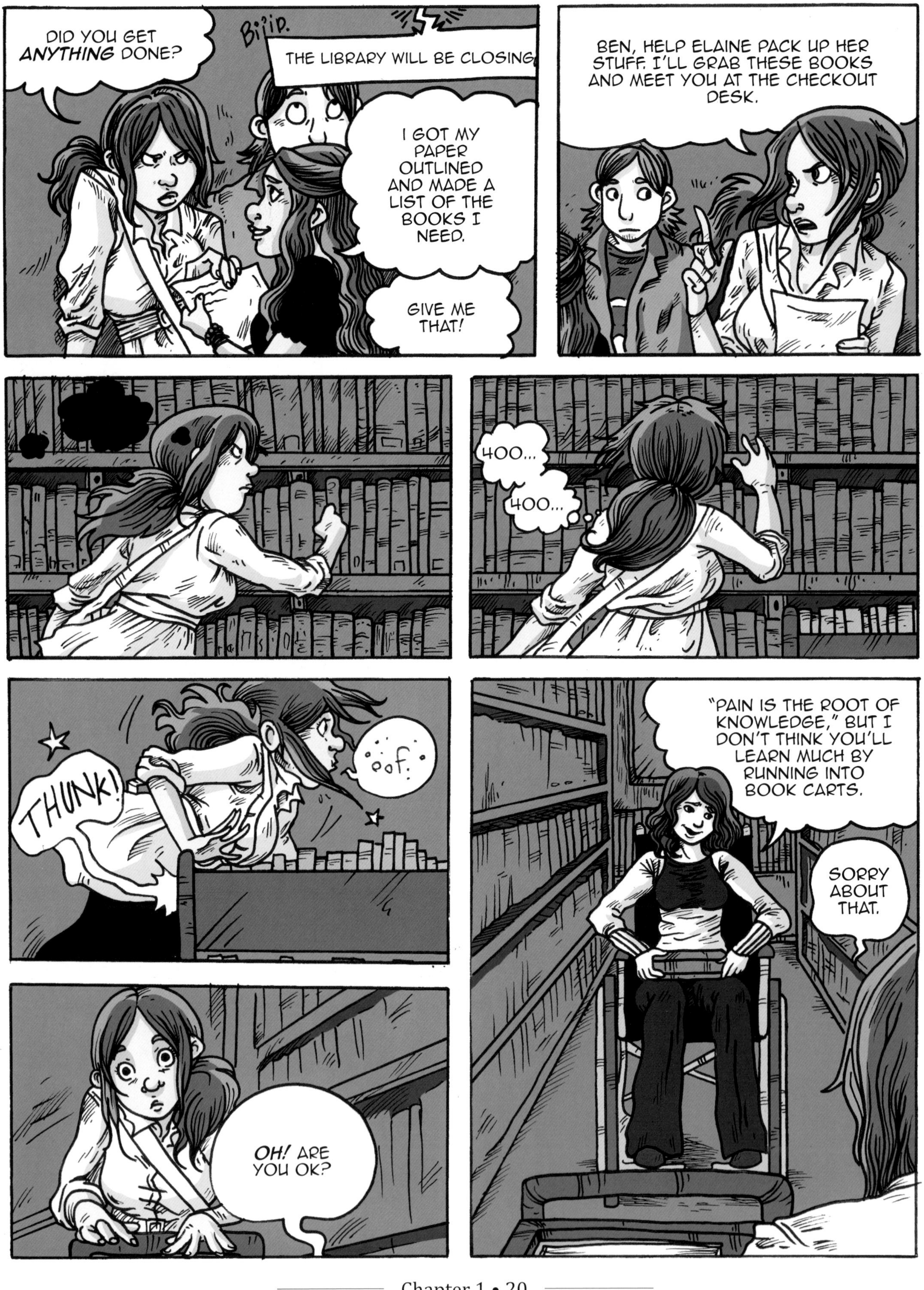
DID YOU GET ANYTHING DONE?
BIIIP.
THE LIBRARY WILL BE CLOSING
I GOT MY PAPER OUTLINED AND MADE A LIST OF THE BOOKS I NEED.
GIVE ME THAT!
BEN, HELP ELAINE PACK UP HER STUFF. I'LL GRAB THESE BOOKS AND MEET YOU AT THE CHECKOUT DESK.
400...
400...
THUNK!
oof.
OH! ARE YOU OK?
"PAIN IS THE ROOT OF KNOWLEDGE," BUT I DON'T THINK YOU'LL LEARN MUCH BY RUNNING INTO BOOK CARTS.
SORRY ABOUT THAT.

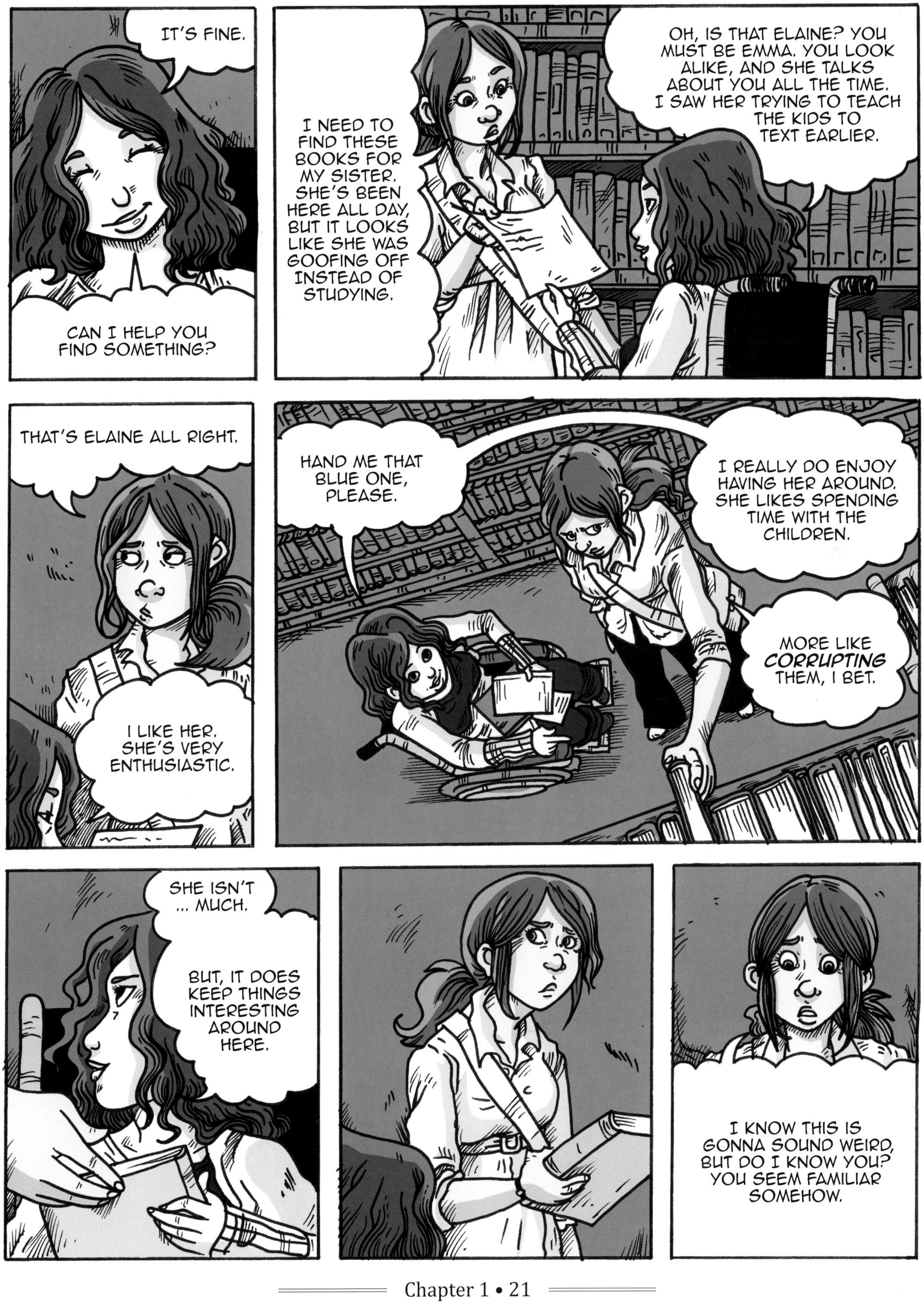
IT'S FINE.
CAN I HELP YOU FIND SOMETHING?
I NEED TO FIND THESE BOOKS FOR MY SISTER. SHE'S BEEN HERE ALL DAY, BUT IT LOOKS LIKE SHE WAS GOOFING OFF INSTEAD OF STUDYING.
OH, IS THAT ELAINE? YOU MUST BE EMMA. YOU LOOK ALIKE, AND SHE TALKS ABOUT YOU ALL THE TIME. I SAW HER TRYING TO TEACH THE KIDS TO TEXT EARLIER.
THAT'S ELAINE ALL RIGHT.
I LIKE HER. SHE'S VERY ENTHUSIASTIC.
HAND ME THAT BLUE ONE, PLEASE.
I REALLY DO ENJOY HAVING HER AROUND. SHE LIKES SPENDING TIME WITH THE CHILDREN.
MORE LIKE CORRUPTING THEM, I BET.
SHE ISN'T ... MUCH.
BUT, IT DOES KEEP THINGS INTERESTING AROUND HERE.
I KNOW THIS IS GONNA SOUND WEIRD, BUT DO I KNOW YOU? YOU SEEM FAMILIAR SOMEHOW.

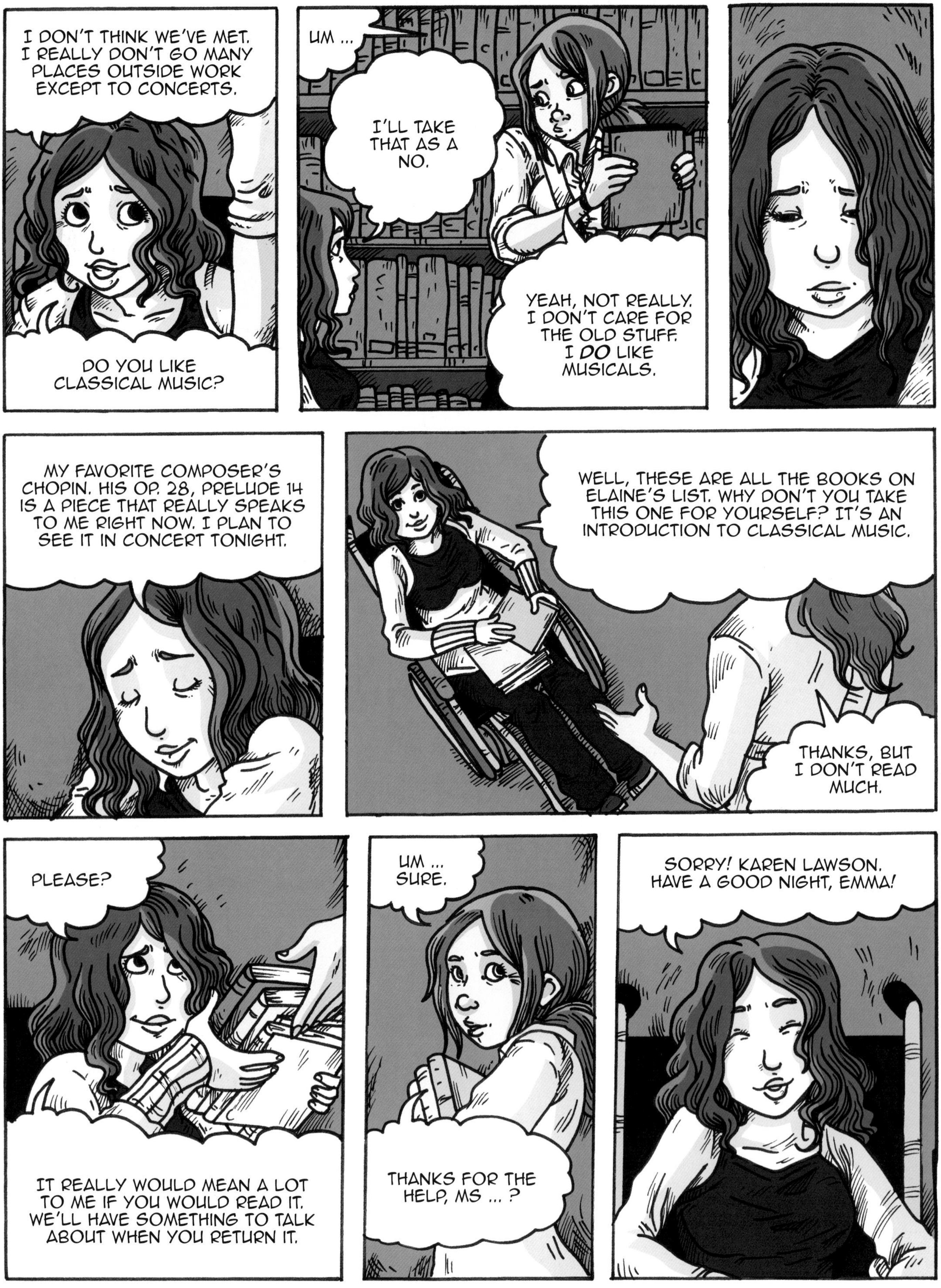
I DON'T THINK WE'VE MET. I REALLY DON'T GO MANY PLACES OUTSIDE WORK EXCEPT TO CONCERTS.
DO YOU LIKE CLASSICAL MUSIC?
UM ...
I'LL TAKE THAT AS A NO.
YEAH, NOT REALLY. I DON'T CARE FOR THE OLD STUFF. I DO LIKE MUSICALS.
MY FAVORITE COMPOSER'S CHOPIN. HIS OP. 28, PRELUDE 14 IS A PIECE THAT REALLY SPEAKS TO ME RIGHT NOW. I PLAN TO SEE IT IN CONCERT TONIGHT.
WELL, THESE ARE ALL THE BOOKS ON ELAINE'S LIST. WHY DON'T YOU TAKE THIS ONE FOR YOURSELF? IT'S AN INTRODUCTION TO CLASSICAL MUSIC.
THANKS, BUT I DON'T READ MUCH.
PLEASE?
IT REALLY WOULD MEAN A LOT TO ME IF YOU WOULD READ IT. WE'LL HAVE SOMETHING TO TALK ABOUT WHEN YOU RETURN IT.
UM ... SURE.
THANKS FOR THE HELP, MS ... ?
SORRY! KAREN LAWSON. HAVE A GOOD NIGHT, EMMA!

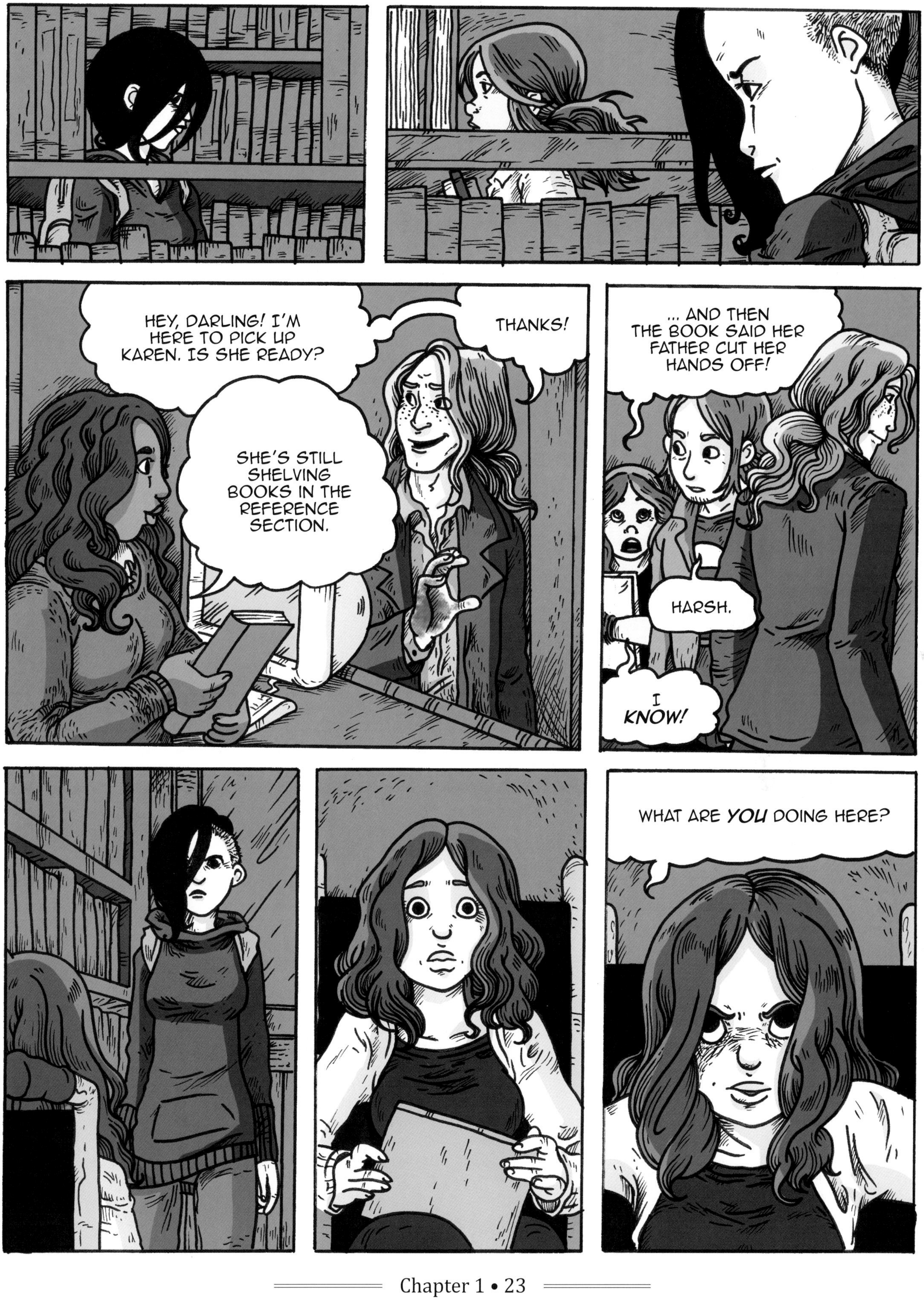
HEY, DARLING! I'M HERE TO PICK UP KAREN. IS SHE READY?
SHE'S STILL SHELVING BOOKS IN THE REFERENCE SECTION.
THANKS!
... AND THEN THE BOOK SAID HER FATHER CUT HER HANDS OFF!
HARSH.
I *KNOW!*
WHAT ARE *YOU* DOING HERE?

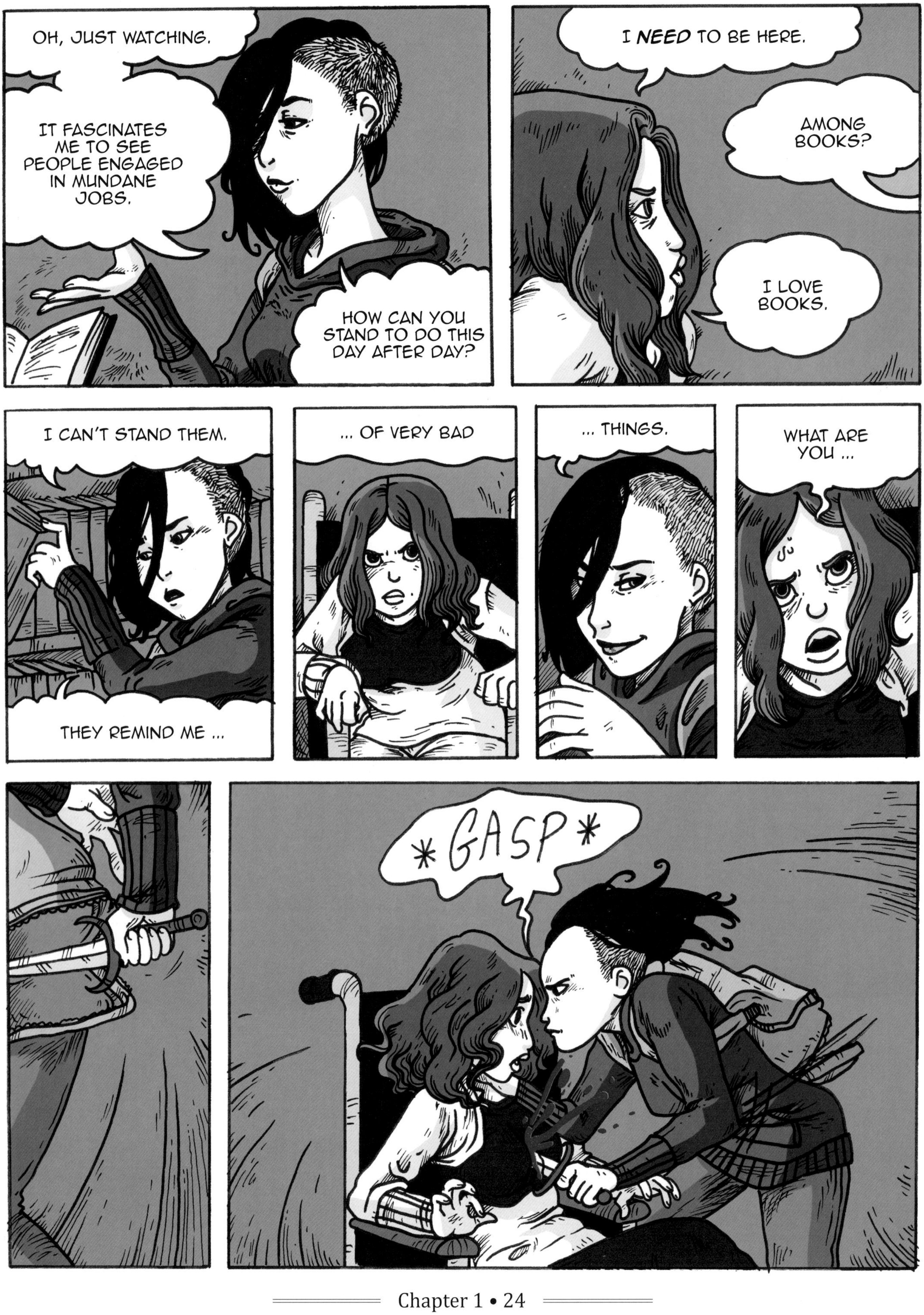
OH, JUST WATCHING.
IT FASCINATES ME TO SEE PEOPLE ENGAGED IN MUNDANE JOBS.
HOW CAN YOU STAND TO DO THIS DAY AFTER DAY?
I NEED TO BE HERE.
AMONG BOOKS?
I LOVE BOOKS.
I CAN'T STAND THEM.
THEY REMIND ME ...
... OF VERY BAD
... THINGS.
WHAT ARE YOU ...
GASP

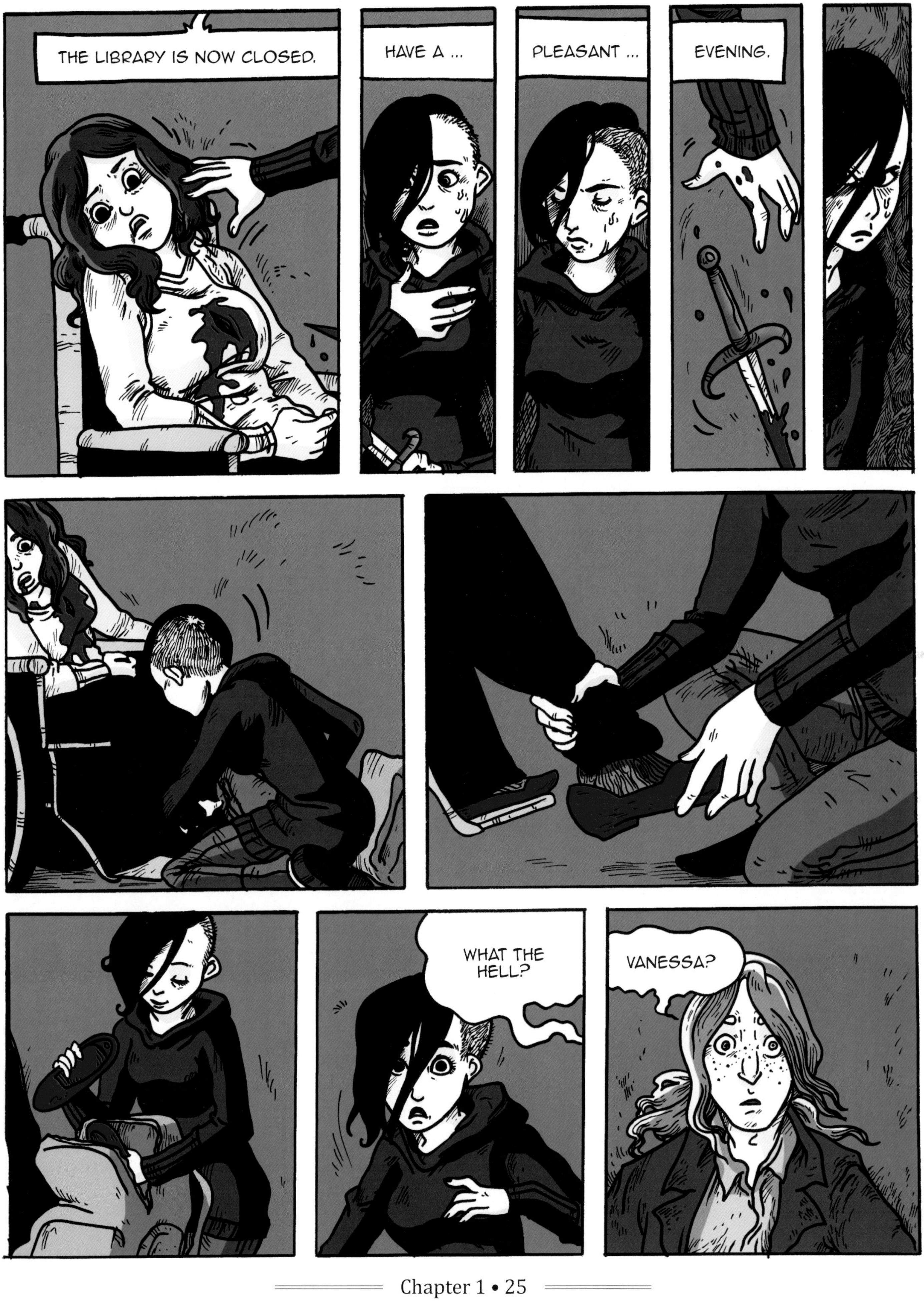
THE LIBRARY IS NOW CLOSED.
HAVE A ...
PLEASANT ...
EVENING.
WHAT THE HELL?
VANESSA?

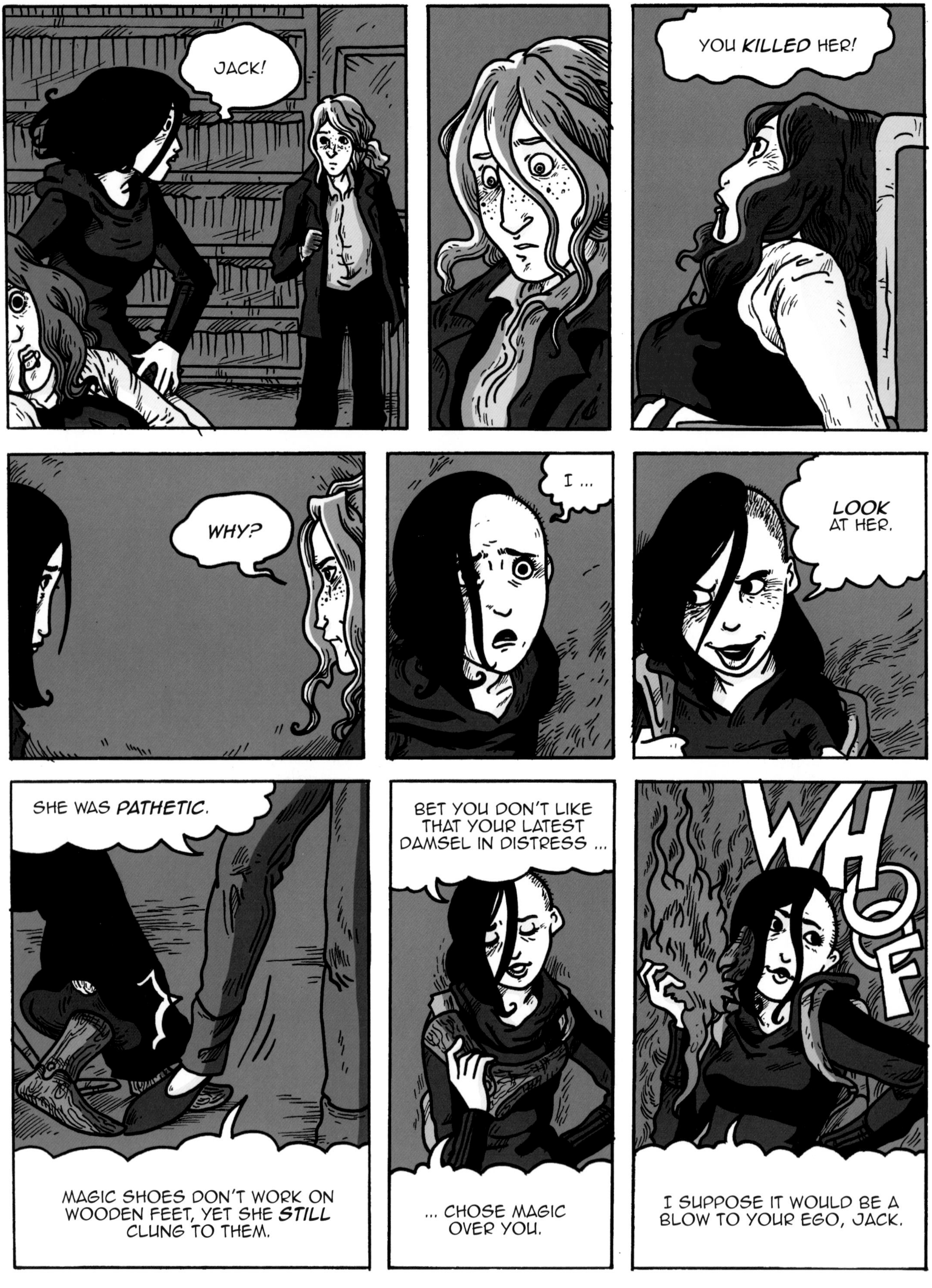
JACK!
YOU KILLED HER!
WHY?
I ...
LOOK AT HER.
SHE WAS PATHETIC.
MAGIC SHOES DON'T WORK ON WOODEN FEET, YET SHE STILL CLUNG TO THEM.
BET YOU DON'T LIKE THAT YOUR LATEST DAMSEL IN DISTRESS ...
... CHOSE MAGIC OVER YOU.
WHOOF
I SUPPOSE IT WOULD BE A BLOW TO YOUR EGO, JACK.

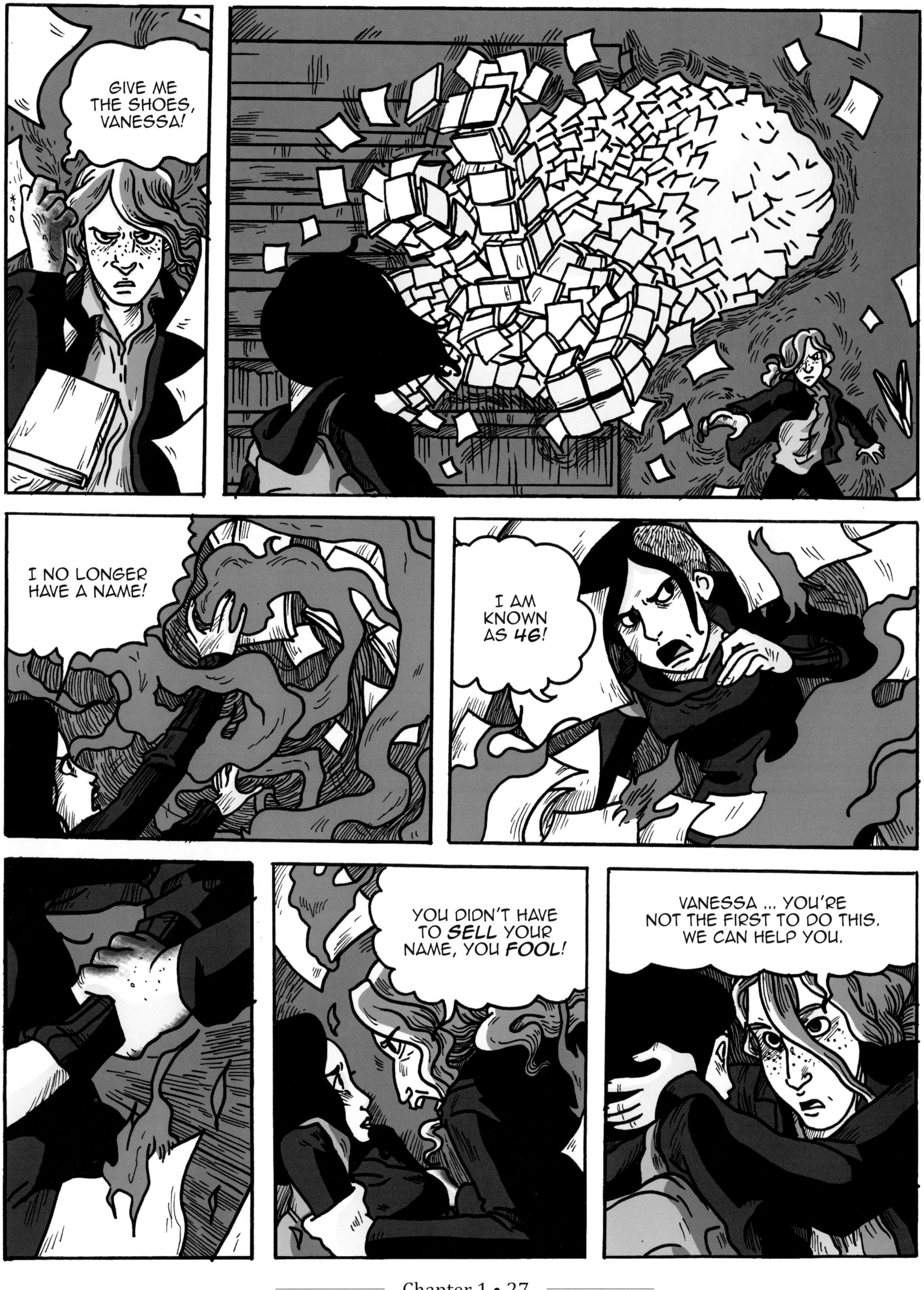
GIVE ME THE SHOES, VANESSA!
I NO LONGER HAVE A NAME!
I AM KNOWN AS 46!
YOU DIDN'T HAVE TO SELL YOUR NAME, YOU FOOL!
VANESSA ... YOU'RE NOT THE FIRST TO DO THIS. WE CAN HELP YOU.

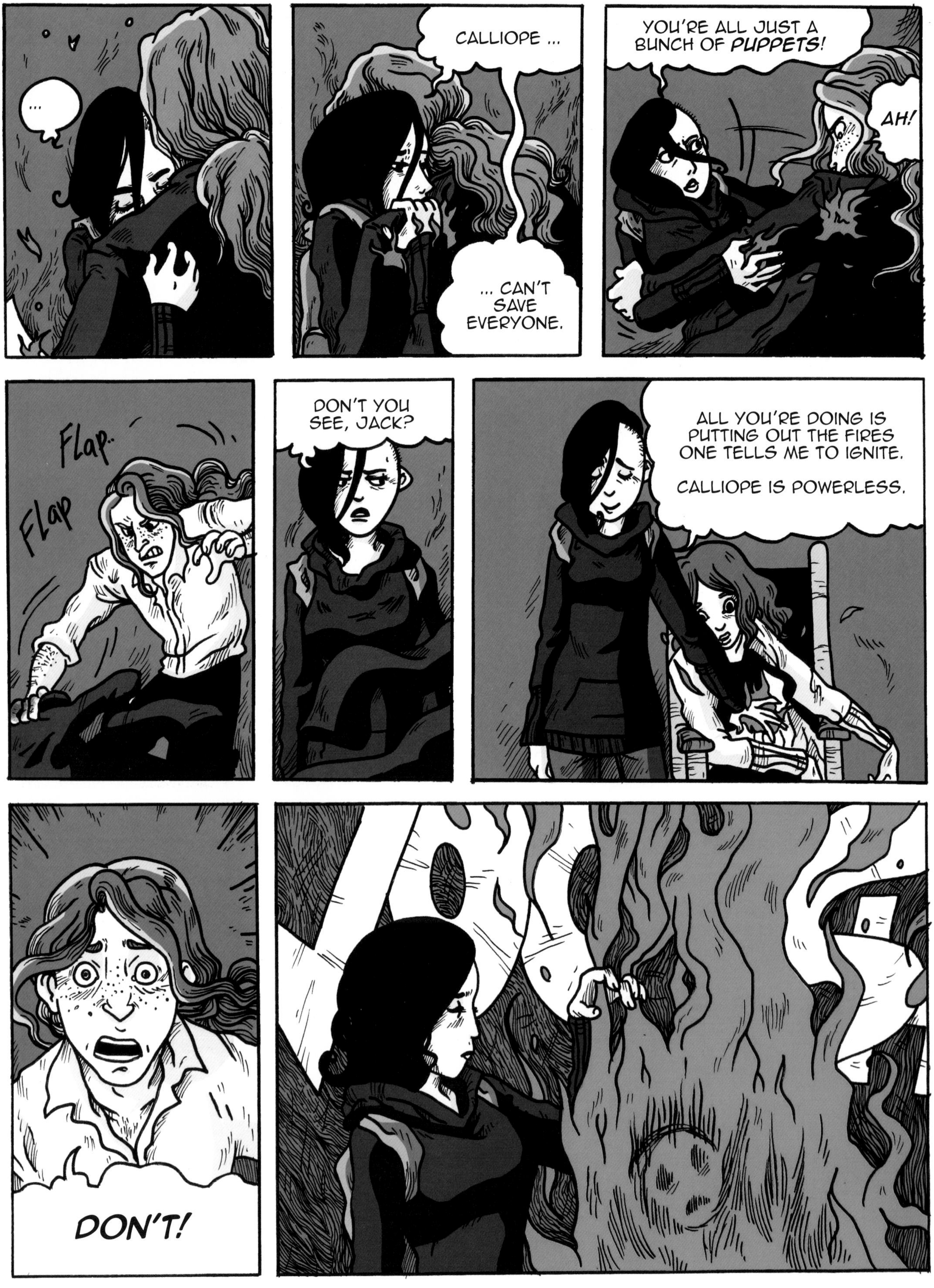
...
CALLIOPE ...
... CAN'T SAVE EVERYONE.
YOU'RE ALL JUST A BUNCH OF PUPPETS!
AH!
FLAP.. FLAP
DON'T YOU SEE, JACK?
ALL YOU'RE DOING IS PUTTING OUT THE FIRES ONE TELLS ME TO IGNITE.
CALLIOPE IS POWERLESS.
DON'T!

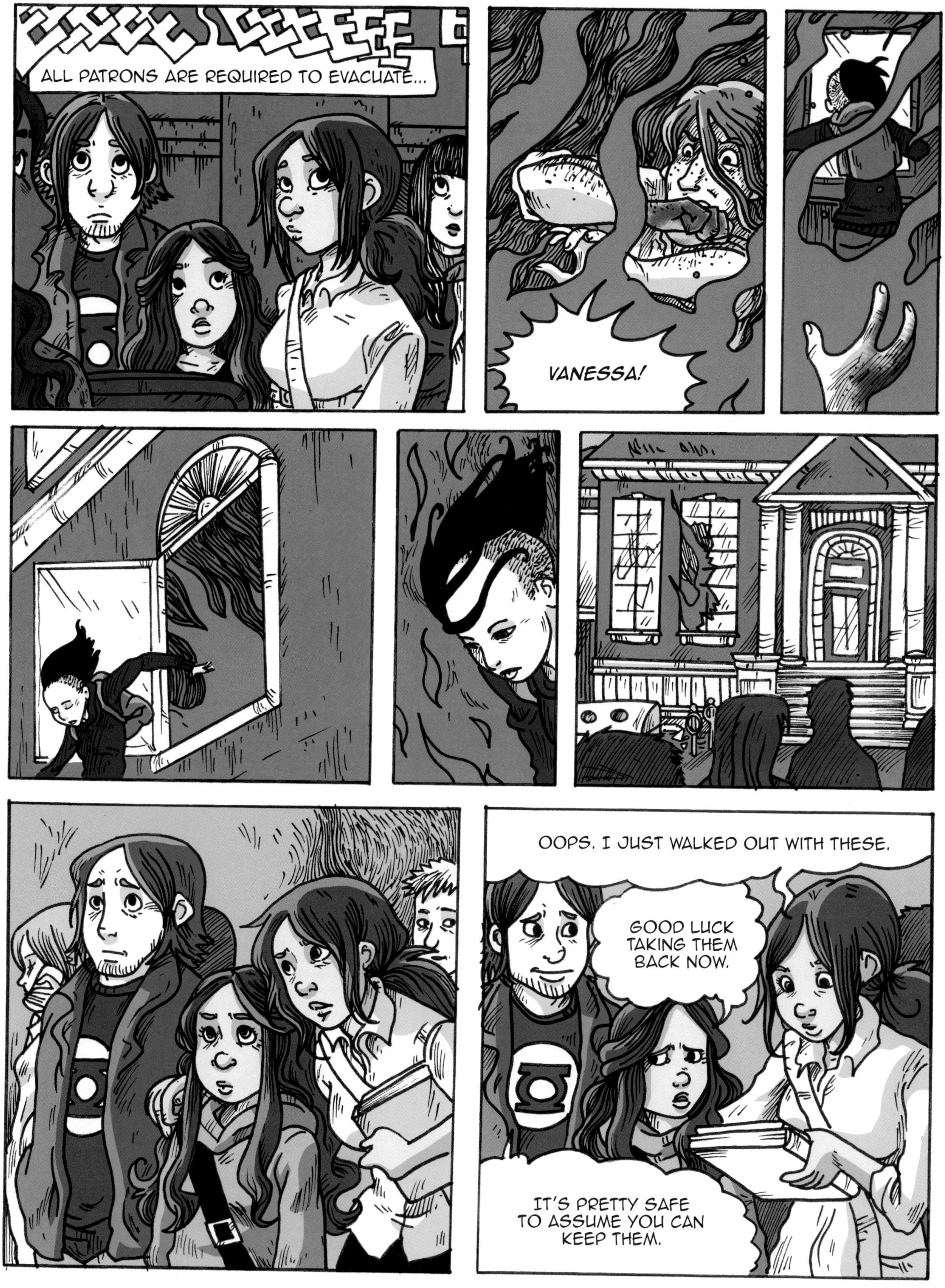
ALL PATRONS ARE REQUIRED TO EVACUATE...
VANESSA!
OOPS. I JUST WALKED OUT WITH THESE.
GOOD LUCK TAKING THEM BACK NOW.
IT'S PRETTY SAFE TO ASSUME YOU CAN KEEP THEM.

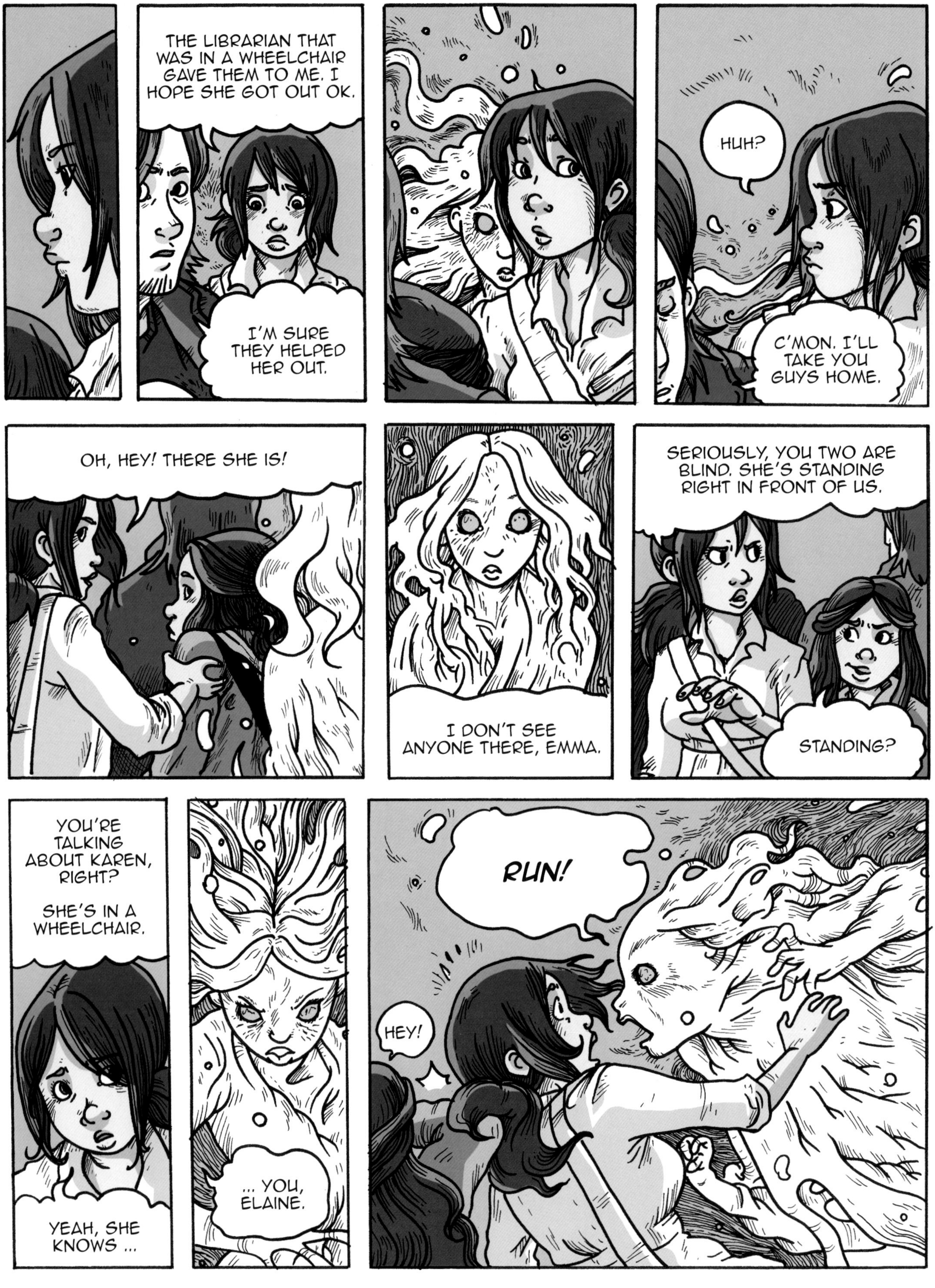
THE LIBRARIAN THAT WAS IN A WHEELCHAIR GAVE THEM TO ME. I HOPE SHE GOT OUT OK.
I'M SURE THEY HELPED HER OUT.
HUH?
C'MON. I'LL TAKE YOU GUYS HOME.
OH, HEY! THERE SHE IS!
I DON'T SEE ANYONE THERE, EMMA.
SERIOUSLY, YOU TWO ARE BLIND. SHE'S STANDING RIGHT IN FRONT OF US.
STANDING?
YOU'RE TALKING ABOUT KAREN, RIGHT?
SHE'S IN A WHEELCHAIR.
YEAH, SHE KNOWS ...
... YOU, ELAINE.
RUN!
HEY!

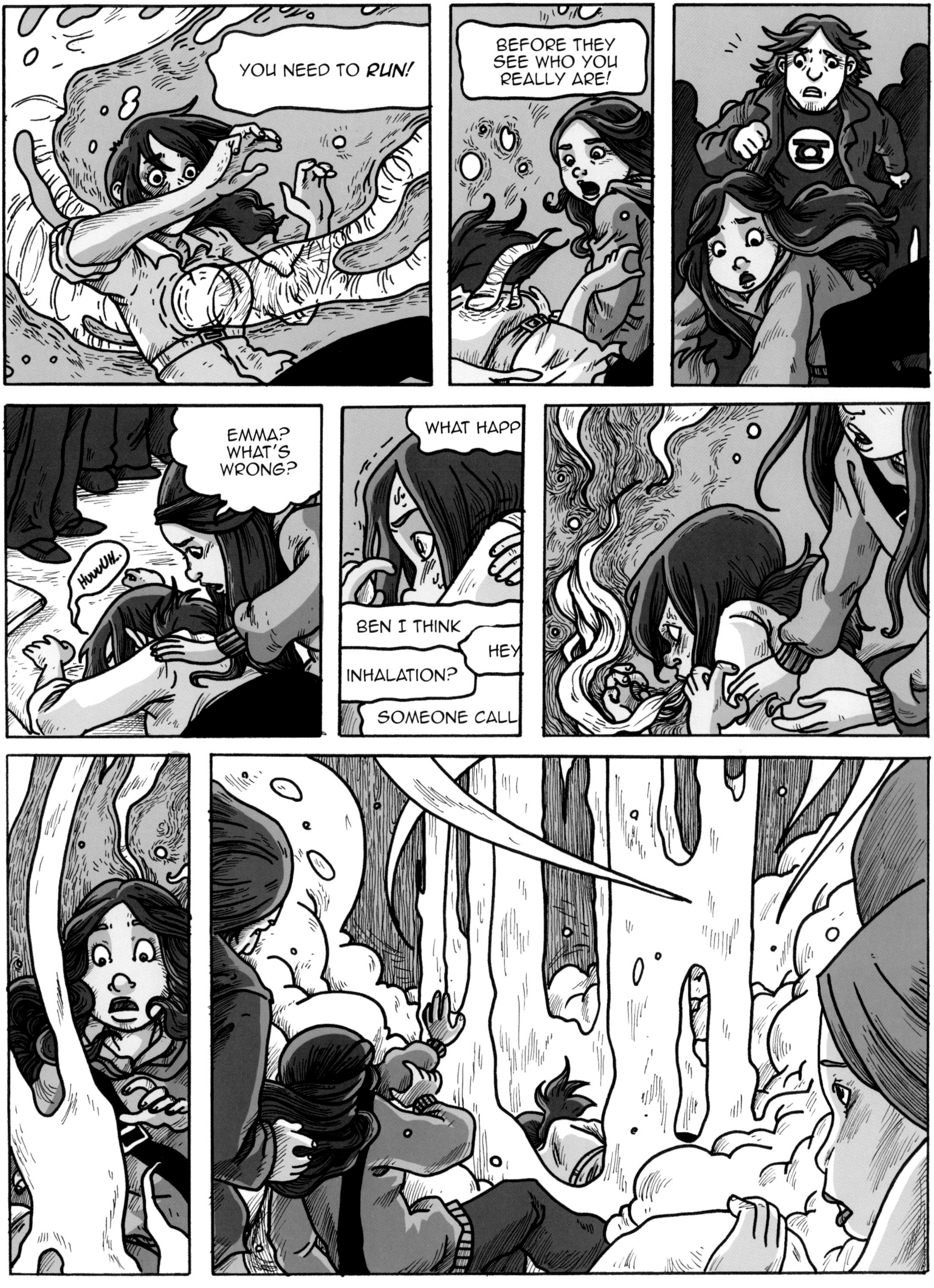
YOU NEED TO *RUN!*
BEFORE THEY SEE WHO YOU REALLY ARE!
EMMA? WHAT'S WRONG?
HuuUH..
WHAT HAPP
BEN I THINK
HEY
INHALATION?
SOMEONE CALL

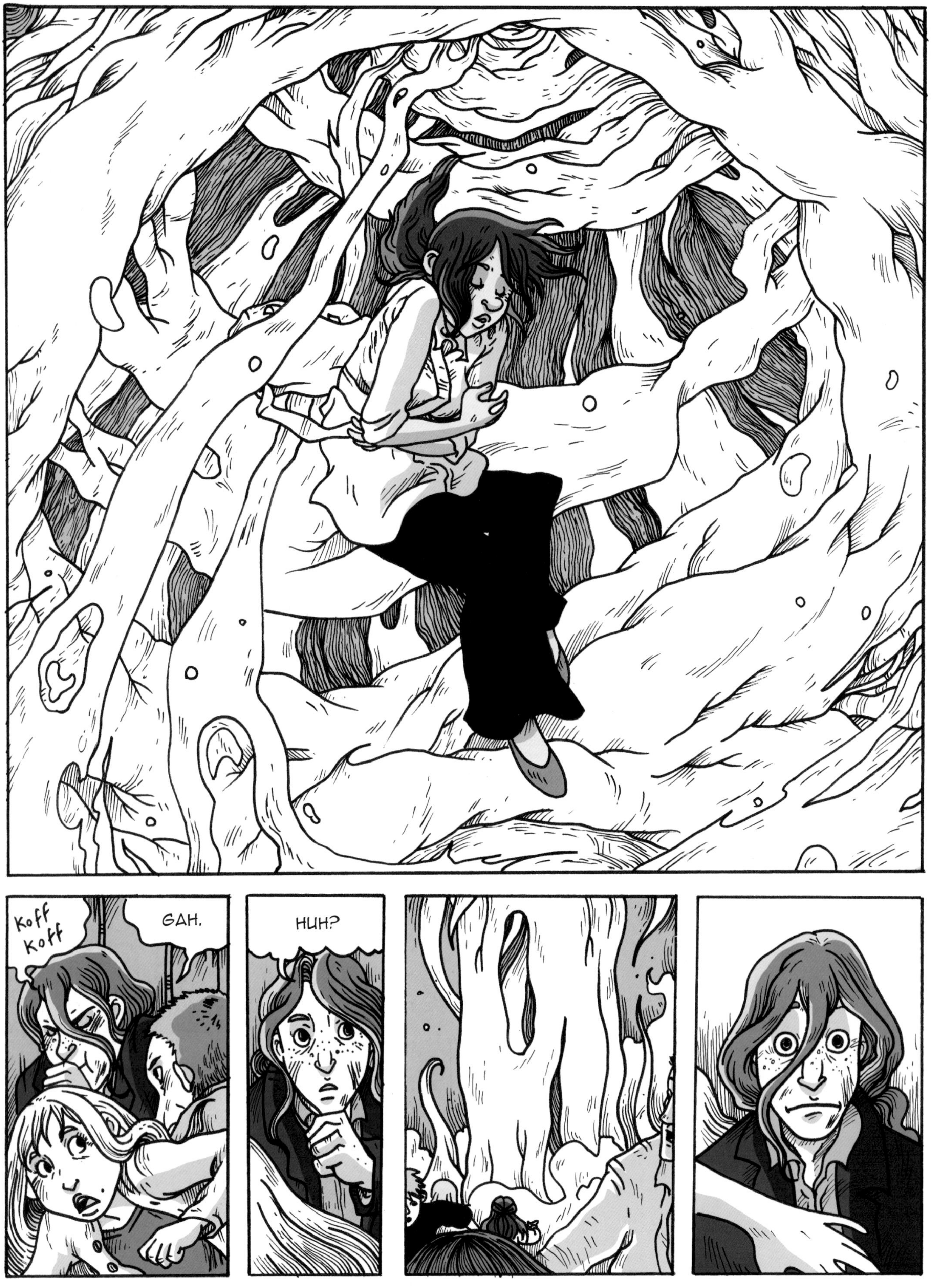
Koff Koff
GAH.
HUH?

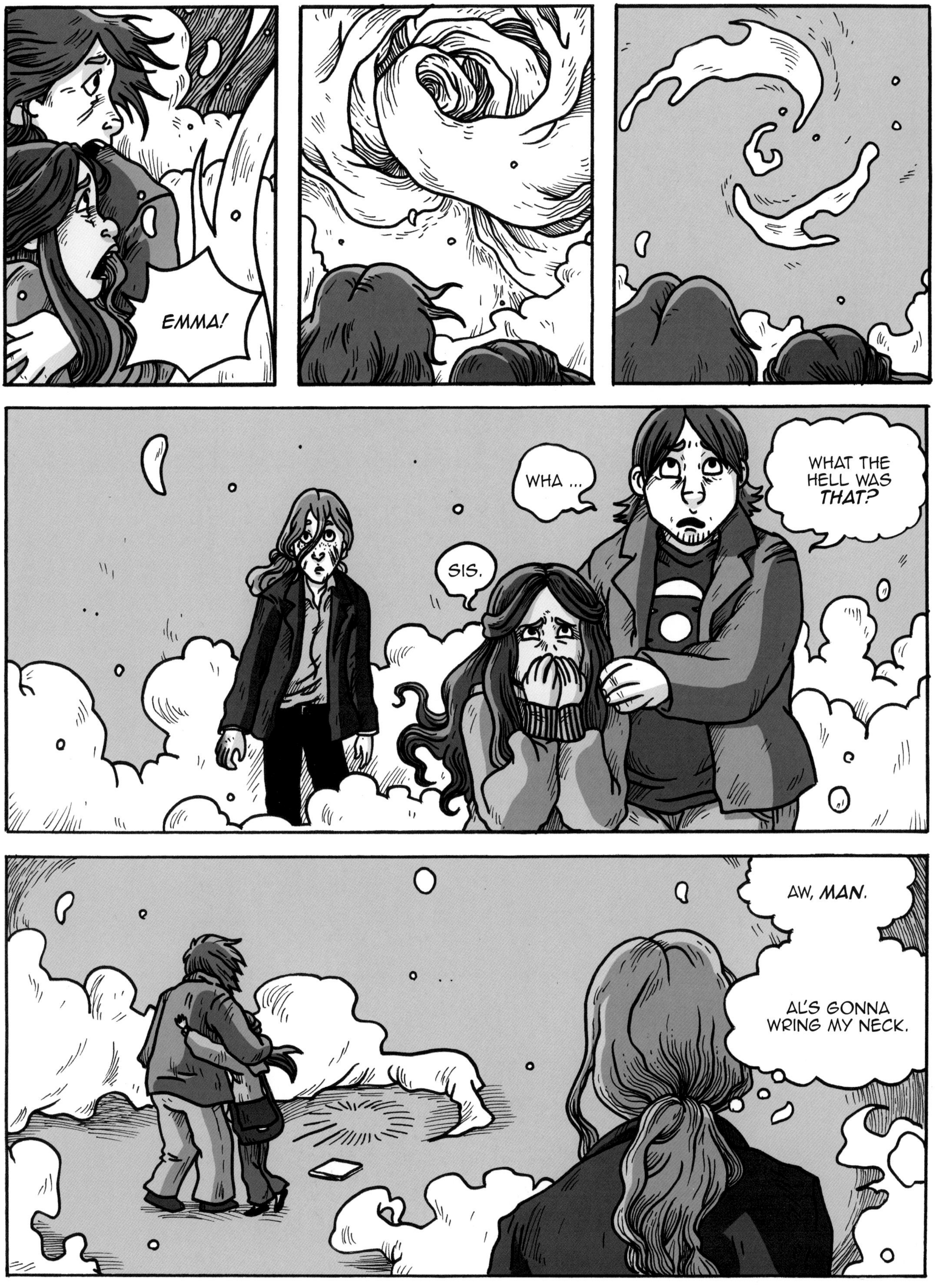
EMMA!
WHA ...
SIS.
WHAT THE HELL WAS *THAT?*
AW, *MAN*.
AL'S GONNA WRING MY NECK.

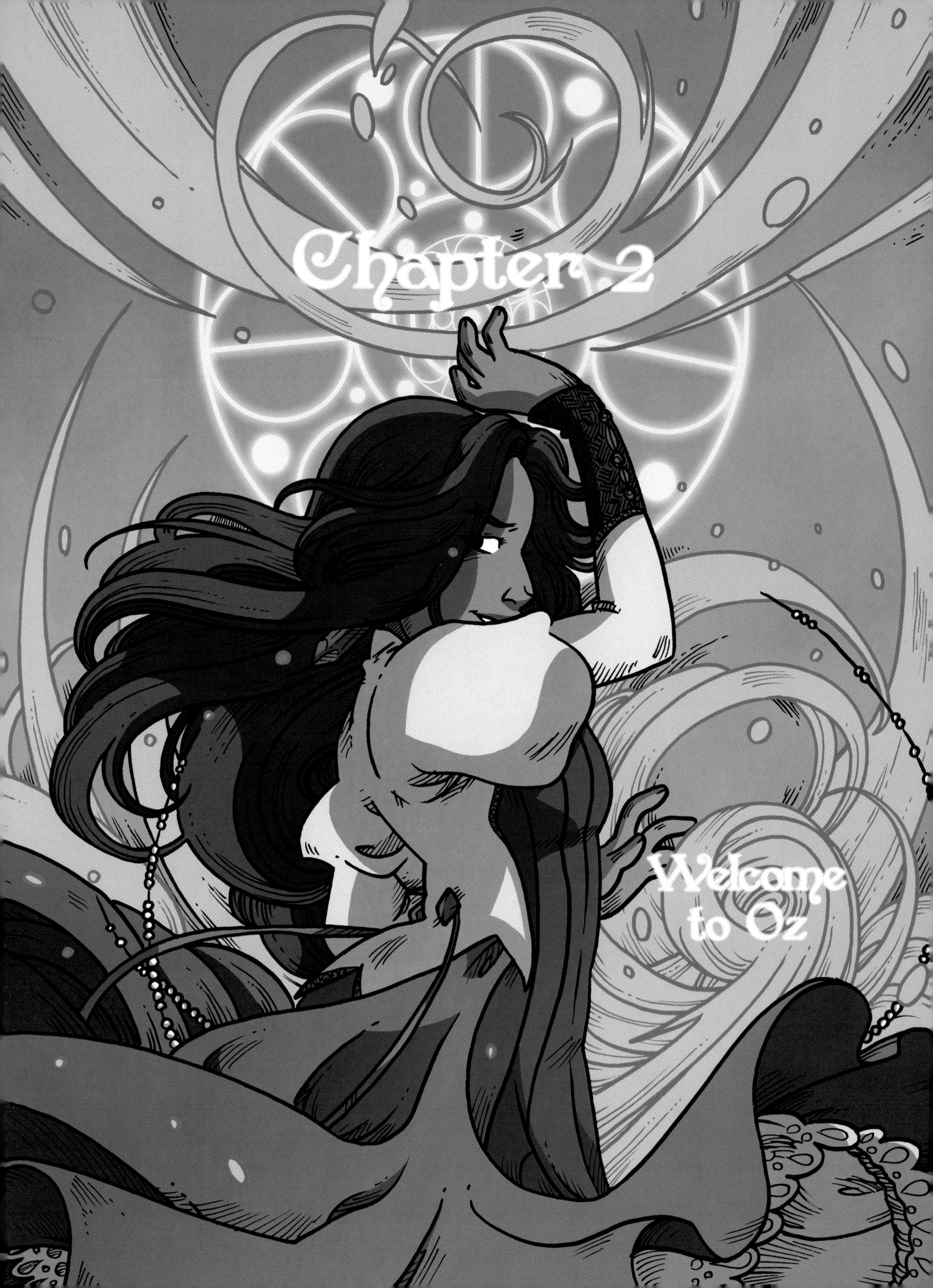
Chapter 2
Welcome to Oz

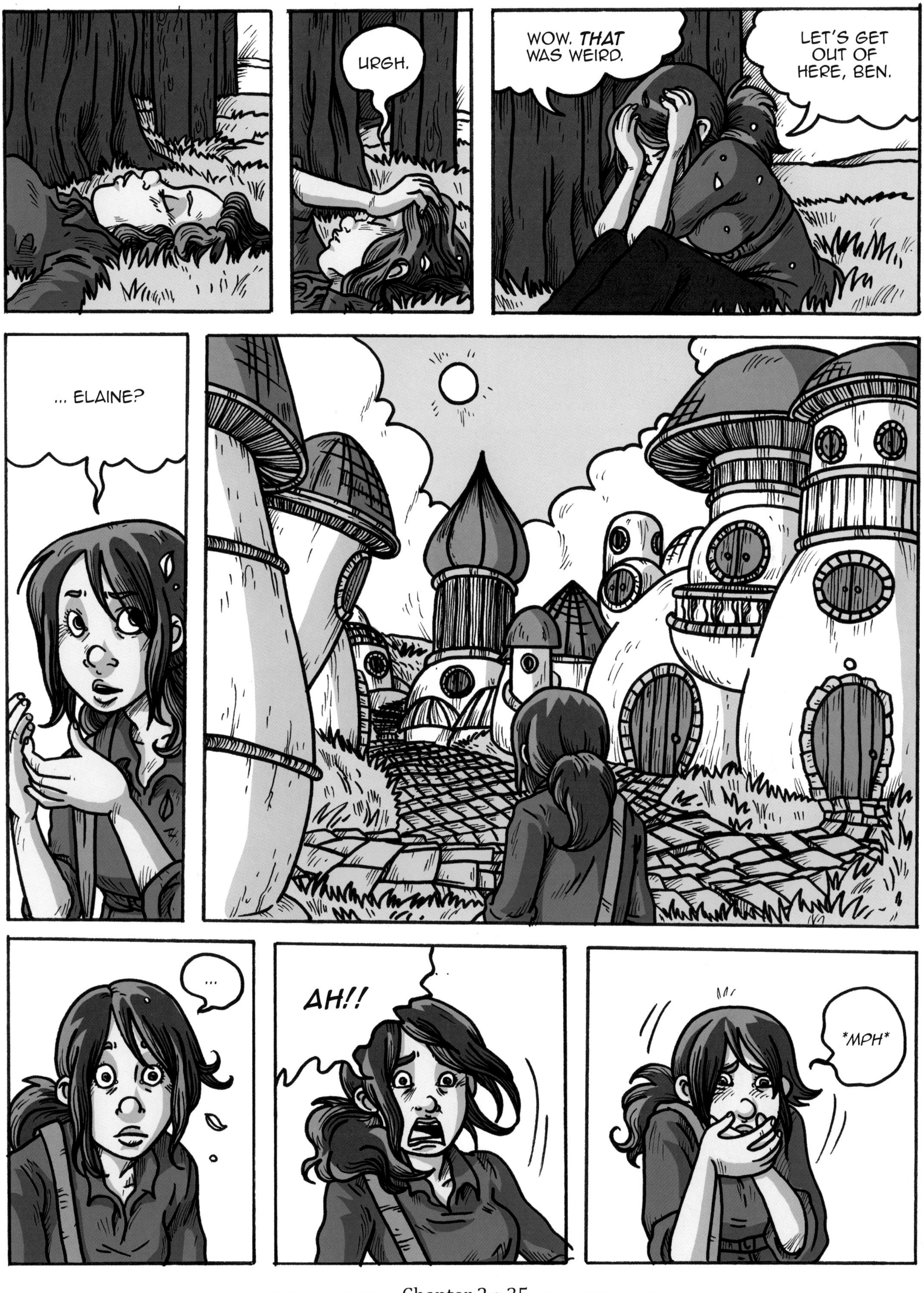
URGH.
WOW. THAT WAS WEIRD.
LET'S GET OUT OF HERE, BEN.
... ELAINE?
...
AH!!
MPH

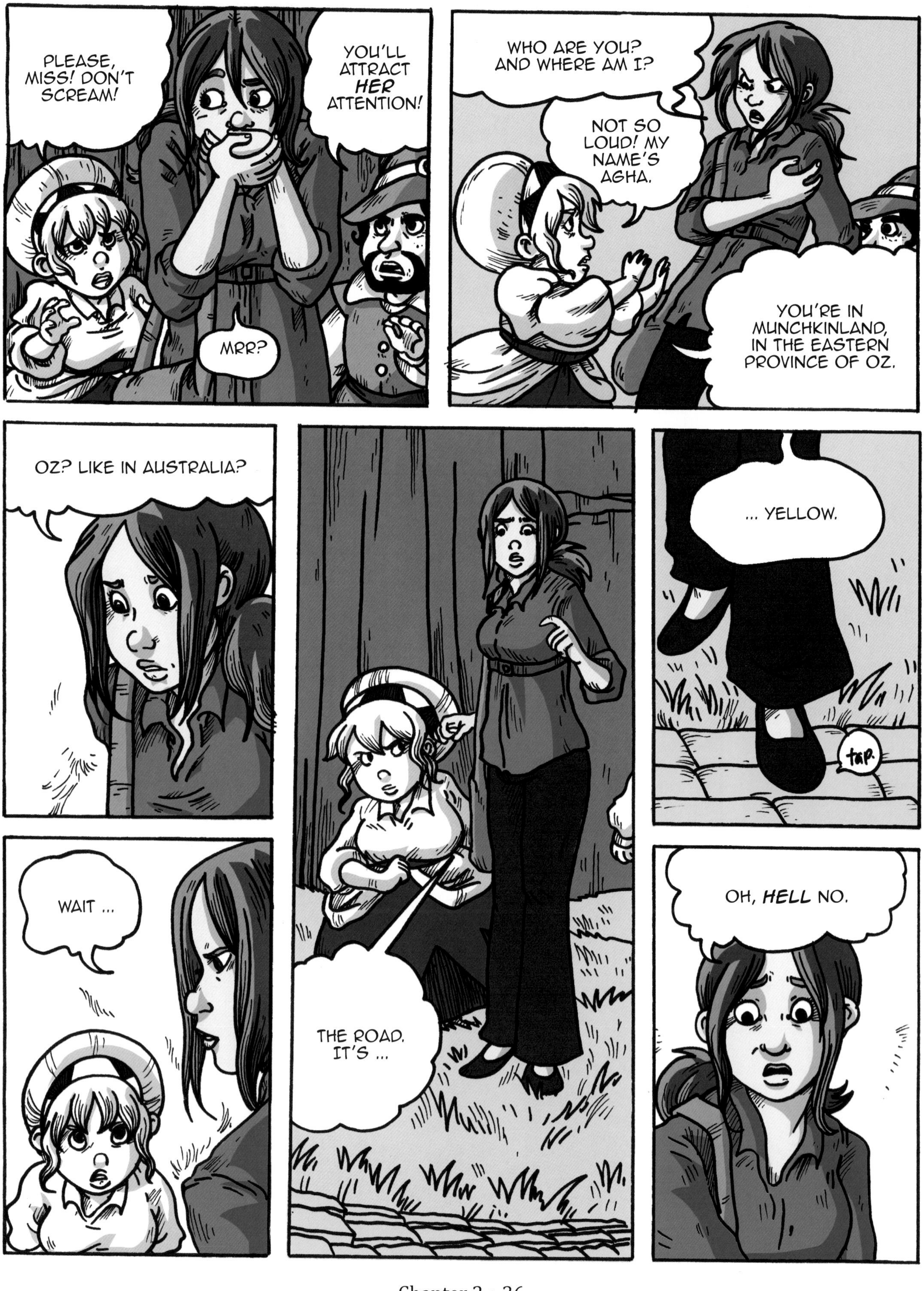
PLEASE, MISS! DON'T SCREAM!
YOU'LL ATTRACT **HER** ATTENTION!
MRR?
WHO ARE YOU? AND WHERE AM I?
NOT SO LOUD! MY NAME'S AGHA.
YOU'RE IN MUNCHKINLAND, IN THE EASTERN PROVINCE OF OZ.
OZ? LIKE IN AUSTRALIA?
WAIT ...
THE ROAD. IT'S ...
... YELLOW.
tap.
OH, **HELL** NO.

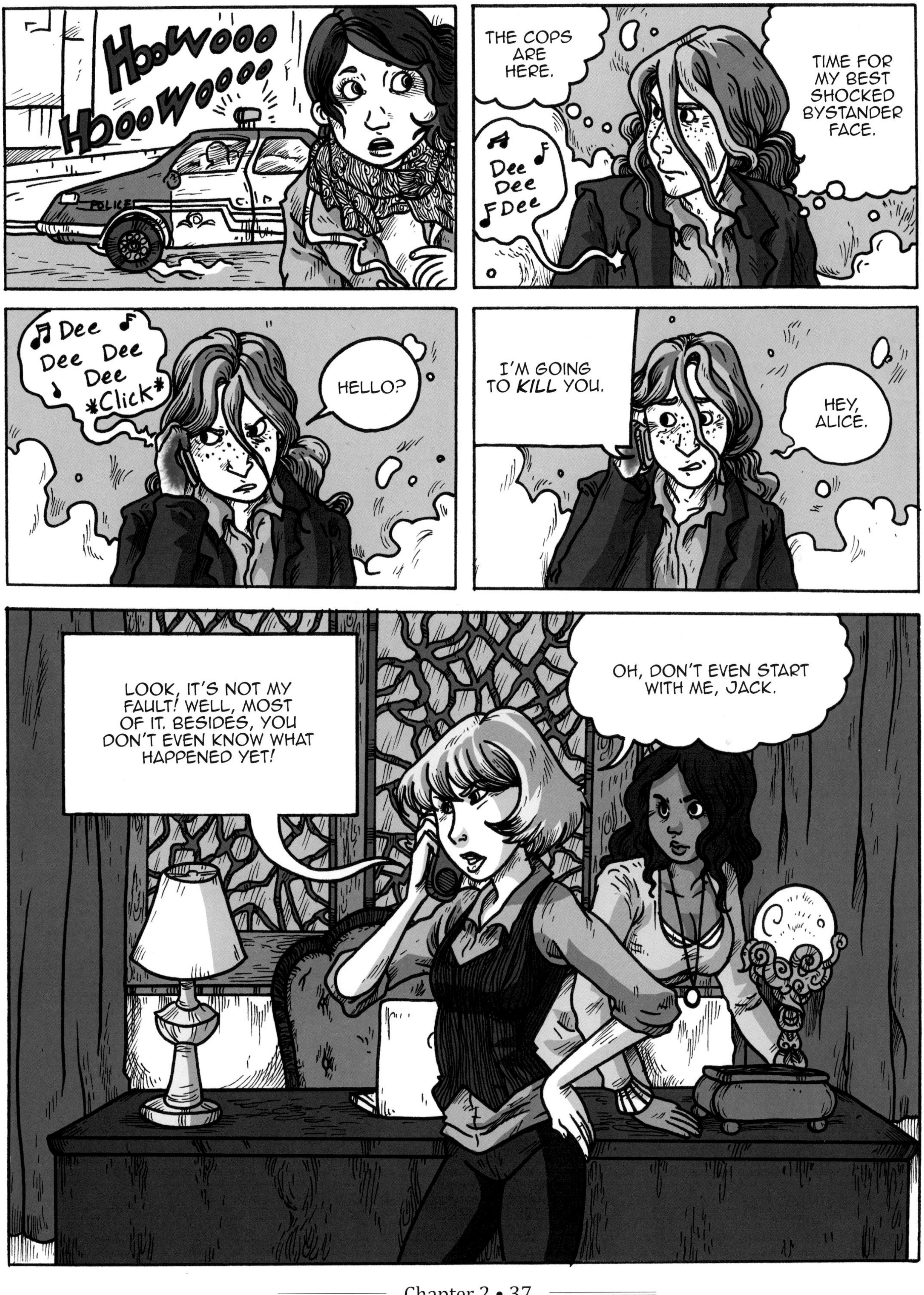

HOOWOOO
HOOOWOOOO
THE COPS ARE HERE.
TIME FOR MY BEST SHOCKED BYSTANDER FACE.
Dee Dee Dee
Dee Dee Dee Dee *Click*
HELLO?
I'M GOING TO KILL YOU.
HEY, ALICE.
LOOK, IT'S NOT MY FAULT! WELL, MOST OF IT. BESIDES, YOU DON'T EVEN KNOW WHAT HAPPENED YET!
OH, DON'T EVEN START WITH ME, JACK.

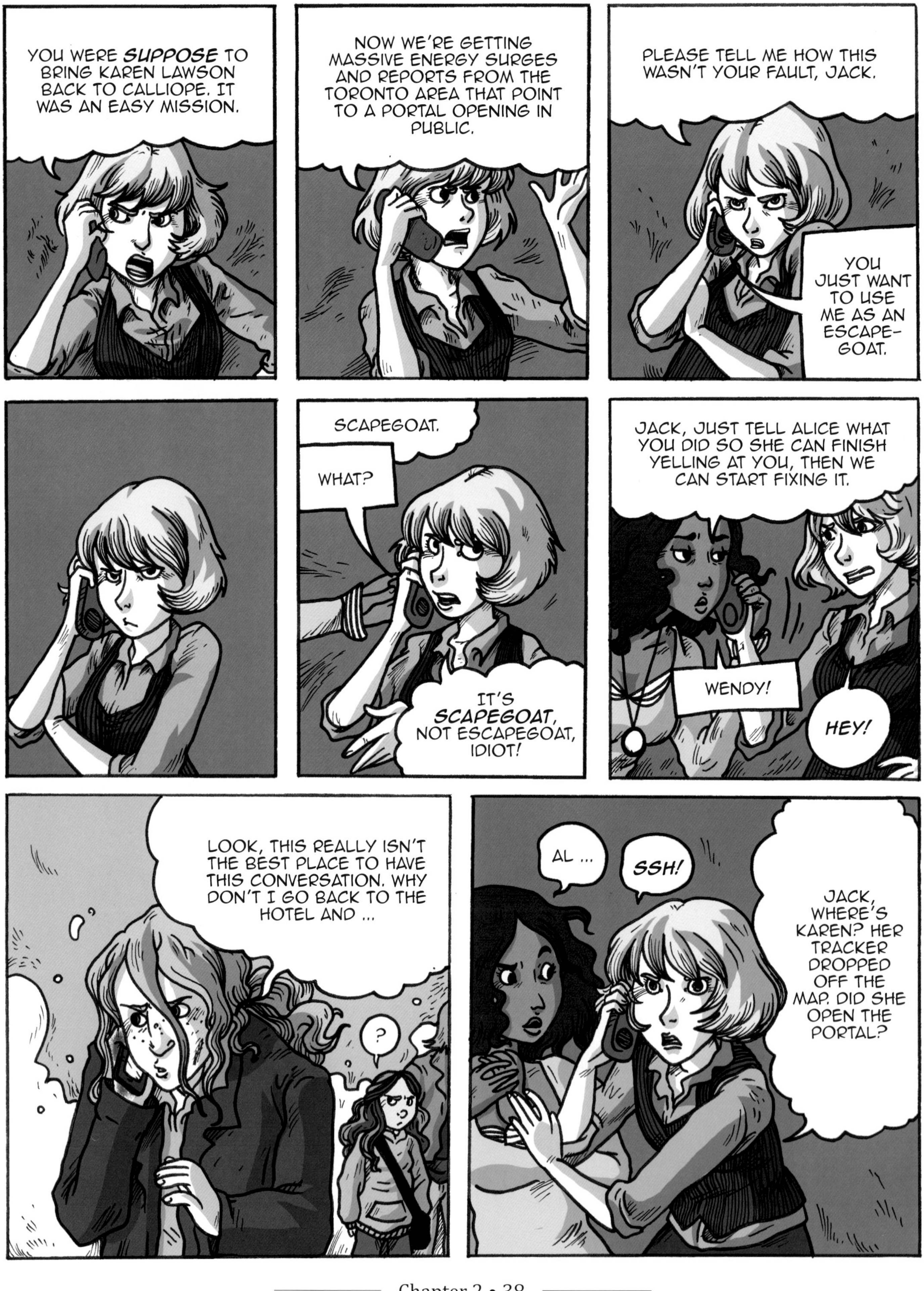
YOU WERE SUPPOSE TO BRING KAREN LAWSON BACK TO CALLIOPE. IT WAS AN EASY MISSION.
NOW WE'RE GETTING MASSIVE ENERGY SURGES AND REPORTS FROM THE TORONTO AREA THAT POINT TO A PORTAL OPENING IN PUBLIC.
PLEASE TELL ME HOW THIS WASN'T YOUR FAULT, JACK.
YOU JUST WANT TO USE ME AS AN ESCAPE-GOAT.
SCAPEGOAT.
WHAT?
IT'S SCAPEGOAT, NOT ESCAPEGOAT, IDIOT!
JACK, JUST TELL ALICE WHAT YOU DID SO SHE CAN FINISH YELLING AT YOU, THEN WE CAN START FIXING IT.
WENDY!
HEY!
LOOK, THIS REALLY ISN'T THE BEST PLACE TO HAVE THIS CONVERSATION. WHY DON'T I GO BACK TO THE HOTEL AND ...
?
AL ...
SSH!
JACK, WHERE'S KAREN? HER TRACKER DROPPED OFF THE MAP. DID SHE OPEN THE PORTAL?

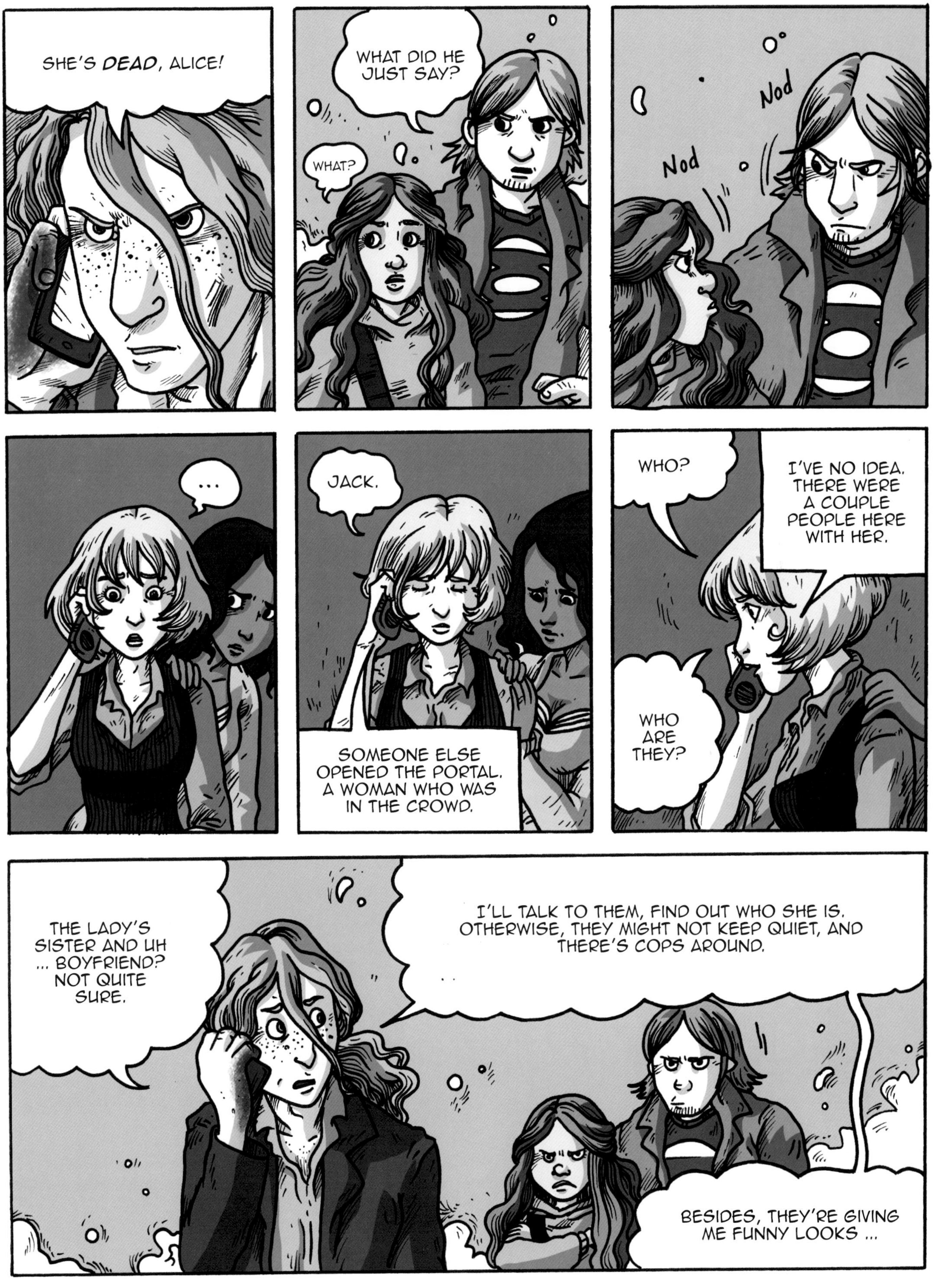
SHE'S *DEAD*, ALICE!
WHAT DID HE JUST SAY?
WHAT?
Nod
Nod
...
JACK.
SOMEONE ELSE OPENED THE PORTAL. A WOMAN WHO WAS IN THE CROWD.
WHO?
I'VE NO IDEA. THERE WERE A COUPLE PEOPLE HERE WITH HER.
WHO ARE THEY?
THE LADY'S SISTER AND UH ... BOYFRIEND? NOT QUITE SURE.
I'LL TALK TO THEM, FIND OUT WHO SHE IS. OTHERWISE, THEY MIGHT NOT KEEP QUIET, AND THERE'S COPS AROUND.
BESIDES, THEY'RE GIVING ME FUNNY LOOKS ...

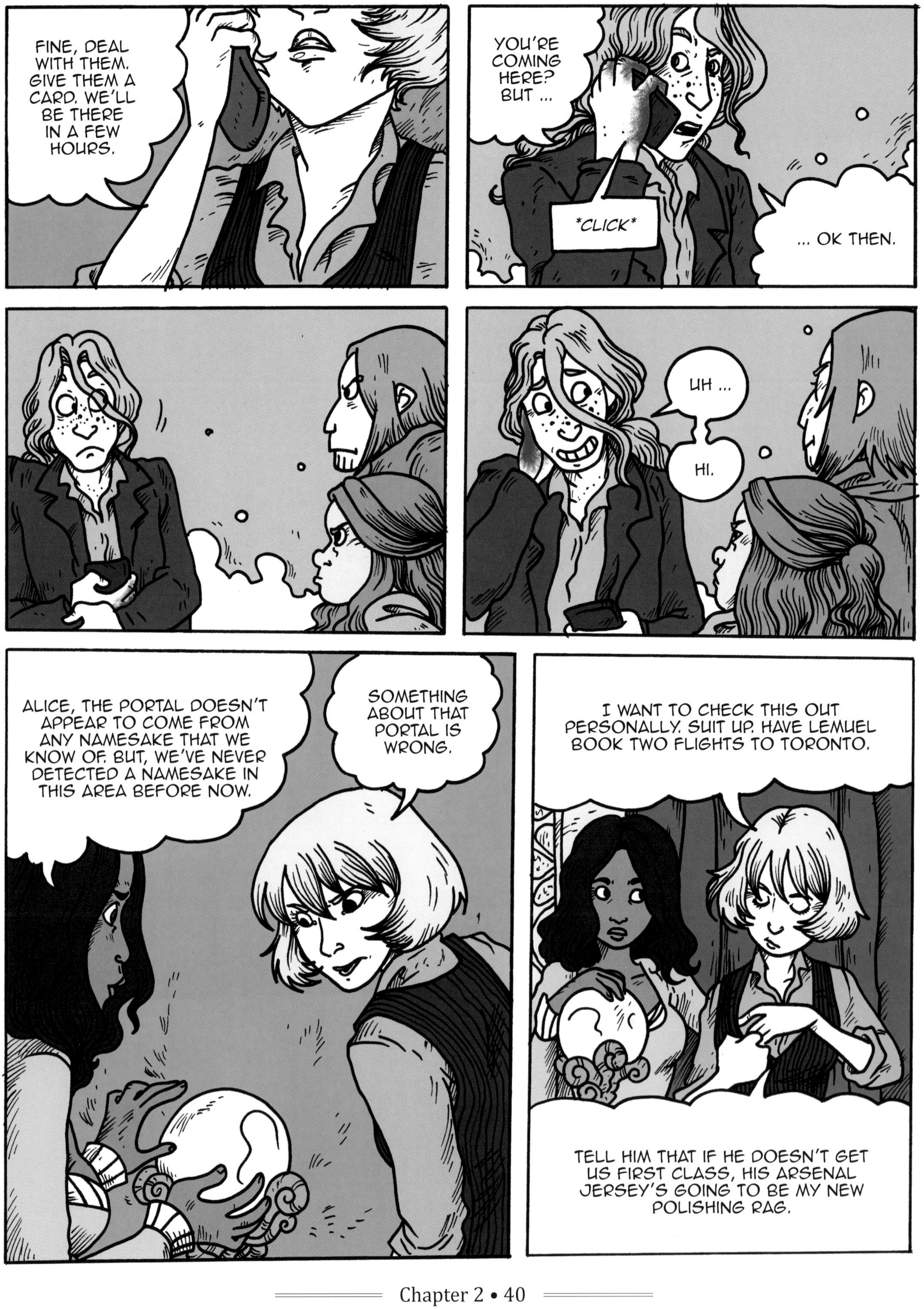
FINE, DEAL WITH THEM. GIVE THEM A CARD. WE'LL BE THERE IN A FEW HOURS.
YOU'RE COMING HERE? BUT ...
CLICK
... OK THEN.
UH ...
HI.
ALICE, THE PORTAL DOESN'T APPEAR TO COME FROM ANY NAMESAKE THAT WE KNOW OF. BUT, WE'VE NEVER DETECTED A NAMESAKE IN THIS AREA BEFORE NOW.
SOMETHING ABOUT THAT PORTAL IS WRONG.
I WANT TO CHECK THIS OUT PERSONALLY. SUIT UP. HAVE LEMUEL BOOK TWO FLIGHTS TO TORONTO.
TELL HIM THAT IF HE DOESN'T GET US FIRST CLASS, HIS ARSENAL JERSEY'S GOING TO BE MY NEW POLISHING RAG.

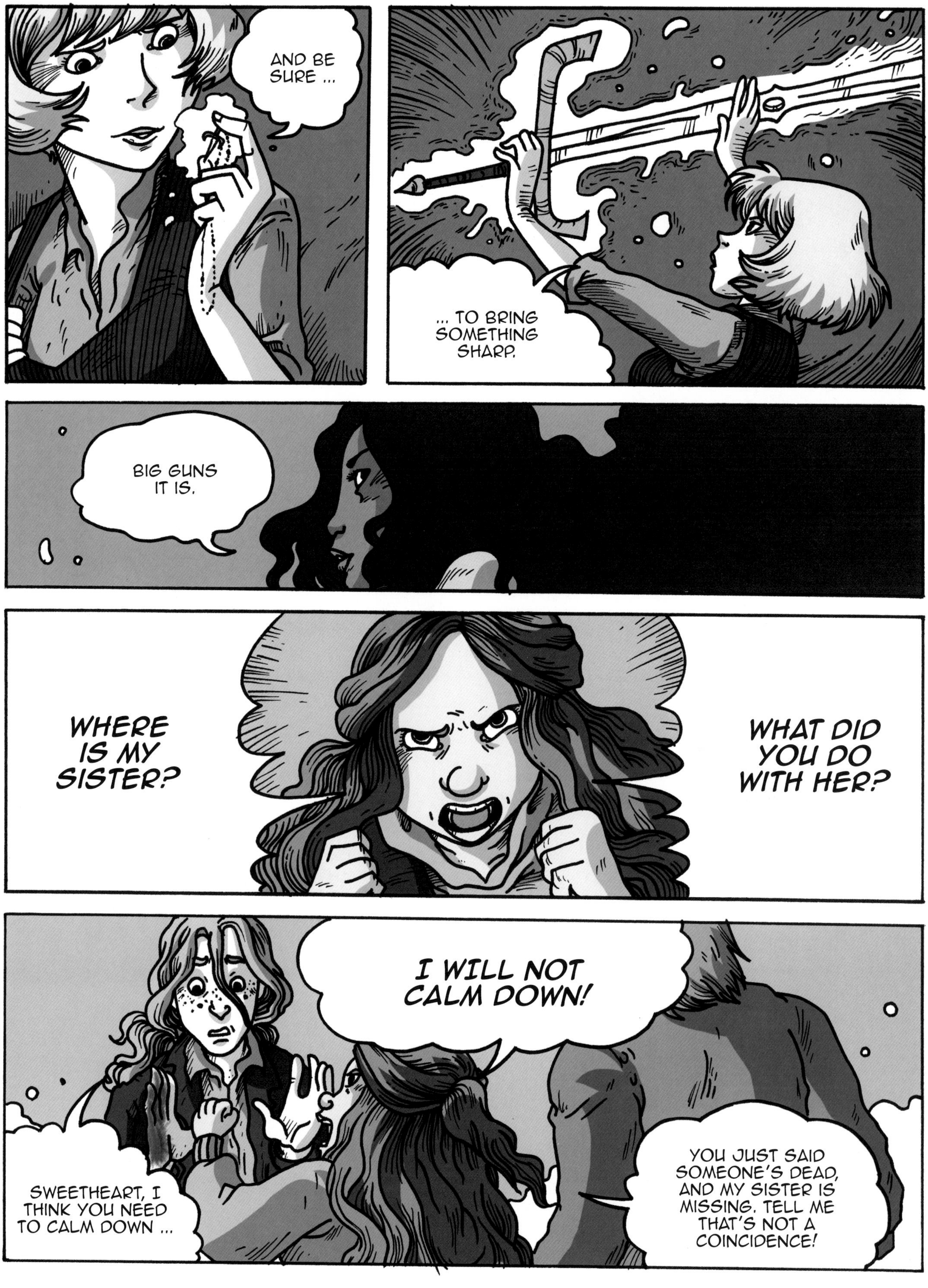
AND BE SURE ...
... TO BRING SOMETHING SHARP.
BIG GUNS IT IS.
WHERE IS MY SISTER?
WHAT DID YOU DO WITH HER?
SWEETHEART, I THINK YOU NEED TO CALM DOWN ...
I WILL NOT CALM DOWN!
YOU JUST SAID SOMEONE'S DEAD, AND MY SISTER IS MISSING. TELL ME THAT'S NOT A COINCIDENCE!

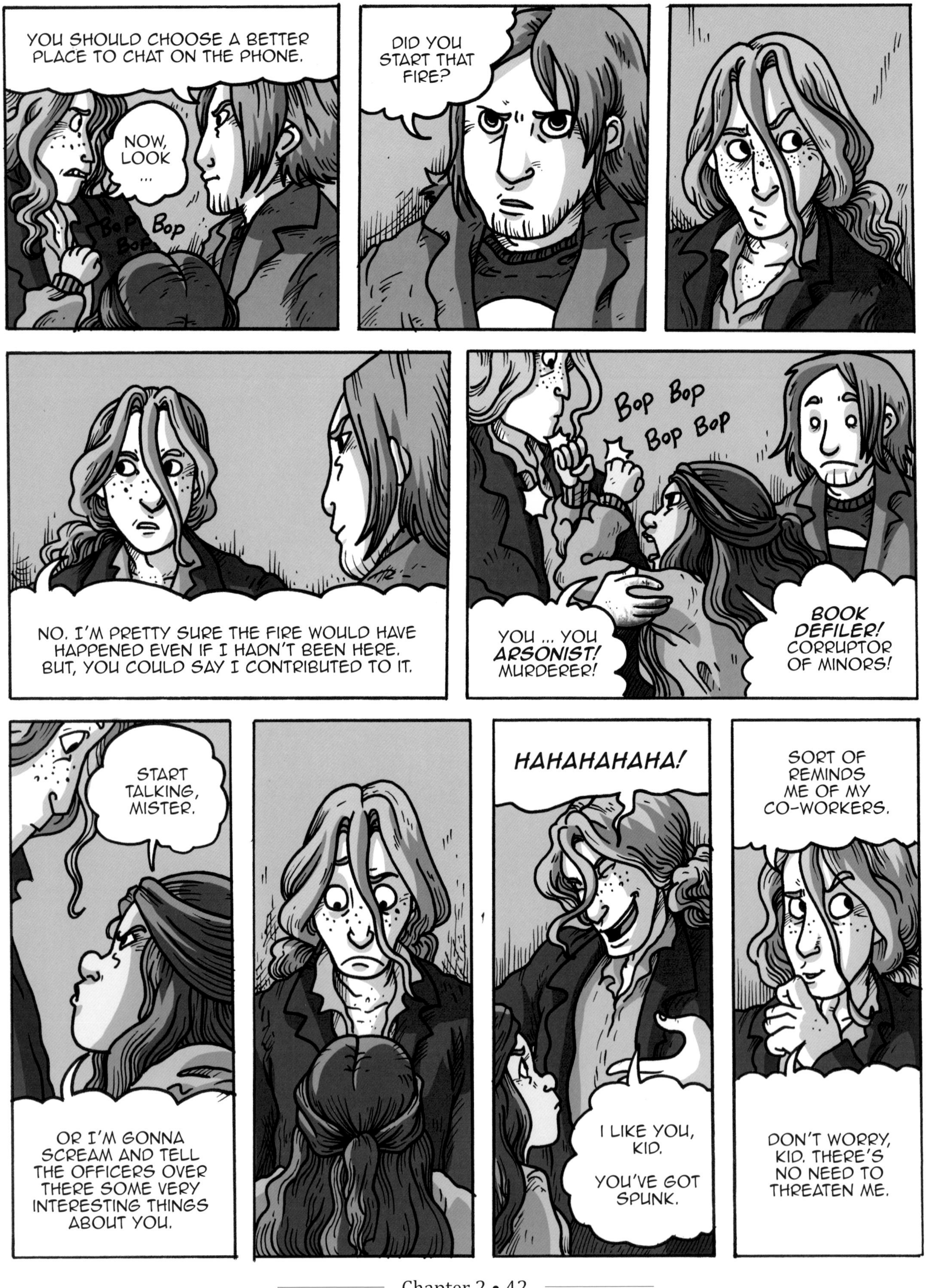
YOU SHOULD CHOOSE A BETTER PLACE TO CHAT ON THE PHONE.
NOW, LOOK ...
Bop Bop Bop
DID YOU START THAT FIRE?
NO. I'M PRETTY SURE THE FIRE WOULD HAVE HAPPENED EVEN IF I HADN'T BEEN HERE. BUT, YOU COULD SAY I CONTRIBUTED TO IT.
Bop Bop Bop Bop
YOU ... YOU ARSONIST! MURDERER!
BOOK DEFILER! CORRUPTOR OF MINORS!
START TALKING, MISTER.
OR I'M GONNA SCREAM AND TELL THE OFFICERS OVER THERE SOME VERY INTERESTING THINGS ABOUT YOU.
HAHAHAHAHA!
I LIKE YOU, KID.
YOU'VE GOT SPUNK.
SORT OF REMINDS ME OF MY CO-WORKERS.
DON'T WORRY, KID. THERE'S NO NEED TO THREATEN ME.

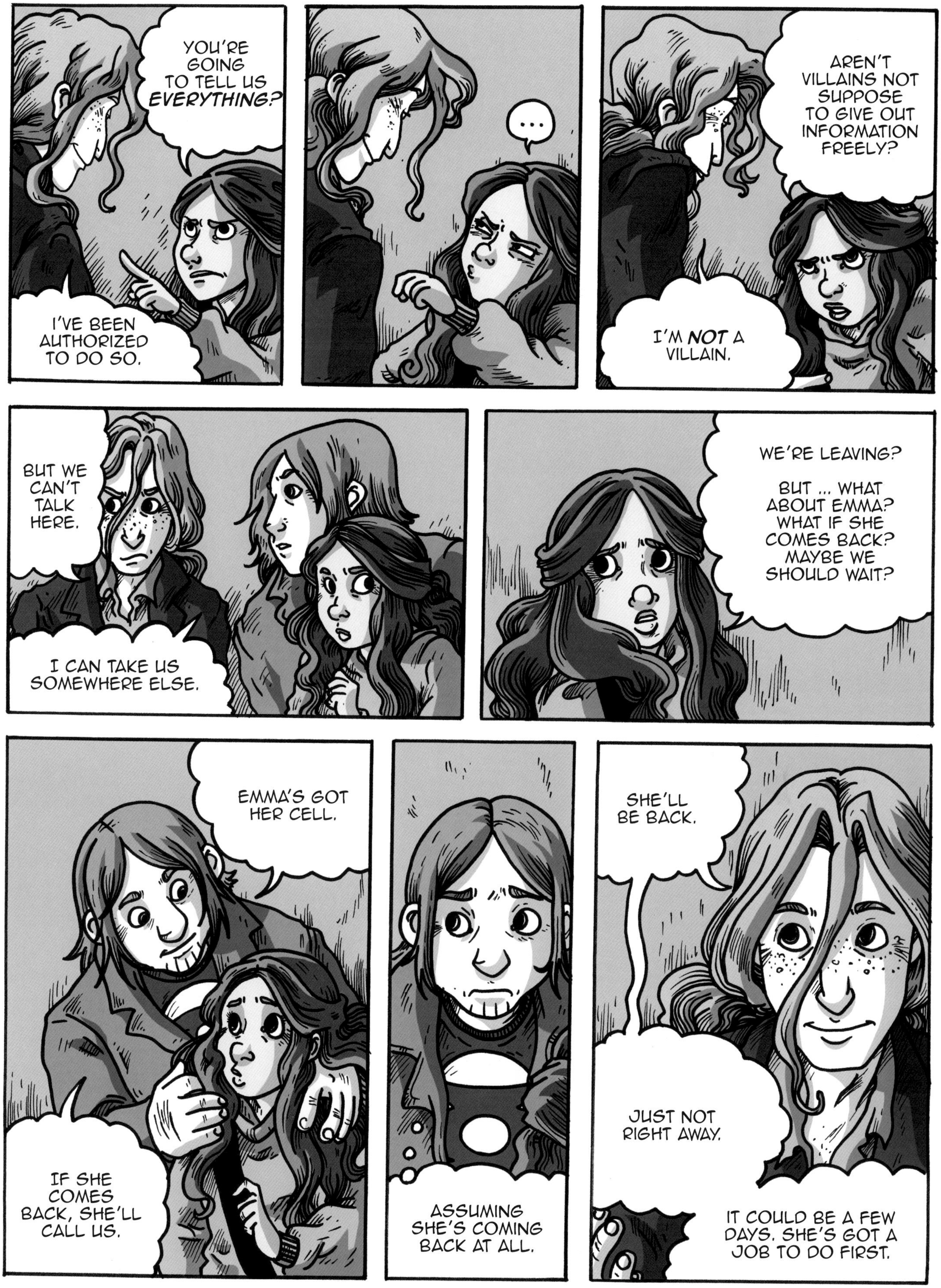
YOU'RE GOING TO TELL US EVERYTHING?
I'VE BEEN AUTHORIZED TO DO SO.
...
AREN'T VILLAINS NOT SUPPOSE TO GIVE OUT INFORMATION FREELY?
I'M NOT A VILLAIN.
BUT WE CAN'T TALK HERE.
I CAN TAKE US SOMEWHERE ELSE.
WE'RE LEAVING?
BUT ... WHAT ABOUT EMMA? WHAT IF SHE COMES BACK? MAYBE WE SHOULD WAIT?
EMMA'S GOT HER CELL.
IF SHE COMES BACK, SHE'LL CALL US.
ASSUMING SHE'S COMING BACK AT ALL.
SHE'LL BE BACK.
JUST NOT RIGHT AWAY.
IT COULD BE A FEW DAYS. SHE'S GOT A JOB TO DO FIRST.

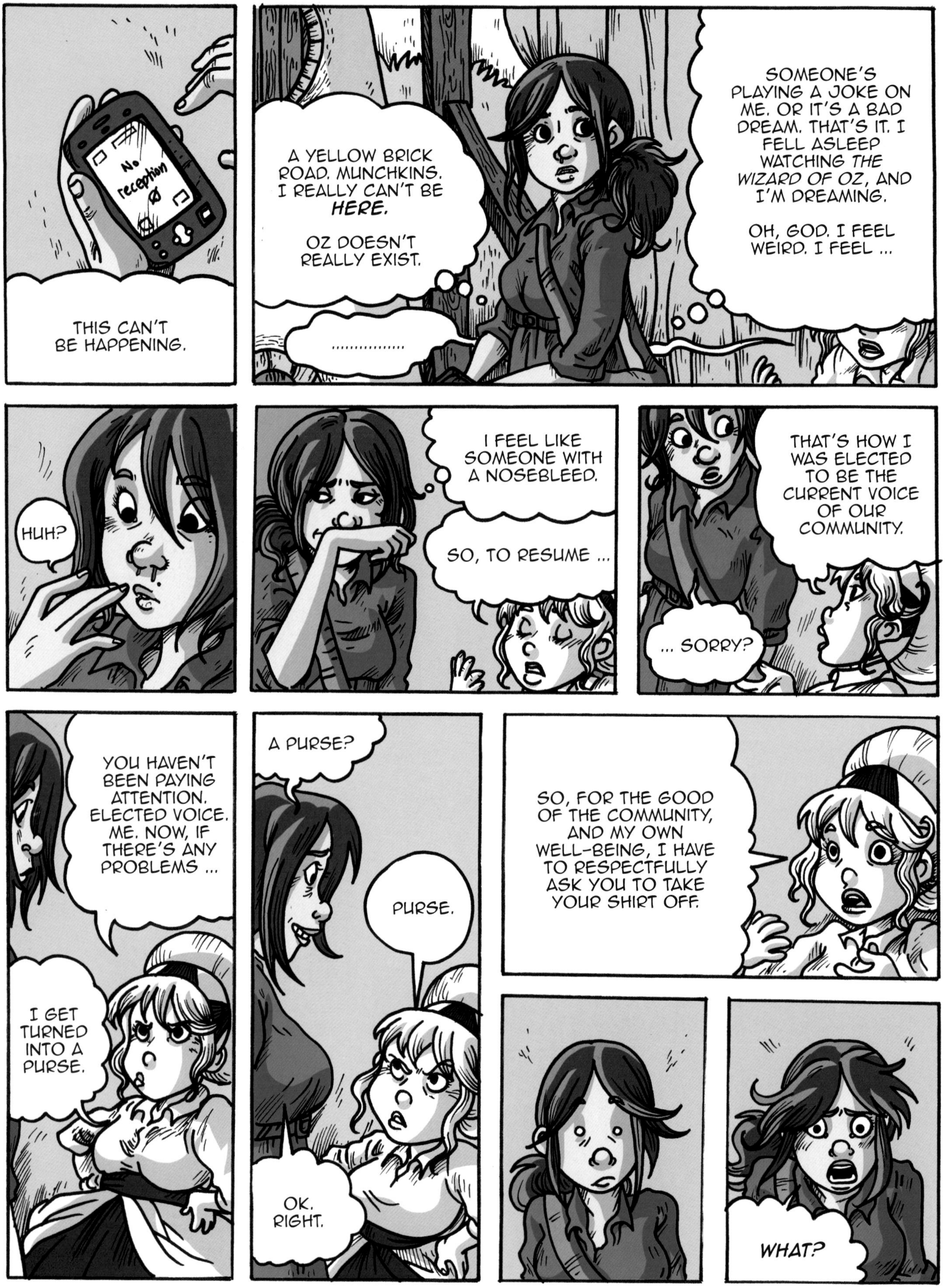
No reception
THIS CAN'T BE HAPPENING.
A YELLOW BRICK ROAD. MUNCHKINS. I REALLY CAN'T BE *HERE.*
OZ DOESN'T REALLY EXIST.
....
SOMEONE'S PLAYING A JOKE ON ME. OR IT'S A BAD DREAM. THAT'S IT. I FELL ASLEEP WATCHING *THE WIZARD OF OZ*, AND I'M DREAMING.
OH, GOD. I FEEL WEIRD. I FEEL ...
HUH?
I FEEL LIKE SOMEONE WITH A NOSEBLEED.
SO, TO RESUME ...
THAT'S HOW I WAS ELECTED TO BE THE CURRENT VOICE OF OUR COMMUNITY.
... SORRY?
YOU HAVEN'T BEEN PAYING ATTENTION. ELECTED VOICE. ME. NOW, IF THERE'S ANY PROBLEMS ...
I GET TURNED INTO A PURSE.
A PURSE?
PURSE.
OK. RIGHT.
SO, FOR THE GOOD OF THE COMMUNITY, AND MY OWN WELL-BEING, I HAVE TO RESPECTFULLY ASK YOU TO TAKE YOUR SHIRT OFF.
WHAT?

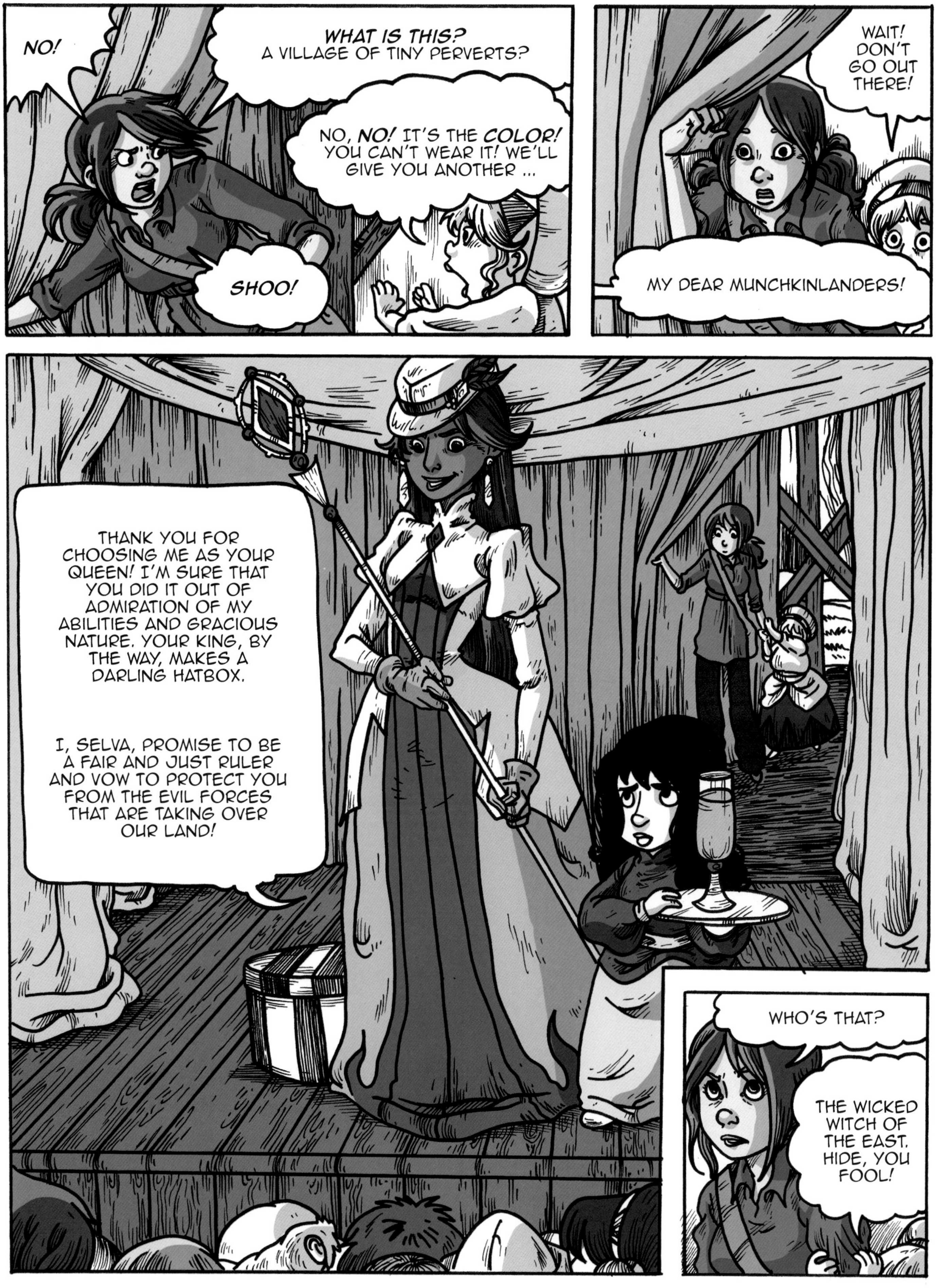
NO!
WHAT IS THIS? A VILLAGE OF TINY PERVERTS?
NO, ***NO!*** IT'S THE ***COLOR!*** YOU CAN'T WEAR IT! WE'LL GIVE YOU ANOTHER ...
SHOO!
WAIT! DON'T GO OUT THERE!
MY DEAR MUNCHKINLANDERS!
THANK YOU FOR CHOOSING ME AS YOUR QUEEN! I'M SURE THAT YOU DID IT OUT OF ADMIRATION OF MY ABILITIES AND GRACIOUS NATURE. YOUR KING, BY THE WAY, MAKES A DARLING HATBOX.
I, SELVA, PROMISE TO BE A FAIR AND JUST RULER AND VOW TO PROTECT YOU FROM THE EVIL FORCES THAT ARE TAKING OVER OUR LAND!
WHO'S THAT?
THE WICKED WITCH OF THE EAST. HIDE, YOU FOOL!

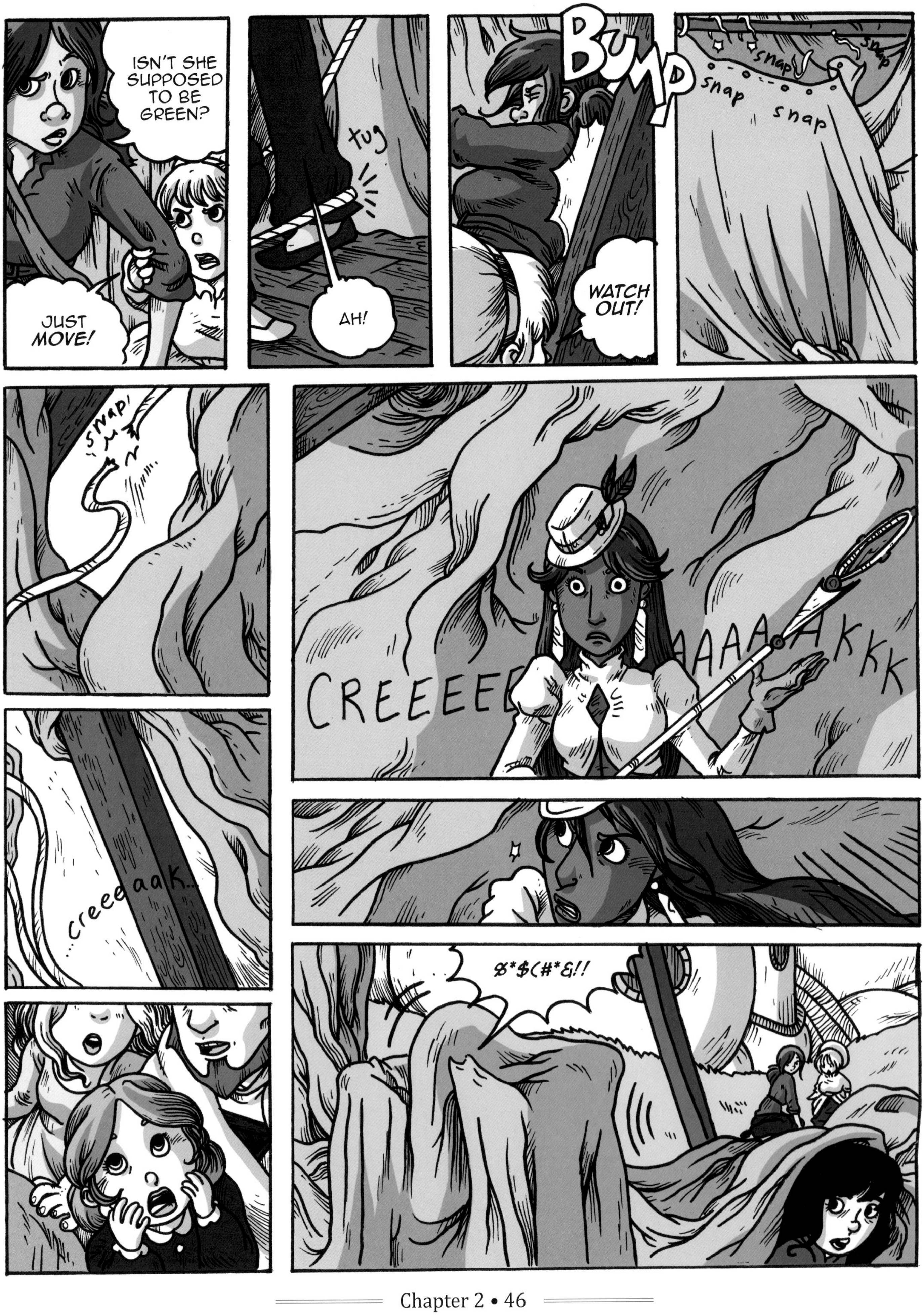
ISN'T SHE SUPPOSED TO BE GREEN?
JUST MOVE!
tug
AH!
BUMP!
WATCH OUT!
snap
snap
snap
snap
snap
SNAP!
CREEEEEAAAAAKKK
creeeaak...
&*$(#*&!!

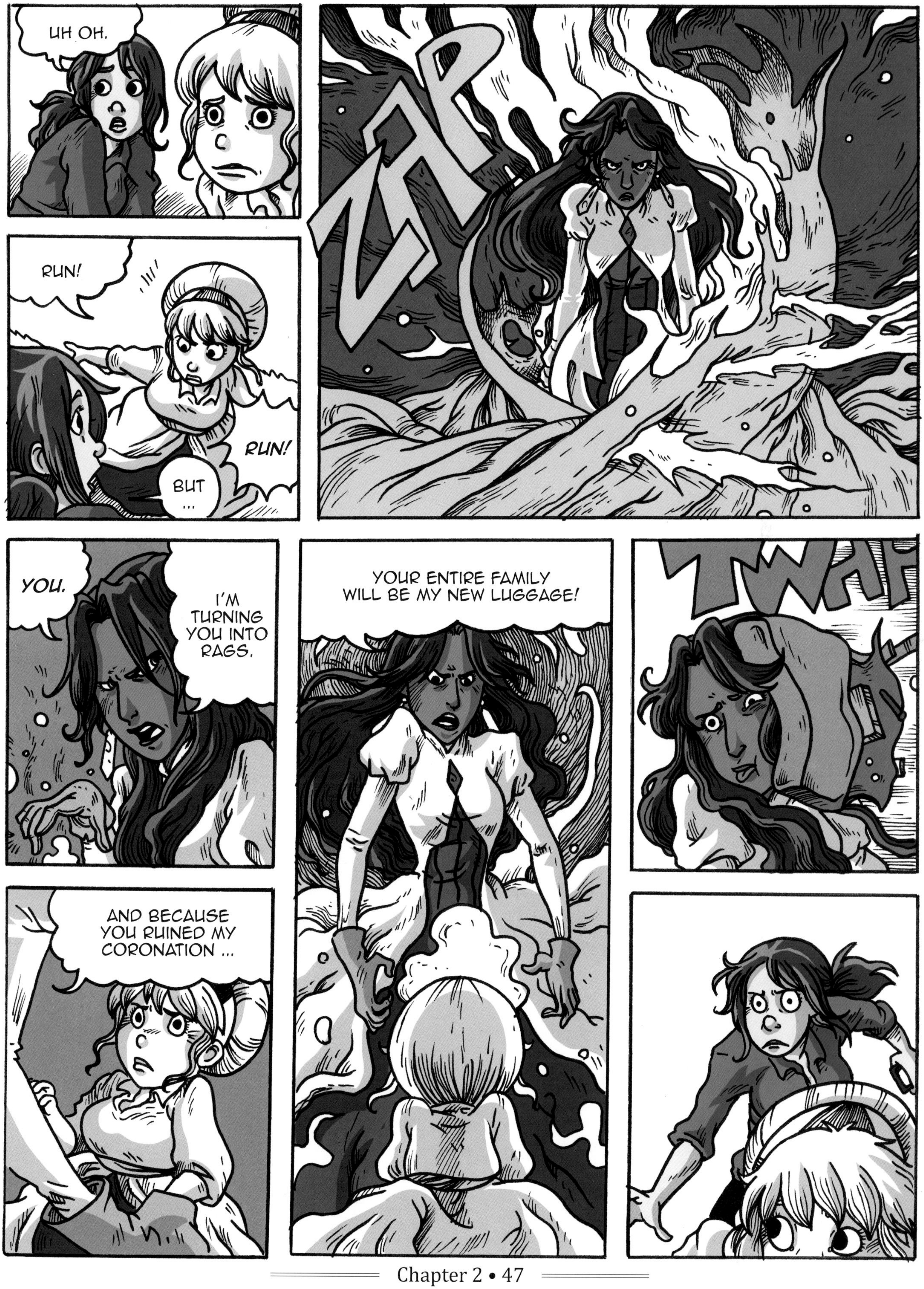
UH OH.
ZAP
RUN!
RUN!
BUT ...
YOU.
I'M TURNING YOU INTO RAGS.
YOUR ENTIRE FAMILY WILL BE MY NEW LUGGAGE!
AND BECAUSE YOU RUINED MY CORONATION ...

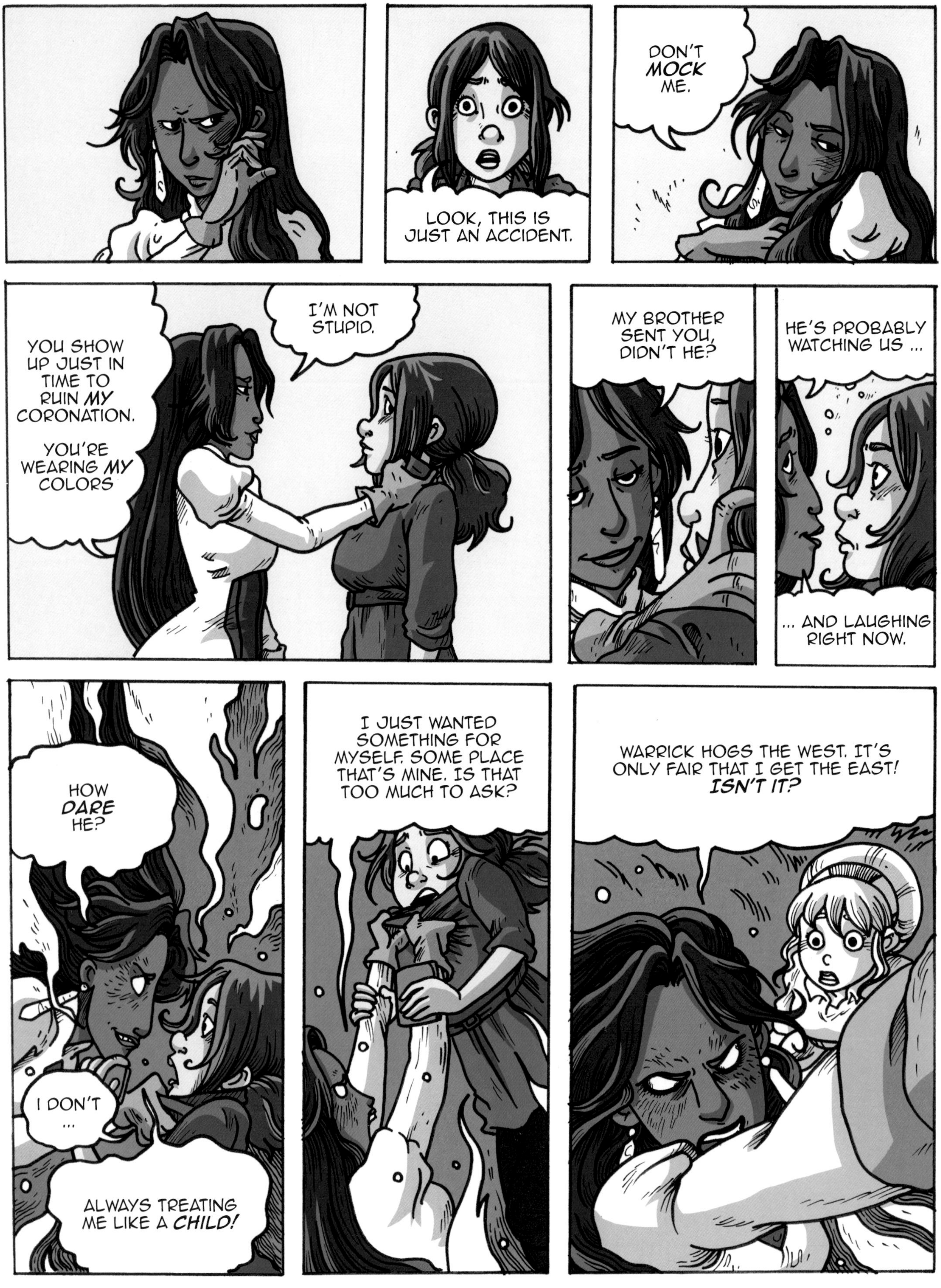

LOOK, THIS IS JUST AN ACCIDENT.
DON'T MOCK ME.
YOU SHOW UP JUST IN TIME TO RUIN MY CORONATION.
YOU'RE WEARING MY COLORS
I'M NOT STUPID.
MY BROTHER SENT YOU, DIDN'T HE?
HE'S PROBABLY WATCHING US ...
... AND LAUGHING RIGHT NOW.
HOW DARE HE?
I DON'T ...
ALWAYS TREATING ME LIKE A CHILD!
I JUST WANTED SOMETHING FOR MYSELF. SOME PLACE THAT'S MINE. IS THAT TOO MUCH TO ASK?
WARRICK HOGS THE WEST. IT'S ONLY FAIR THAT I GET THE EAST! ISN'T IT?

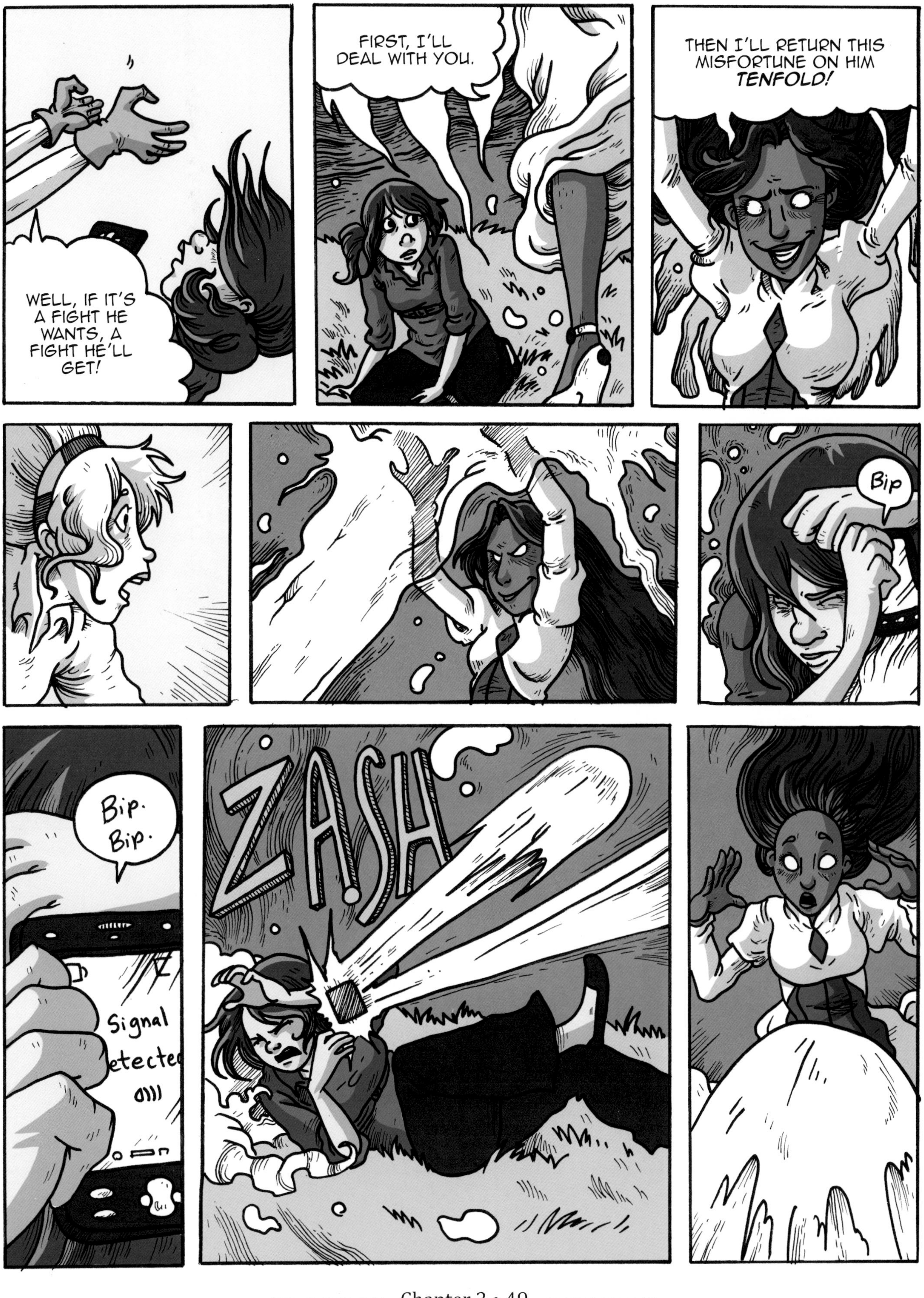
WELL, IF IT'S A FIGHT HE WANTS, A FIGHT HE'LL GET!
FIRST, I'LL DEAL WITH YOU.
THEN I'LL RETURN THIS MISFORTUNE ON HIM *TENFOLD!*
Bip
Bip. Bip.
Signal
etecte
ZASH

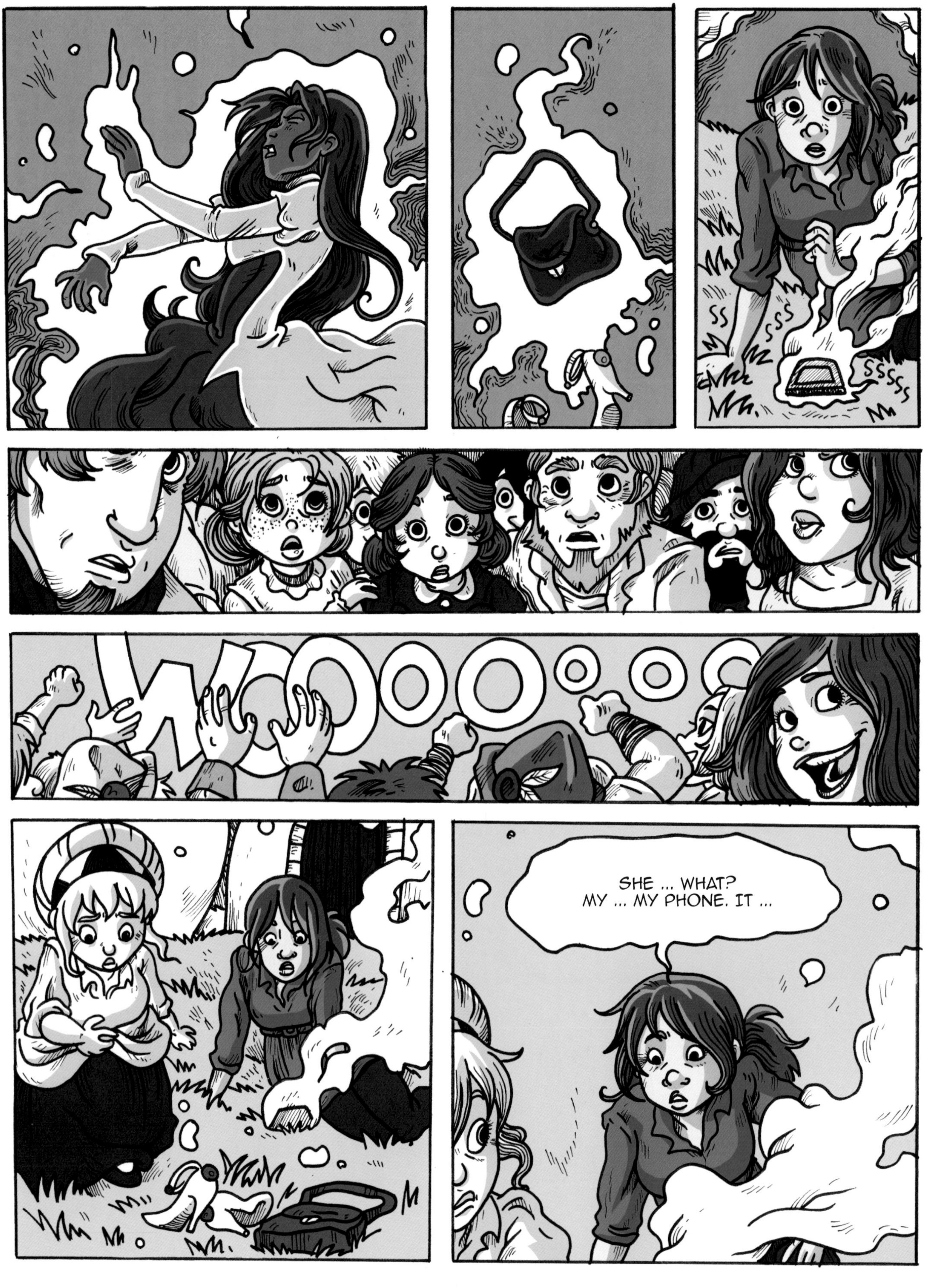
SS
SSS
SSSSS
WOOOOOOO
SHE ... WHAT?
MY ... MY PHONE. IT ...

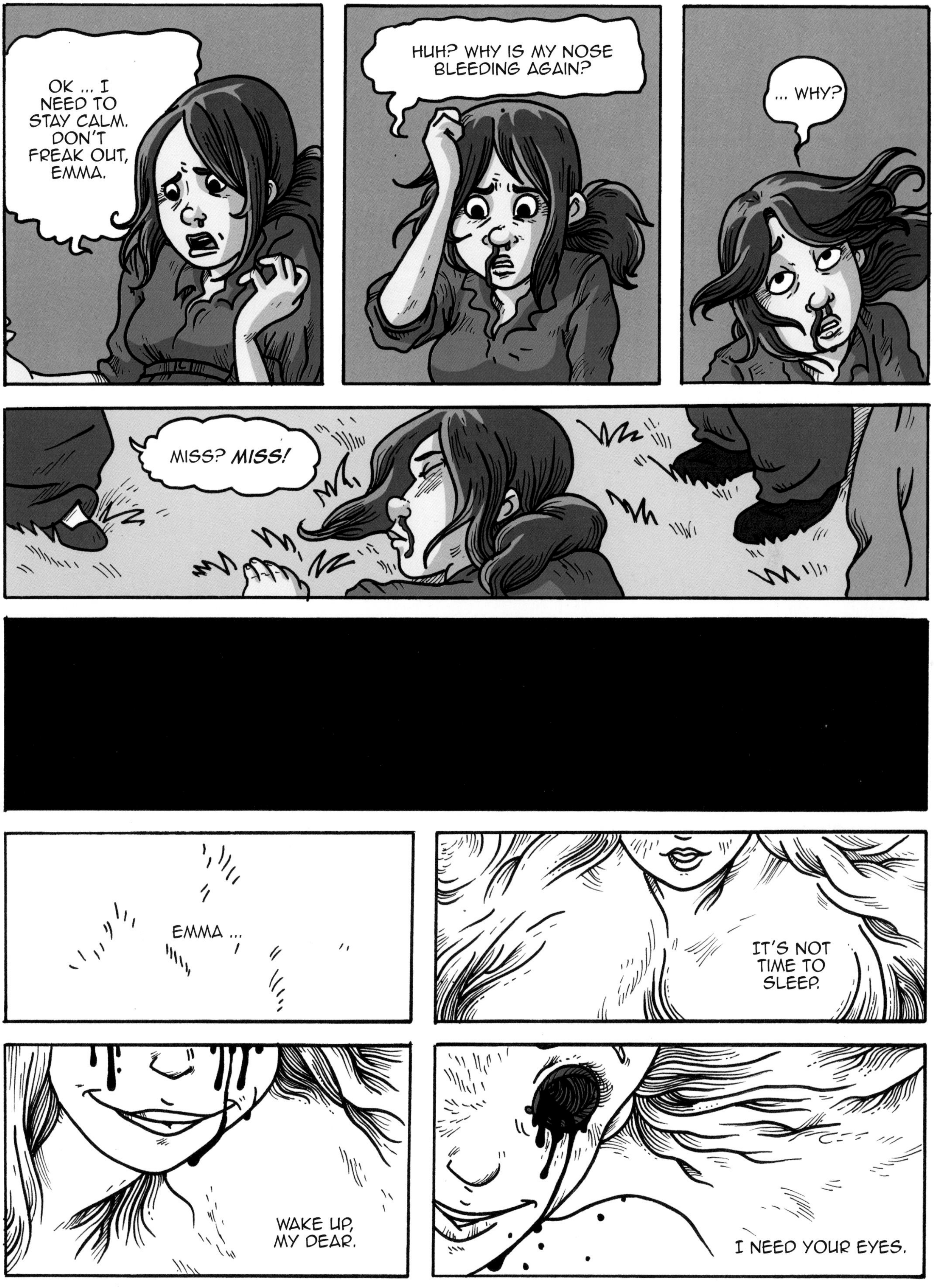
OK ... I NEED TO STAY CALM. DON'T FREAK OUT, EMMA.
HUH? WHY IS MY NOSE BLEEDING AGAIN?
... WHY?
MISS? *MISS!*
EMMA ...
IT'S NOT TIME TO SLEEP.
WAKE UP, MY DEAR.
I NEED YOUR EYES.

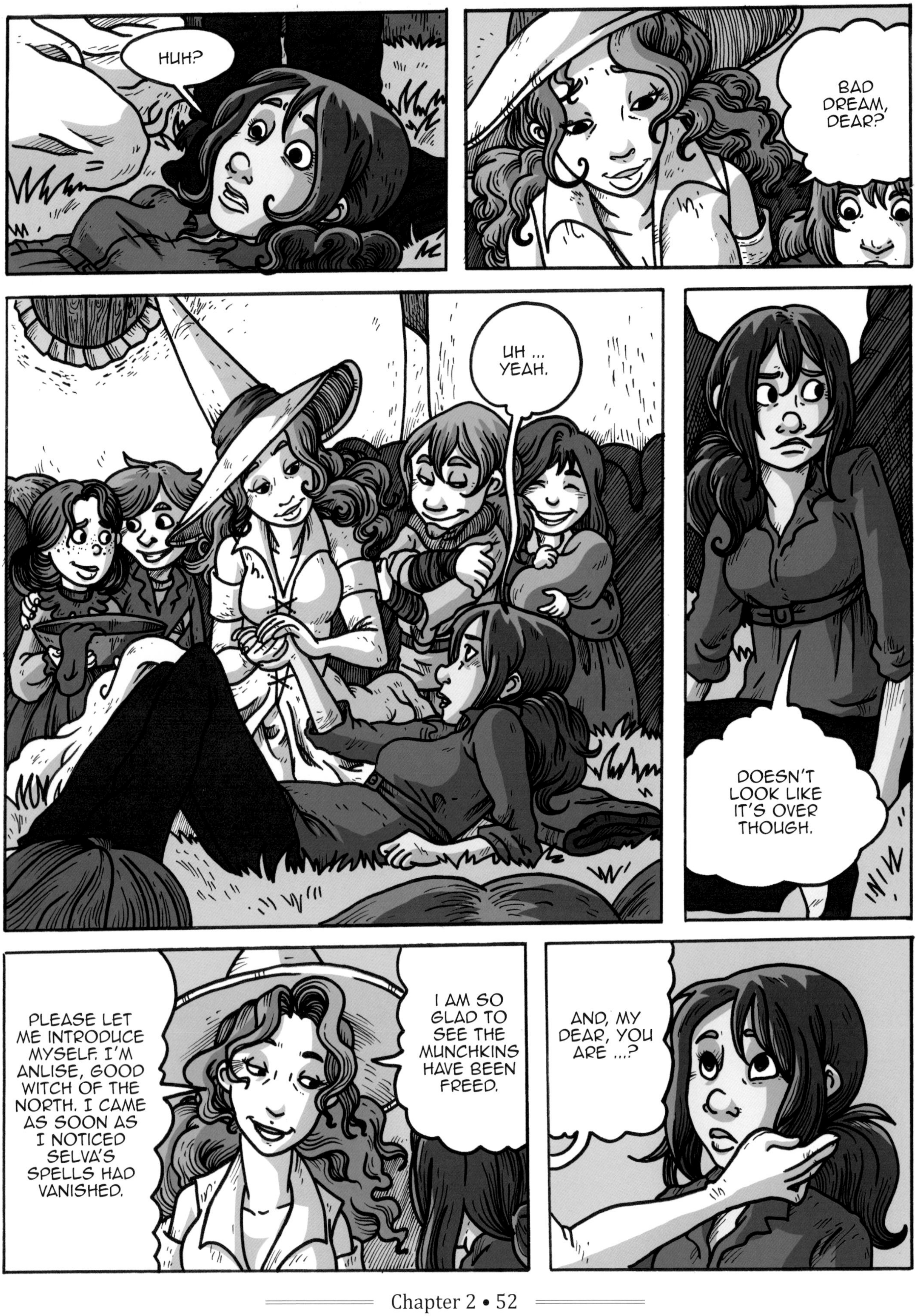
HUH?
BAD DREAM, DEAR?
UH ... YEAH.
DOESN'T LOOK LIKE IT'S OVER THOUGH.
PLEASE LET ME INTRODUCE MYSELF. I'M ANLISE, GOOD WITCH OF THE NORTH. I CAME AS SOON AS I NOTICED SELVA'S SPELLS HAD VANISHED.
I AM SO GLAD TO SEE THE MUNCHKINS HAVE BEEN FREED.
AND, MY DEAR, YOU ARE ...?

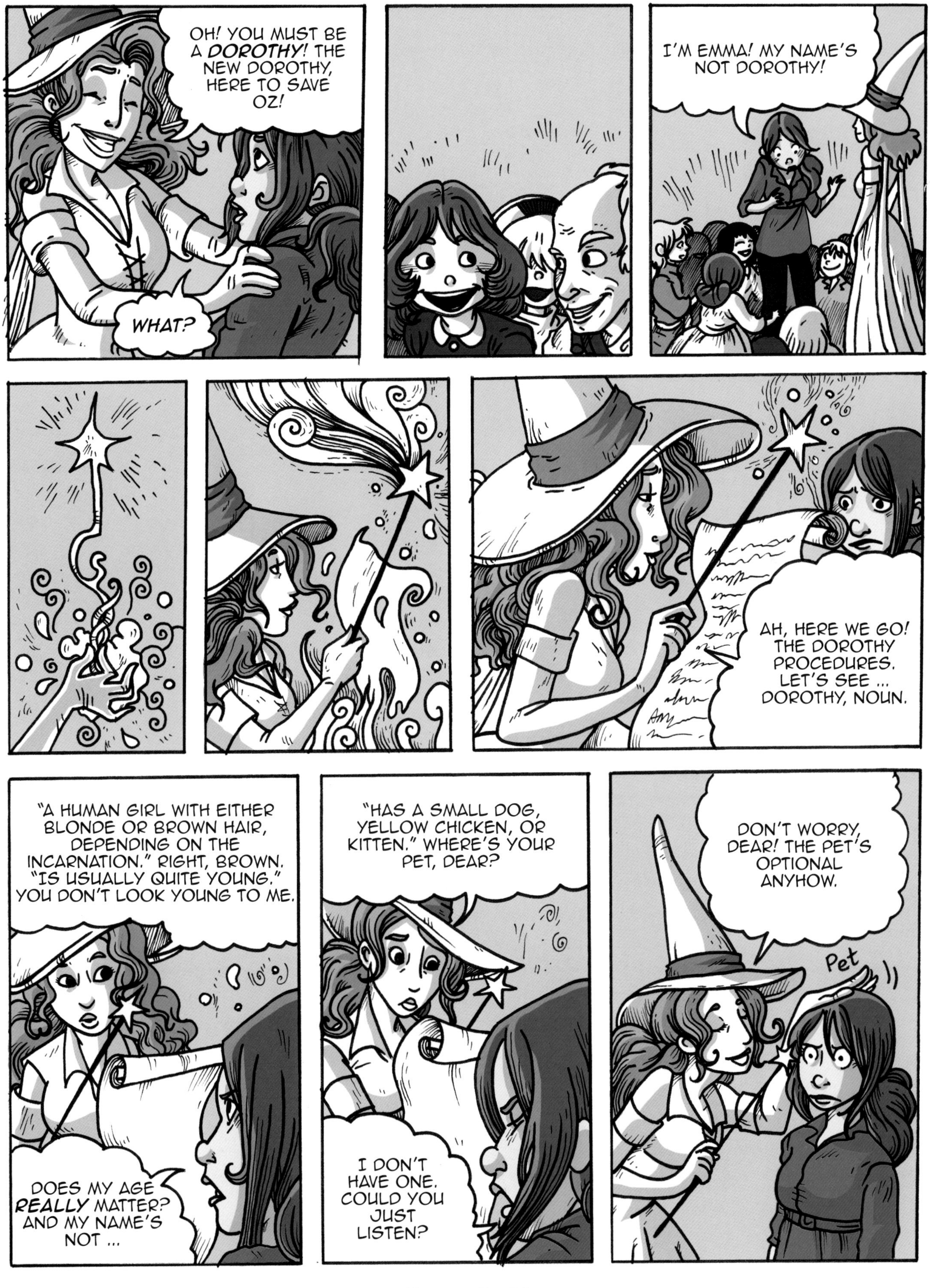
OH! YOU MUST BE A **DOROTHY**! THE NEW DOROTHY, HERE TO SAVE OZ!
WHAT?
I'M EMMA! MY NAME'S NOT DOROTHY!
AH, HERE WE GO! THE DOROTHY PROCEDURES. LET'S SEE ... DOROTHY, NOUN.
"A HUMAN GIRL WITH EITHER BLONDE OR BROWN HAIR, DEPENDING ON THE INCARNATION." RIGHT, BROWN. "IS USUALLY QUITE YOUNG." YOU DON'T LOOK YOUNG TO ME.
DOES MY AGE **REALLY** MATTER? AND MY NAME'S NOT ...
"HAS A SMALL DOG, YELLOW CHICKEN, OR KITTEN." WHERE'S YOUR PET, DEAR?
I DON'T HAVE ONE. COULD YOU JUST LISTEN?
DON'T WORRY, DEAR! THE PET'S OPTIONAL ANYHOW.
Pet

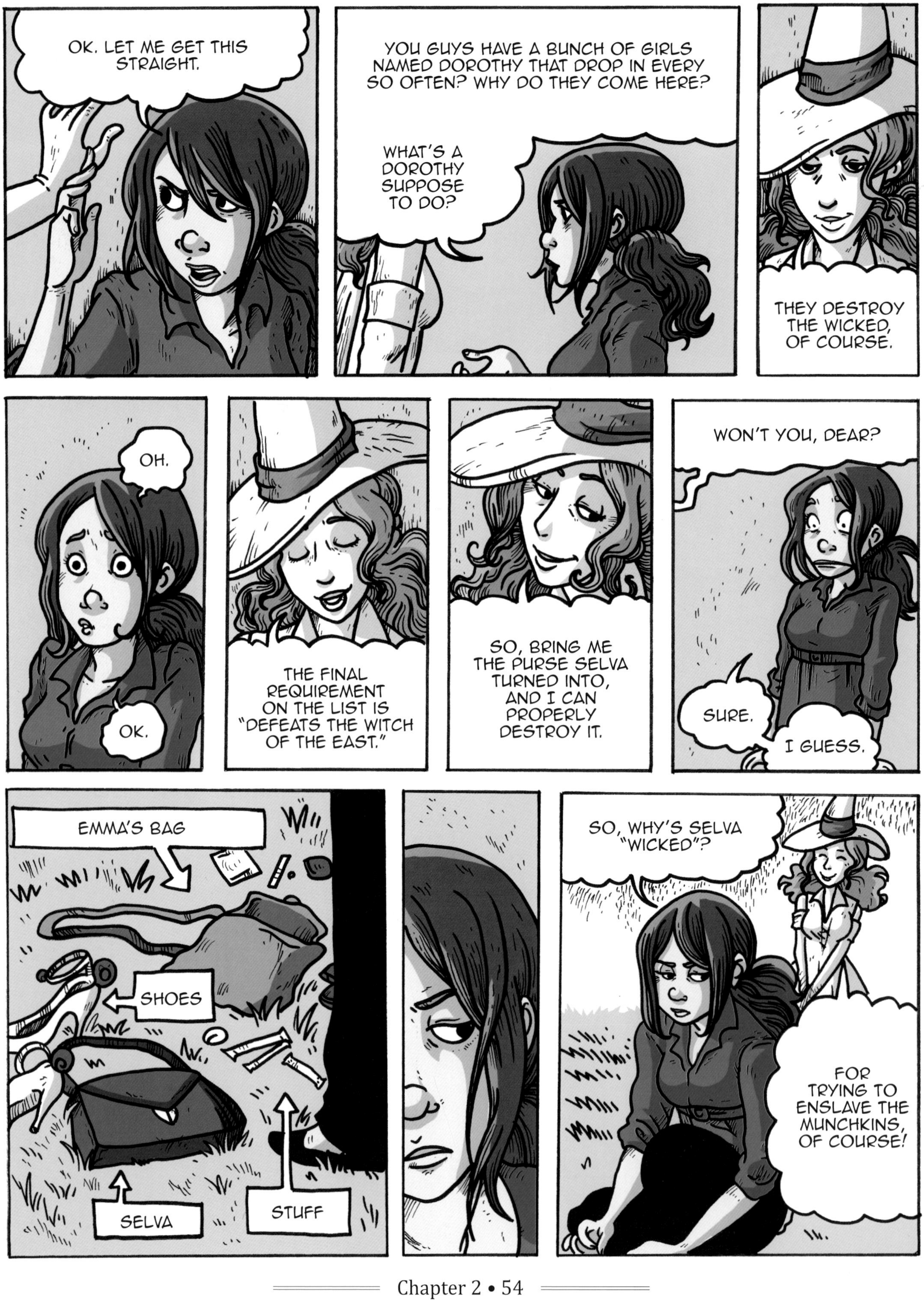

OK. LET ME GET THIS STRAIGHT.
YOU GUYS HAVE A BUNCH OF GIRLS NAMED DOROTHY THAT DROP IN EVERY SO OFTEN? WHY DO THEY COME HERE?
WHAT'S A DOROTHY SUPPOSE TO DO?
THEY DESTROY THE WICKED, OF COURSE.
OH.
OK.
THE FINAL REQUIREMENT ON THE LIST IS "DEFEATS THE WITCH OF THE EAST."
SO, BRING ME THE PURSE SELVA TURNED INTO, AND I CAN PROPERLY DESTROY IT.
WON'T YOU, DEAR?
SURE.
I GUESS.
EMMA'S BAG
SHOES
SELVA
STUFF
SO, WHY'S SELVA "WICKED"?
FOR TRYING TO ENSLAVE THE MUNCHKINS, OF COURSE!

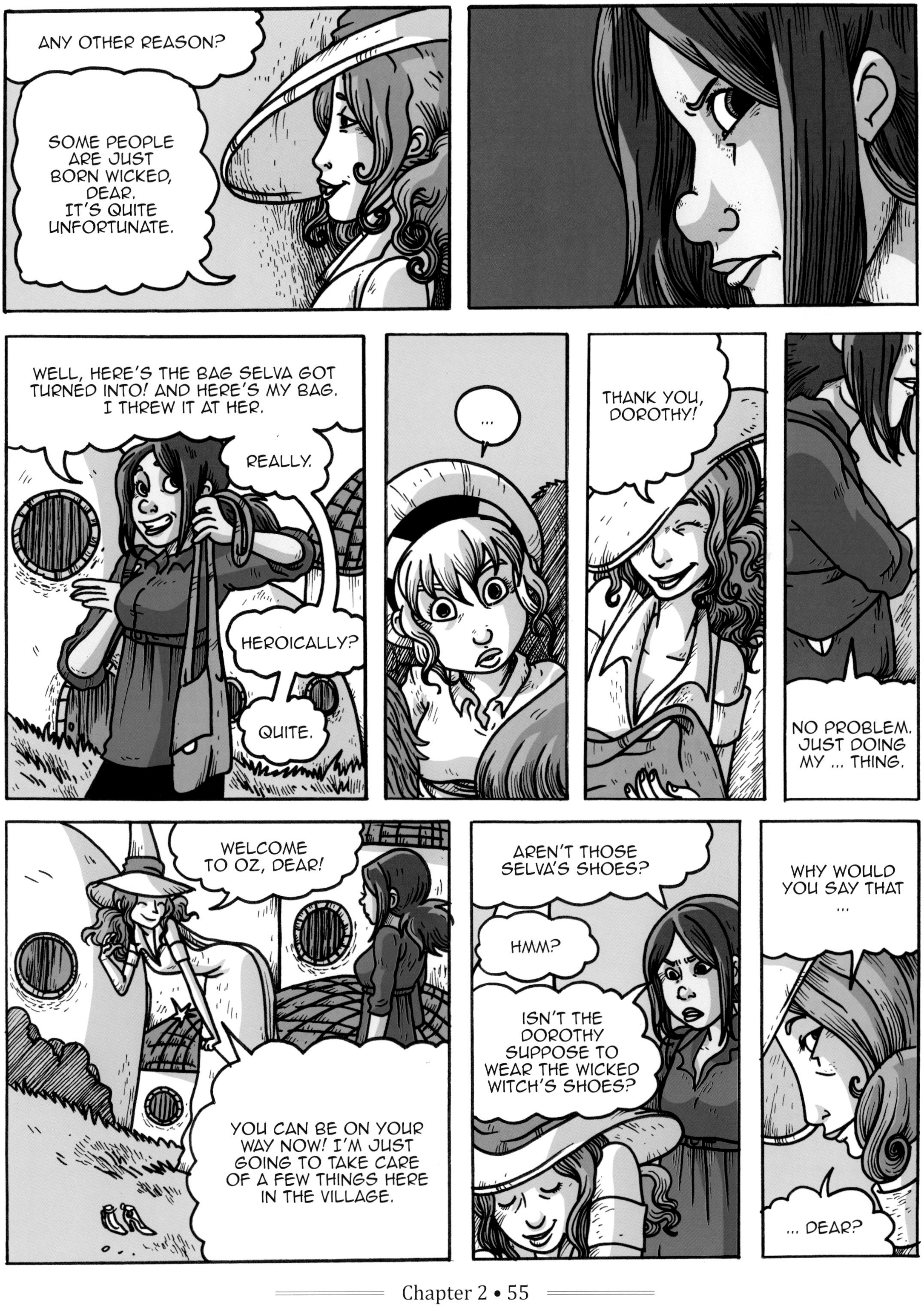
ANY OTHER REASON?
SOME PEOPLE ARE JUST BORN WICKED, DEAR. IT'S QUITE UNFORTUNATE.
WELL, HERE'S THE BAG SELVA GOT TURNED INTO! AND HERE'S MY BAG. I THREW IT AT HER.
REALLY.
HEROICALLY?
QUITE.
...
THANK YOU, DOROTHY!
NO PROBLEM. JUST DOING MY ... THING.
WELCOME TO OZ, DEAR!
YOU CAN BE ON YOUR WAY NOW! I'M JUST GOING TO TAKE CARE OF A FEW THINGS HERE IN THE VILLAGE.
AREN'T THOSE SELVA'S SHOES?
HMM?
ISN'T THE DOROTHY SUPPOSE TO WEAR THE WICKED WITCH'S SHOES?
WHY WOULD YOU SAY THAT ...
... DEAR?

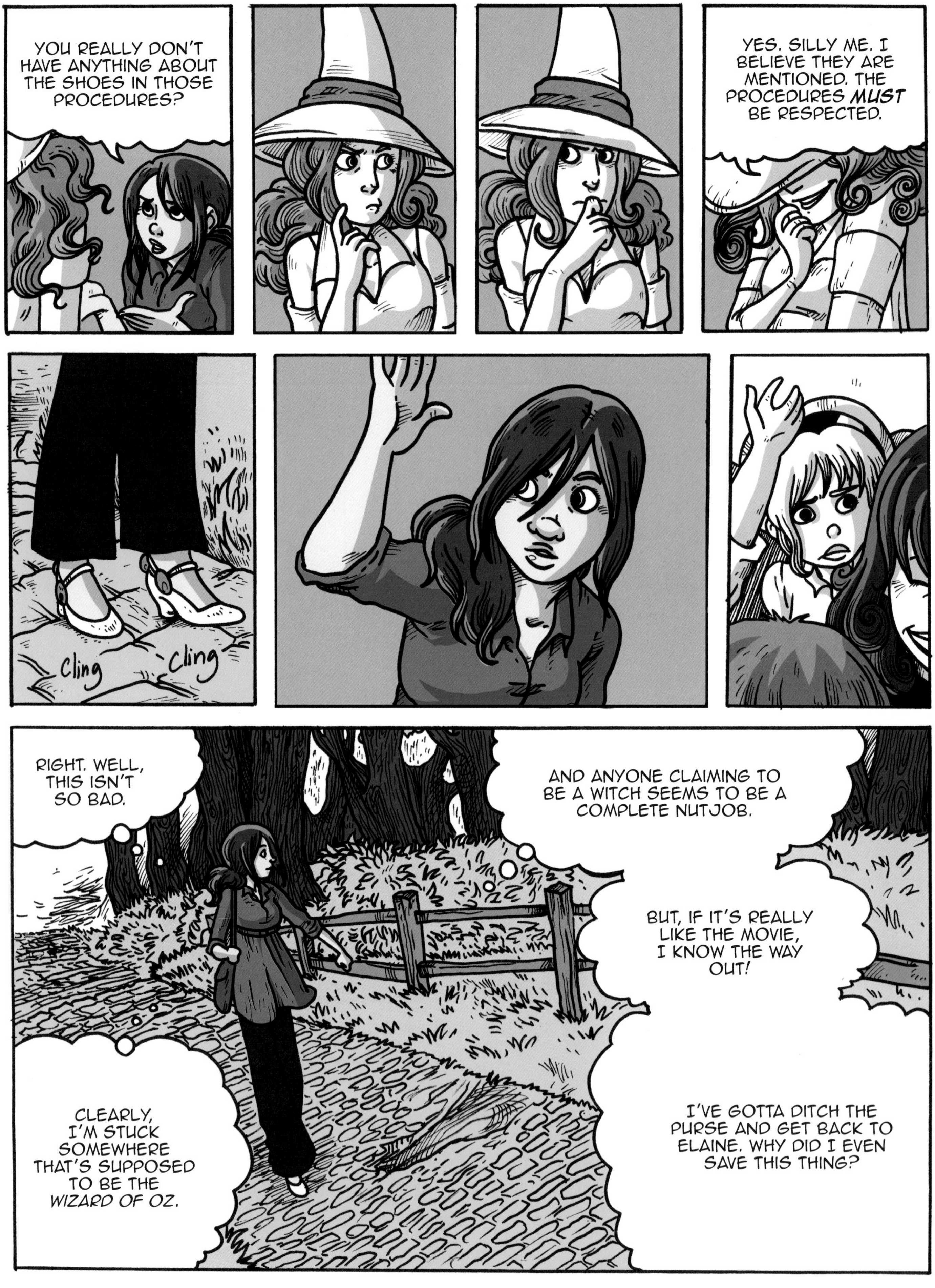
YOU REALLY DON'T HAVE ANYTHING ABOUT THE SHOES IN THOSE PROCEDURES?
YES. SILLY ME. I BELIEVE THEY ARE MENTIONED. THE PROCEDURES MUST BE RESPECTED.
Cling
Cling
RIGHT. WELL, THIS ISN'T SO BAD.
CLEARLY, I'M STUCK SOMEWHERE THAT'S SUPPOSED TO BE THE WIZARD OF OZ.
AND ANYONE CLAIMING TO BE A WITCH SEEMS TO BE A COMPLETE NUTJOB.
BUT, IF IT'S REALLY LIKE THE MOVIE, I KNOW THE WAY OUT!
I'VE GOTTA DITCH THE PURSE AND GET BACK TO ELAINE. WHY DID I EVEN SAVE THIS THING?

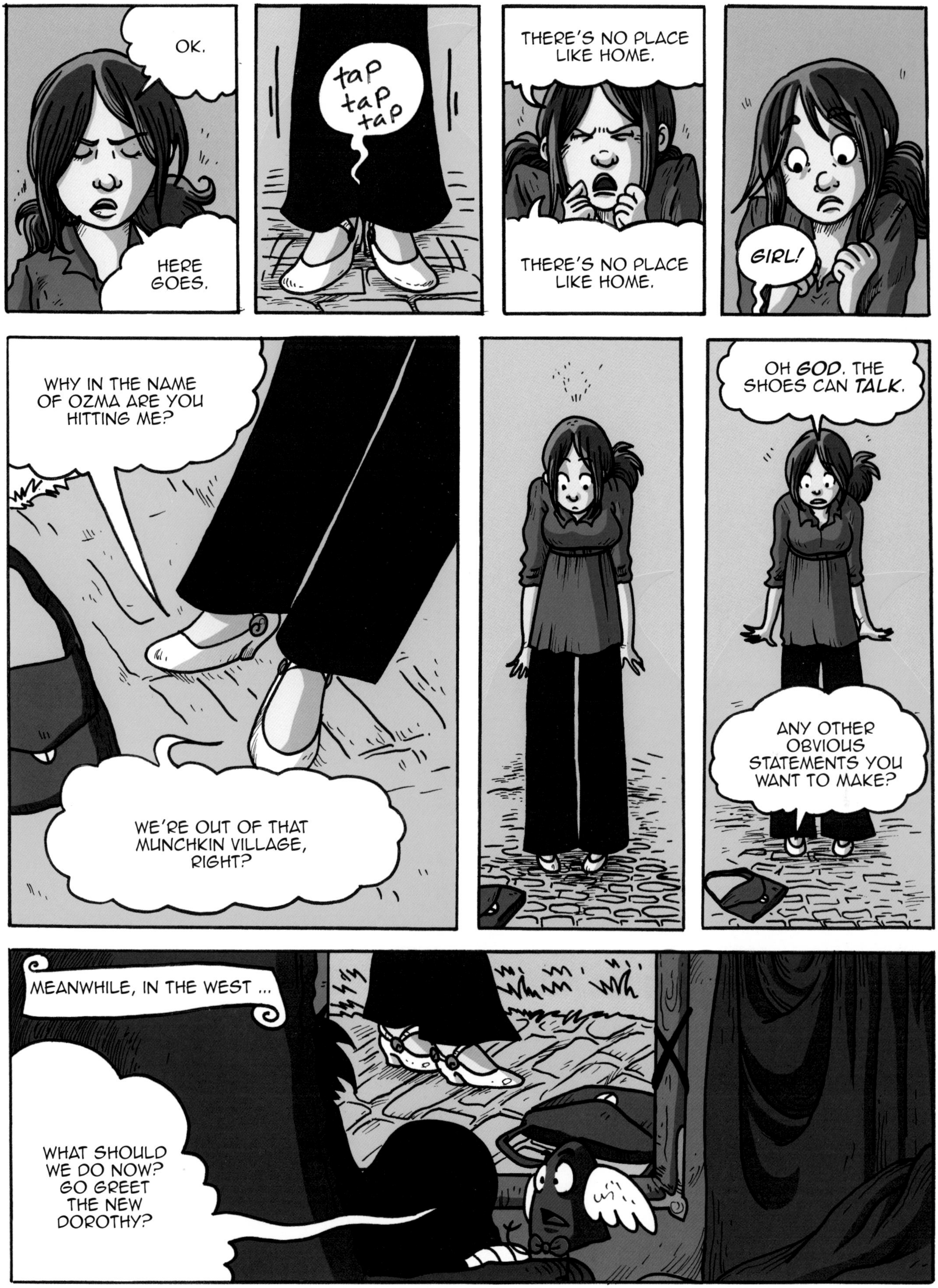
OK.
HERE GOES.
tap tap tap
THERE'S NO PLACE LIKE HOME.
THERE'S NO PLACE LIKE HOME.
GIRL!
WHY IN THE NAME OF OZMA ARE YOU HITTING ME?
WE'RE OUT OF THAT MUNCHKIN VILLAGE, RIGHT?
OH GOD. THE SHOES CAN TALK.
ANY OTHER OBVIOUS STATEMENTS YOU WANT TO MAKE?
MEANWHILE, IN THE WEST ...
WHAT SHOULD WE DO NOW? GO GREET THE NEW DOROTHY?

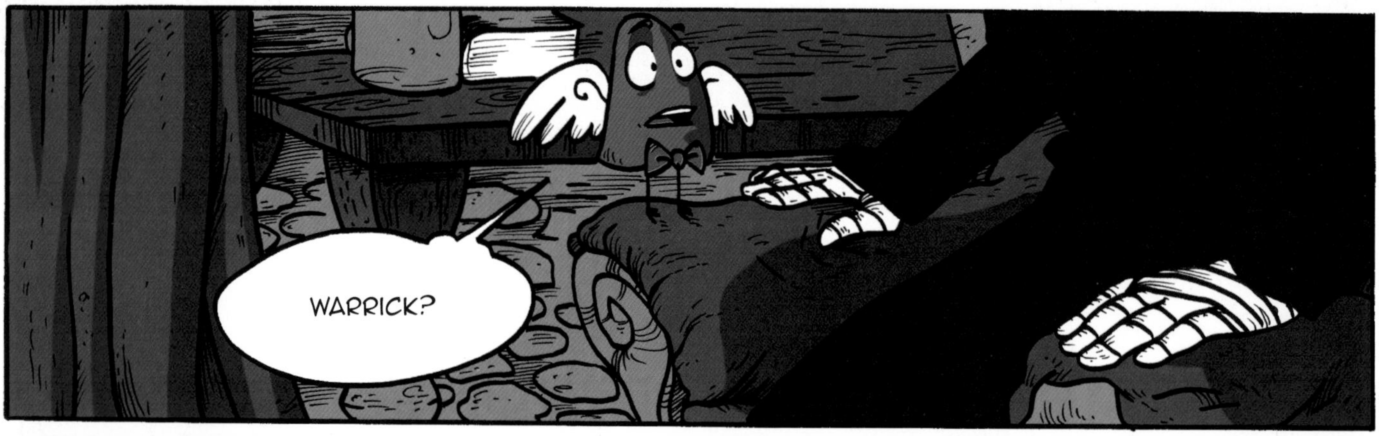
WARRICK?

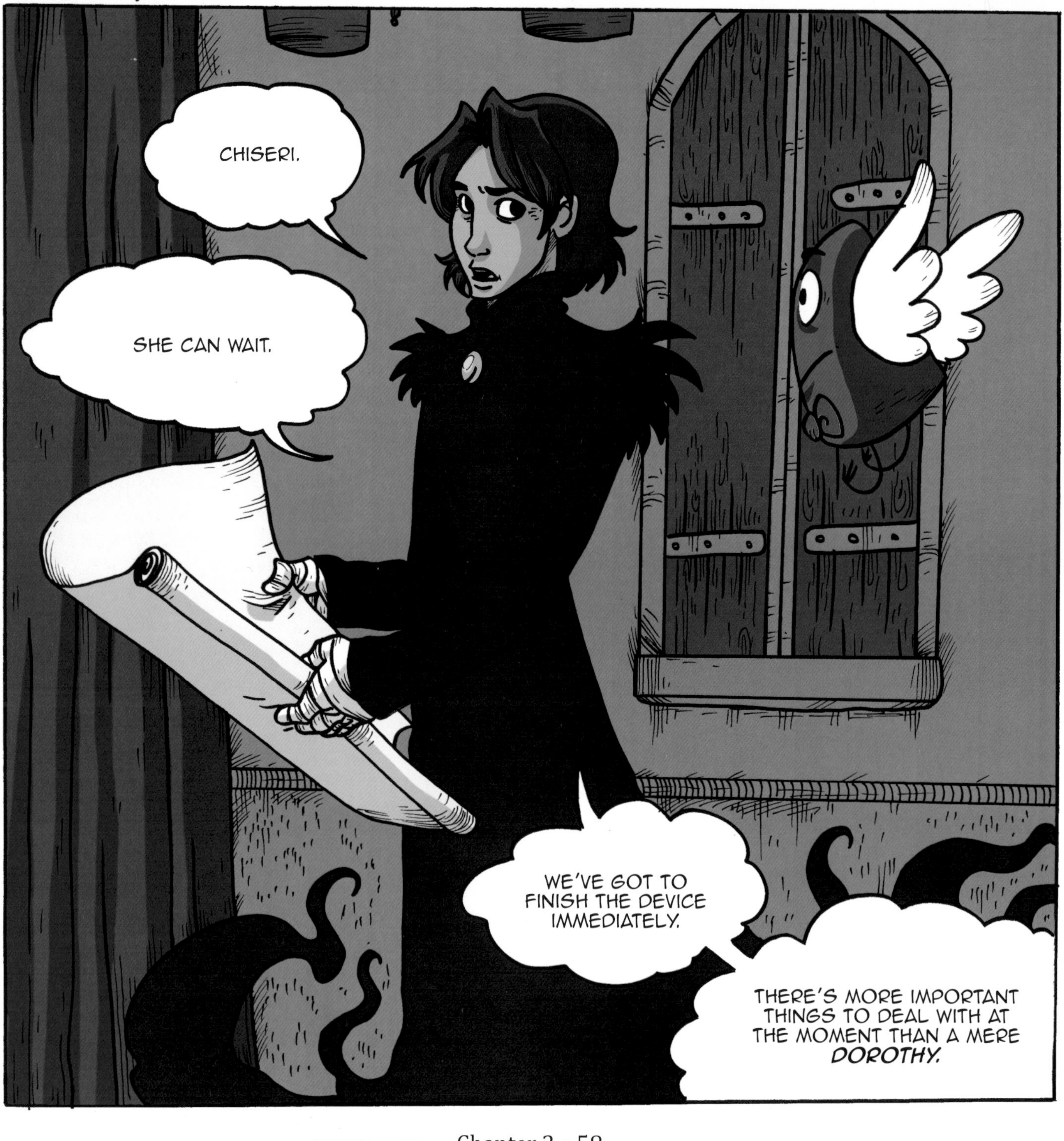
CHISERI.
SHE CAN WAIT.
WE'VE GOT TO FINISH THE DEVICE IMMEDIATELY.
THERE'S MORE IMPORTANT THINGS TO DEAL WITH AT THE MOMENT THAN A MERE *DOROTHY.*

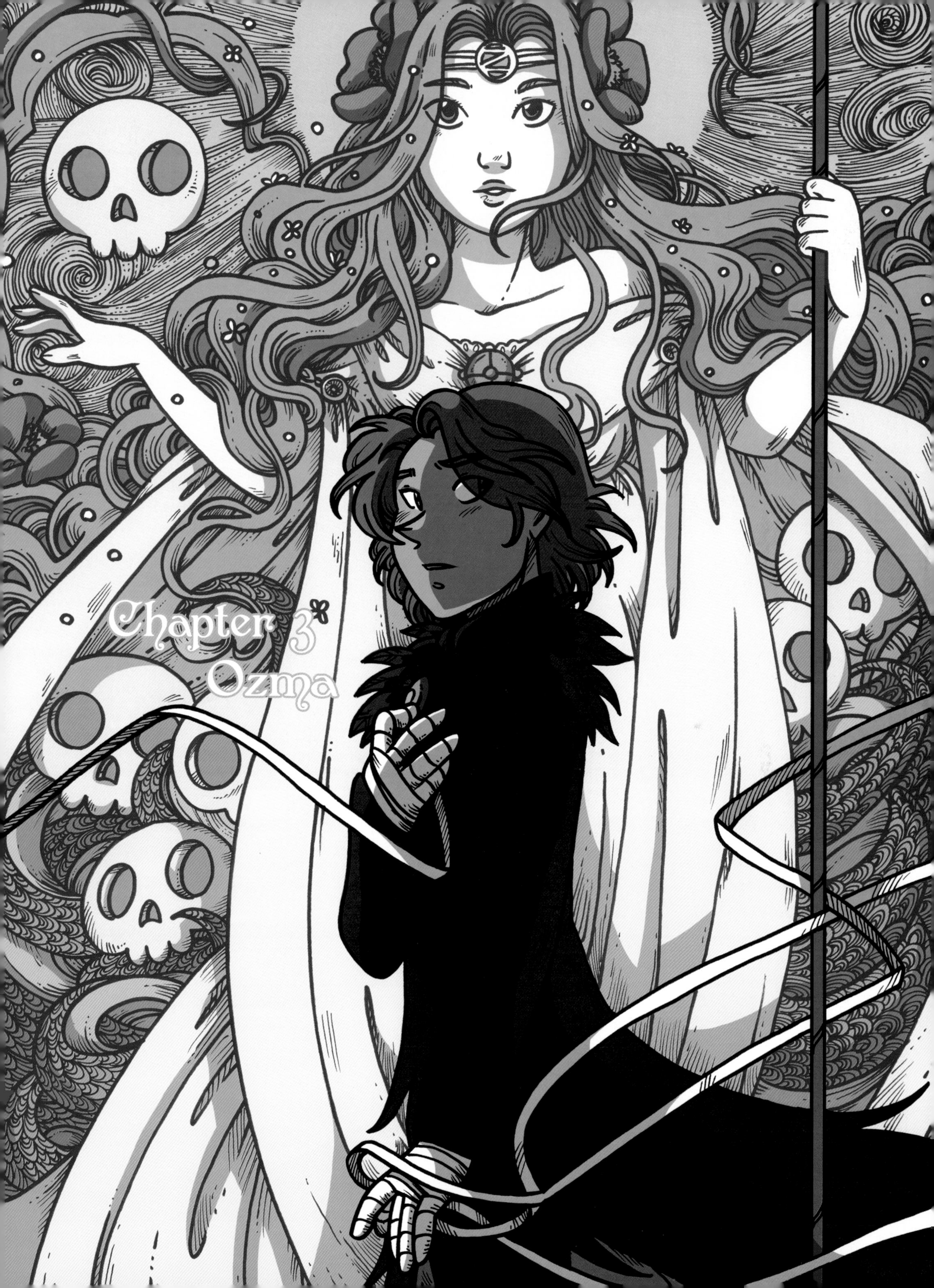
Chapter 3
Ozma

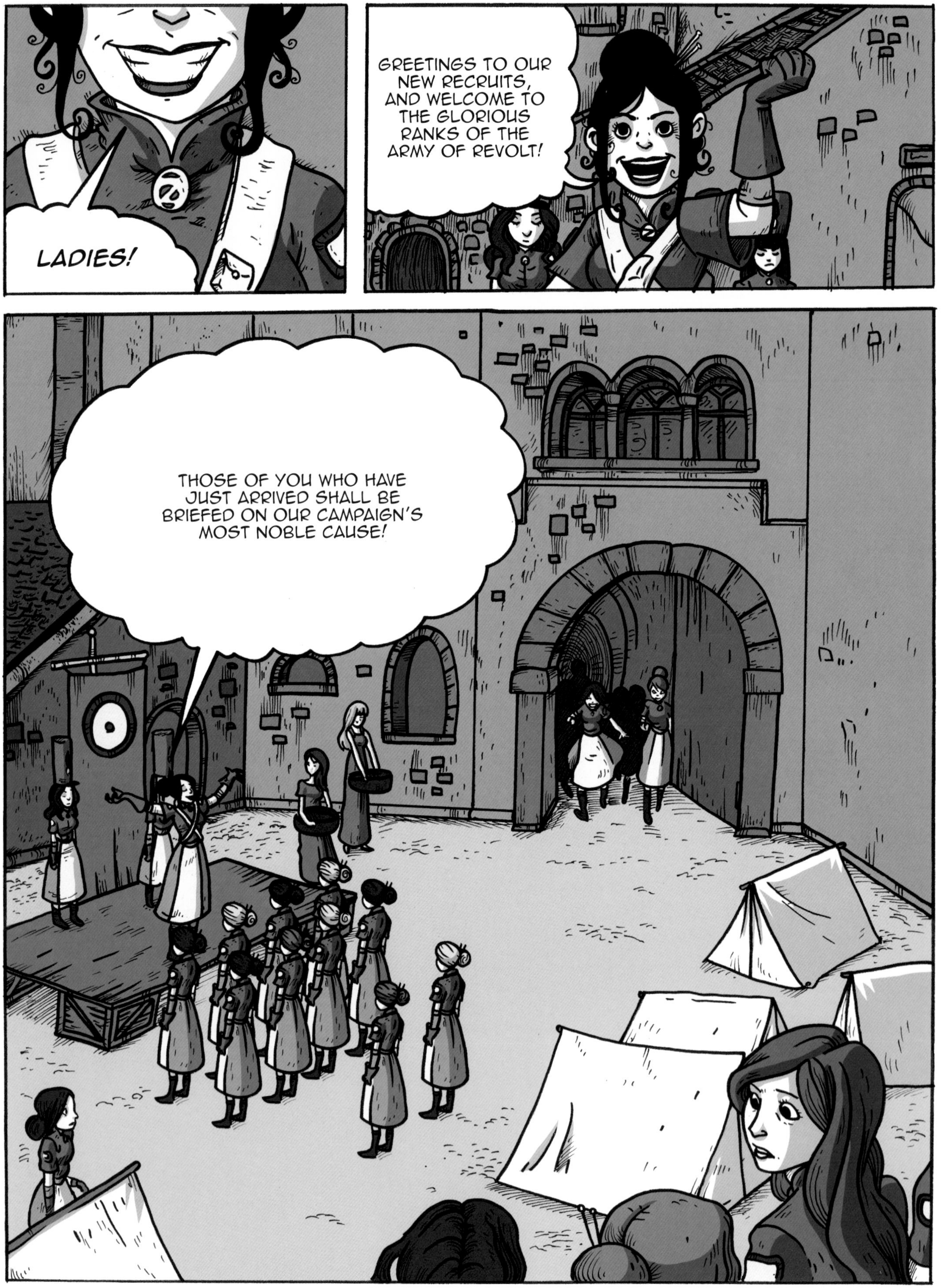
LADIES!
GREETINGS TO OUR NEW RECRUITS, AND WELCOME TO THE GLORIOUS RANKS OF THE ARMY OF REVOLT!
THOSE OF YOU WHO HAVE JUST ARRIVED SHALL BE BRIEFED ON OUR CAMPAIGN'S MOST NOBLE CAUSE!

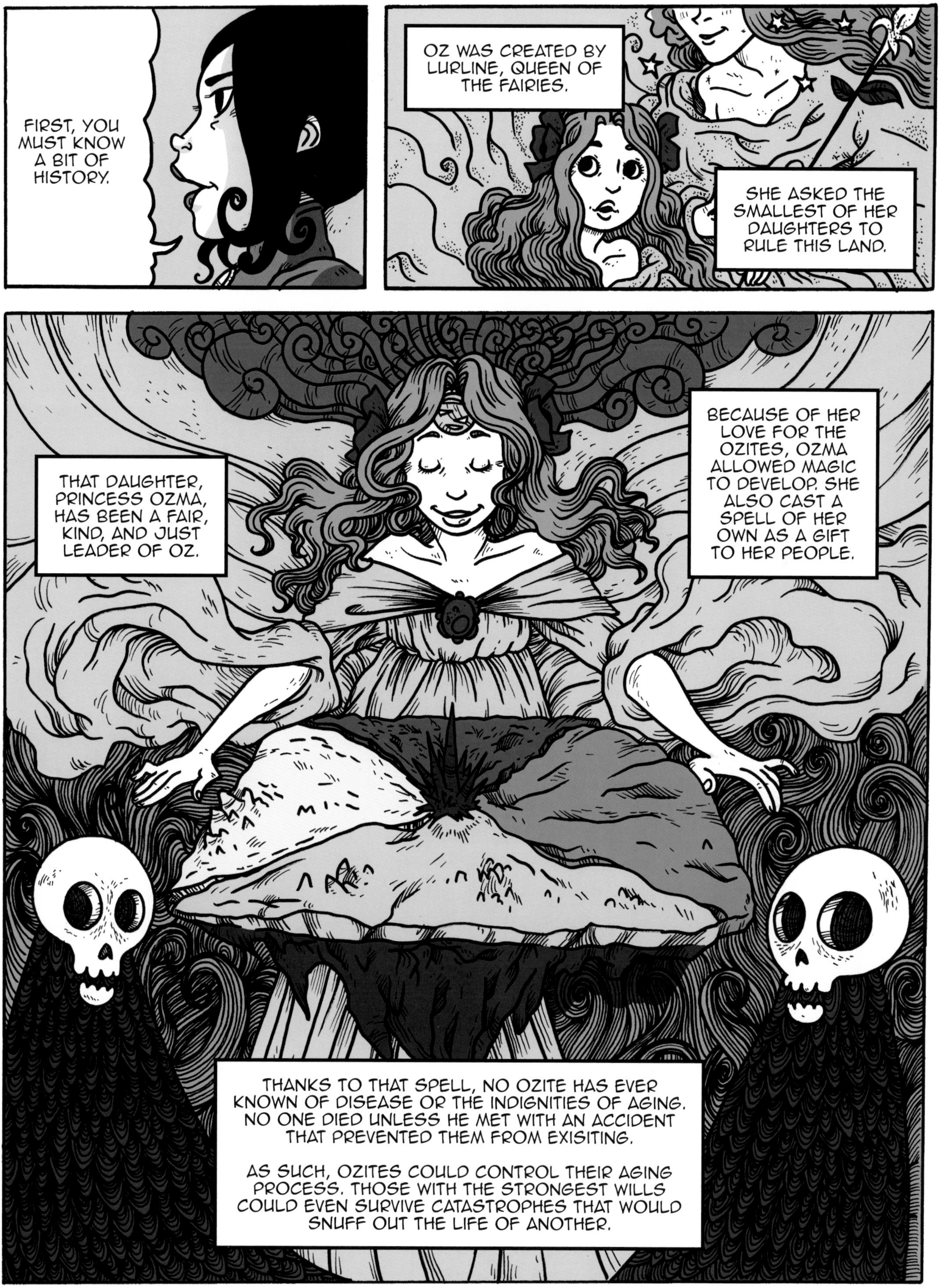
FIRST, YOU MUST KNOW A BIT OF HISTORY.
OZ WAS CREATED BY LURLINE, QUEEN OF THE FAIRIES.
SHE ASKED THE SMALLEST OF HER DAUGHTERS TO RULE THIS LAND.
THAT DAUGHTER, PRINCESS OZMA, HAS BEEN A FAIR, KIND, AND JUST LEADER OF OZ.
BECAUSE OF HER LOVE FOR THE OZITES, OZMA ALLOWED MAGIC TO DEVELOP. SHE ALSO CAST A SPELL OF HER OWN AS A GIFT TO HER PEOPLE.
THANKS TO THAT SPELL, NO OZITE HAS EVER KNOWN OF DISEASE OR THE INDIGNITIES OF AGING. NO ONE DIED UNLESS HE MET WITH AN ACCIDENT THAT PREVENTED THEM FROM EXISITING.
AS SUCH, OZITES COULD CONTROL THEIR AGING PROCESS. THOSE WITH THE STRONGEST WILLS COULD EVEN SURVIVE CATASTROPHES THAT WOULD SNUFF OUT THE LIFE OF ANOTHER.

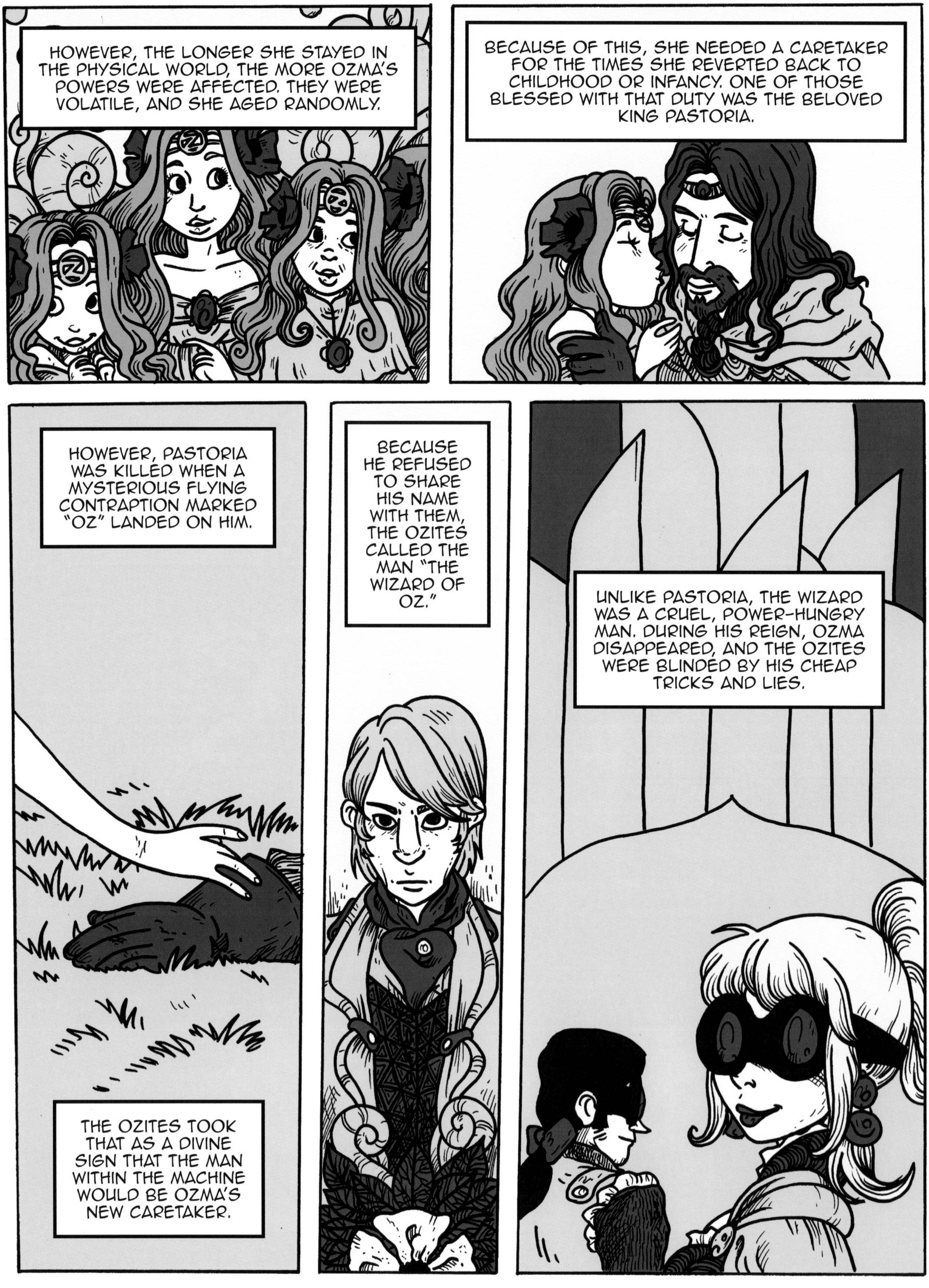
HOWEVER, THE LONGER SHE STAYED IN THE PHYSICAL WORLD, THE MORE OZMA'S POWERS WERE AFFECTED. THEY WERE VOLATILE, AND SHE AGED RANDOMLY.
BECAUSE OF THIS, SHE NEEDED A CARETAKER FOR THE TIMES SHE REVERTED BACK TO CHILDHOOD OR INFANCY. ONE OF THOSE BLESSED WITH THAT DUTY WAS THE BELOVED KING PASTORIA.
HOWEVER, PASTORIA WAS KILLED WHEN A MYSTERIOUS FLYING CONTRAPTION MARKED "OZ" LANDED ON HIM.
THE OZITES TOOK THAT AS A DIVINE SIGN THAT THE MAN WITHIN THE MACHINE WOULD BE OZMA'S NEW CARETAKER.
BECAUSE HE REFUSED TO SHARE HIS NAME WITH THEM, THE OZITES CALLED THE MAN "THE WIZARD OF OZ."
UNLIKE PASTORIA, THE WIZARD WAS A CRUEL, POWER-HUNGRY MAN. DURING HIS REIGN, OZMA DISAPPEARED, AND THE OZITES WERE BLINDED BY HIS CHEAP TRICKS AND LIES.

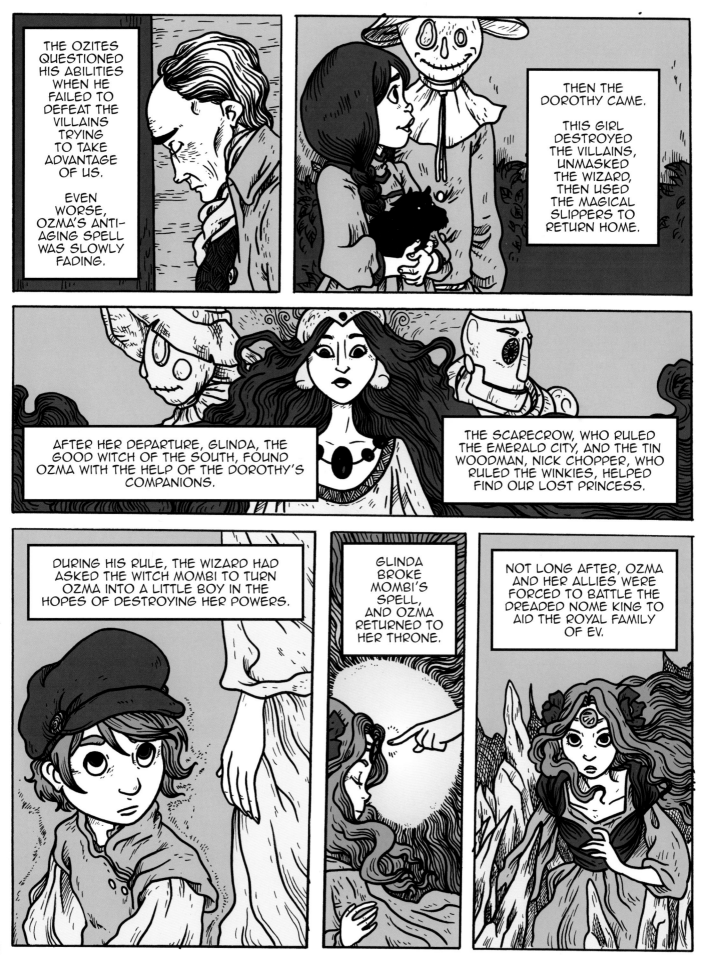

THE OZITES QUESTIONED HIS ABILITIES WHEN HE FAILED TO DEFEAT THE VILLAINS TRYING TO TAKE ADVANTAGE OF US.

EVEN WORSE, OZMA'S ANTI-AGING SPELL WAS SLOWLY FADING.

THEN THE DOROTHY CAME.

THIS GIRL DESTROYED THE VILLAINS, UNMASKED THE WIZARD, THEN USED THE MAGICAL SLIPPERS TO RETURN HOME.

AFTER HER DEPARTURE, GLINDA, THE GOOD WITCH OF THE SOUTH, FOUND OZMA WITH THE HELP OF THE DOROTHY'S COMPANIONS.

THE SCARECROW, WHO RULED THE EMERALD CITY, AND THE TIN WOODMAN, NICK CHOPPER, WHO RULED THE WINKIES, HELPED FIND OUR LOST PRINCESS.

DURING HIS RULE, THE WIZARD HAD ASKED THE WITCH MOMBI TO TURN OZMA INTO A LITTLE BOY IN THE HOPES OF DESTROYING HER POWERS.

GLINDA BROKE MOMBI'S SPELL, AND OZMA RETURNED TO HER THRONE.

NOT LONG AFTER, OZMA AND HER ALLIES WERE FORCED TO BATTLE THE DREADED NOME KING TO AID THE ROYAL FAMILY OF EV.

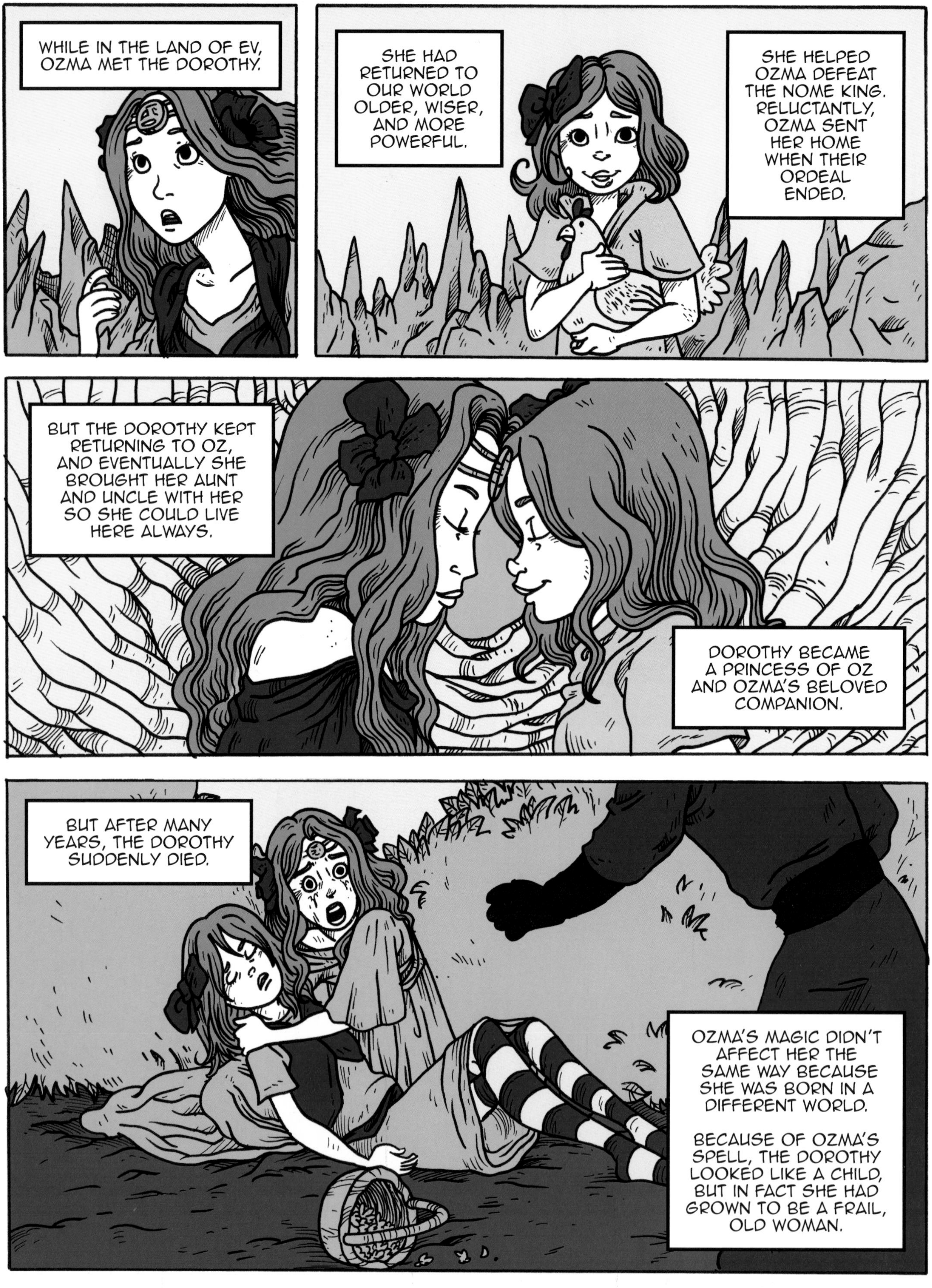
WHILE IN THE LAND OF EV, OZMA MET THE DOROTHY.
SHE HAD RETURNED TO OUR WORLD OLDER, WISER, AND MORE POWERFUL.
SHE HELPED OZMA DEFEAT THE NOME KING. RELUCTANTLY, OZMA SENT HER HOME WHEN THEIR ORDEAL ENDED.
BUT THE DOROTHY KEPT RETURNING TO OZ, AND EVENTUALLY SHE BROUGHT HER AUNT AND UNCLE WITH HER SO SHE COULD LIVE HERE ALWAYS.
DOROTHY BECAME A PRINCESS OF OZ AND OZMA'S BELOVED COMPANION.
BUT AFTER MANY YEARS, THE DOROTHY SUDDENLY DIED.
OZMA'S MAGIC DIDN'T AFFECT HER THE SAME WAY BECAUSE SHE WAS BORN IN A DIFFERENT WORLD.
BECAUSE OF OZMA'S SPELL, THE DOROTHY LOOKED LIKE A CHILD, BUT IN FACT SHE HAD GROWN TO BE A FRAIL, OLD WOMAN.

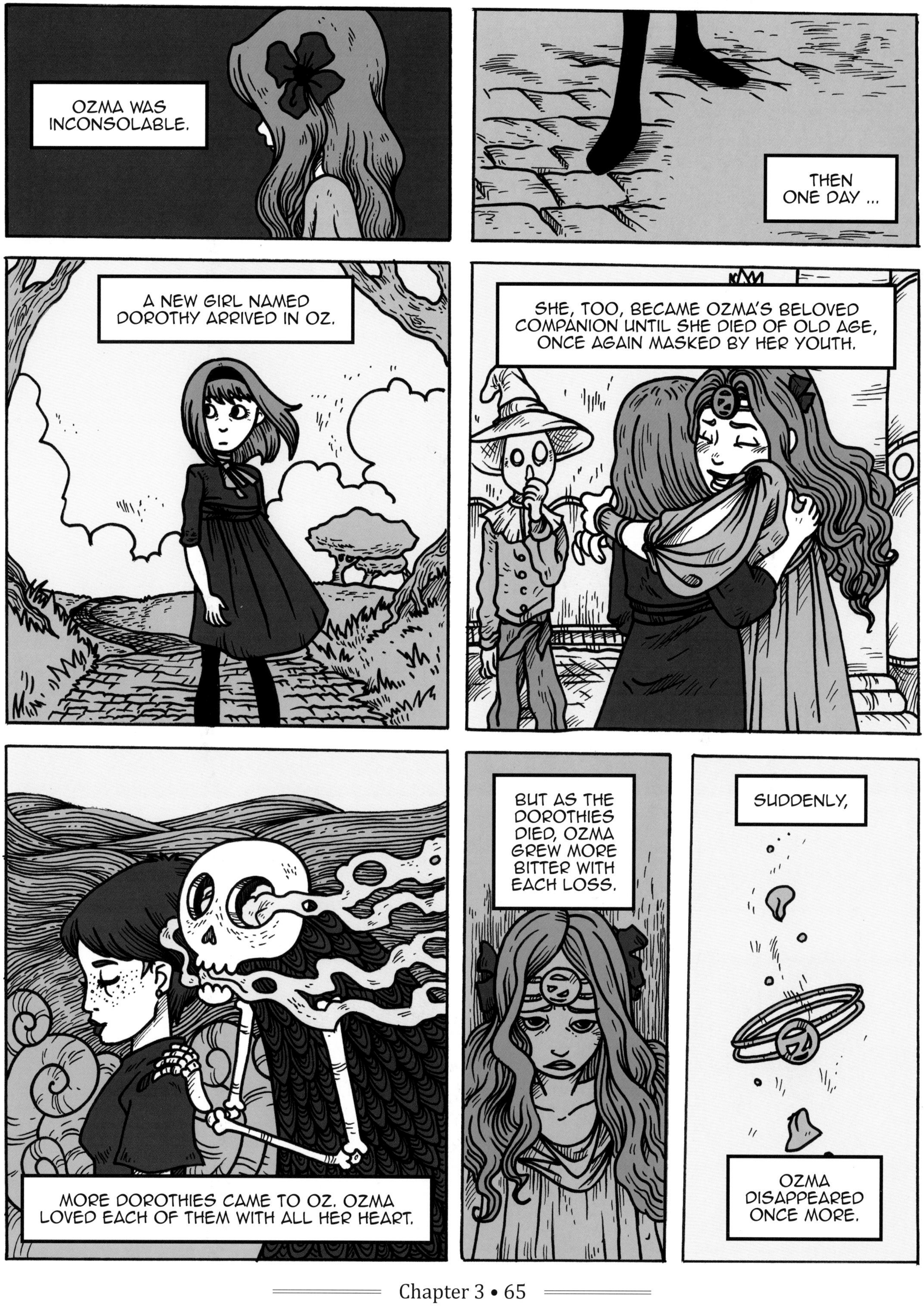

OZMA WAS INCONSOLABLE.
THEN ONE DAY ...
A NEW GIRL NAMED DOROTHY ARRIVED IN OZ.
SHE, TOO, BECAME OZMA'S BELOVED COMPANION UNTIL SHE DIED OF OLD AGE, ONCE AGAIN MASKED BY HER YOUTH.
MORE DOROTHIES CAME TO OZ. OZMA LOVED EACH OF THEM WITH ALL HER HEART.
BUT AS THE DOROTHIES DIED, OZMA GREW MORE BITTER WITH EACH LOSS.
SUDDENLY,
OZMA DISAPPEARED ONCE MORE.

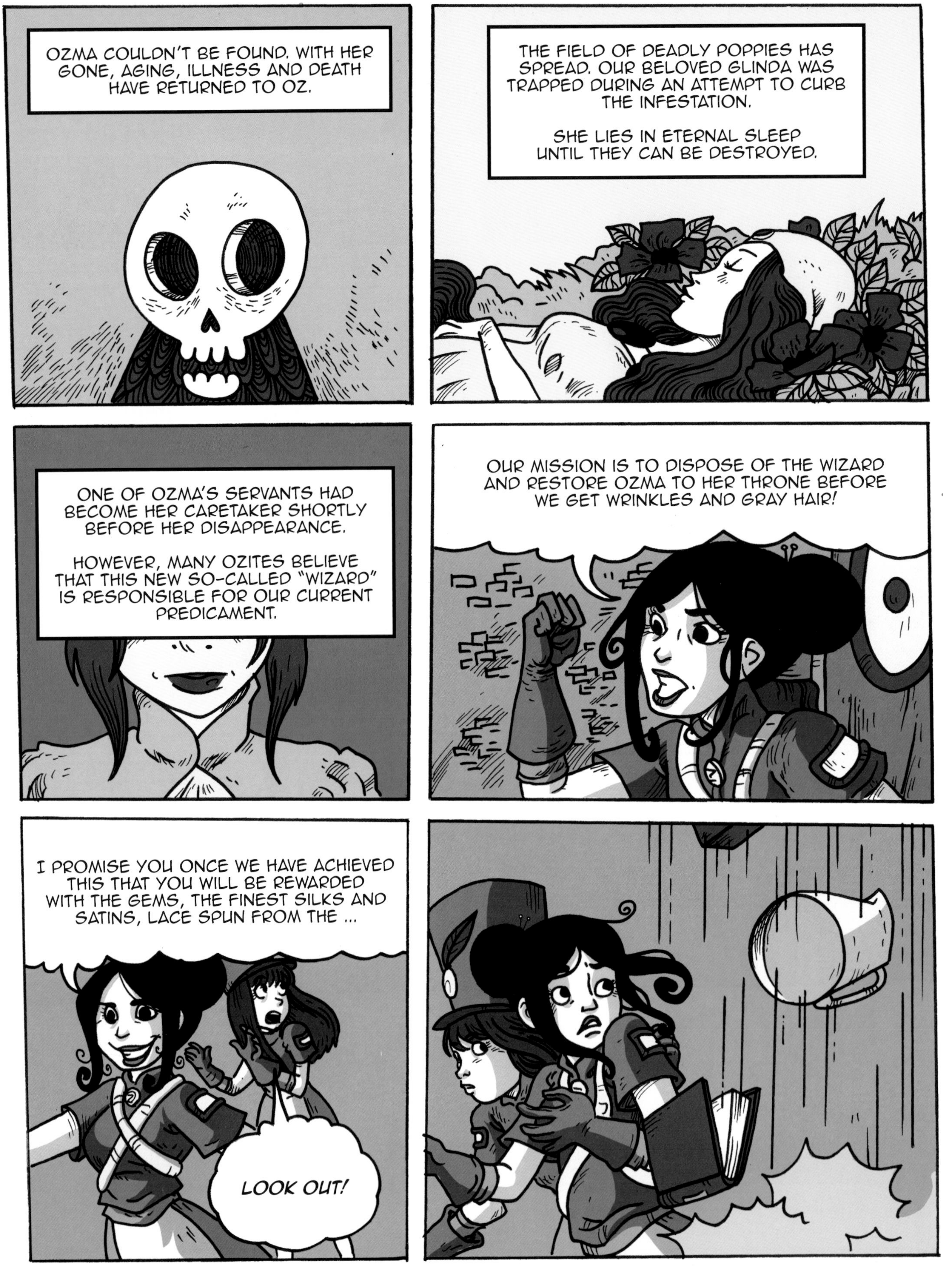
OZMA COULDN'T BE FOUND. WITH HER GONE, AGING, ILLNESS AND DEATH HAVE RETURNED TO OZ.
THE FIELD OF DEADLY POPPIES HAS SPREAD. OUR BELOVED GLINDA WAS TRAPPED DURING AN ATTEMPT TO CURB THE INFESTATION.
SHE LIES IN ETERNAL SLEEP UNTIL THEY CAN BE DESTROYED.
ONE OF OZMA'S SERVANTS HAD BECOME HER CARETAKER SHORTLY BEFORE HER DISAPPEARANCE.
HOWEVER, MANY OZITES BELIEVE THAT THIS NEW SO-CALLED "WIZARD" IS RESPONSIBLE FOR OUR CURRENT PREDICAMENT.
OUR MISSION IS TO DISPOSE OF THE WIZARD AND RESTORE OZMA TO HER THRONE BEFORE WE GET WRINKLES AND GRAY HAIR!
I PROMISE YOU ONCE WE HAVE ACHIEVED THIS THAT YOU WILL BE REWARDED WITH THE GEMS, THE FINEST SILKS AND SATINS, LACE SPUN FROM THE ...
LOOK OUT!

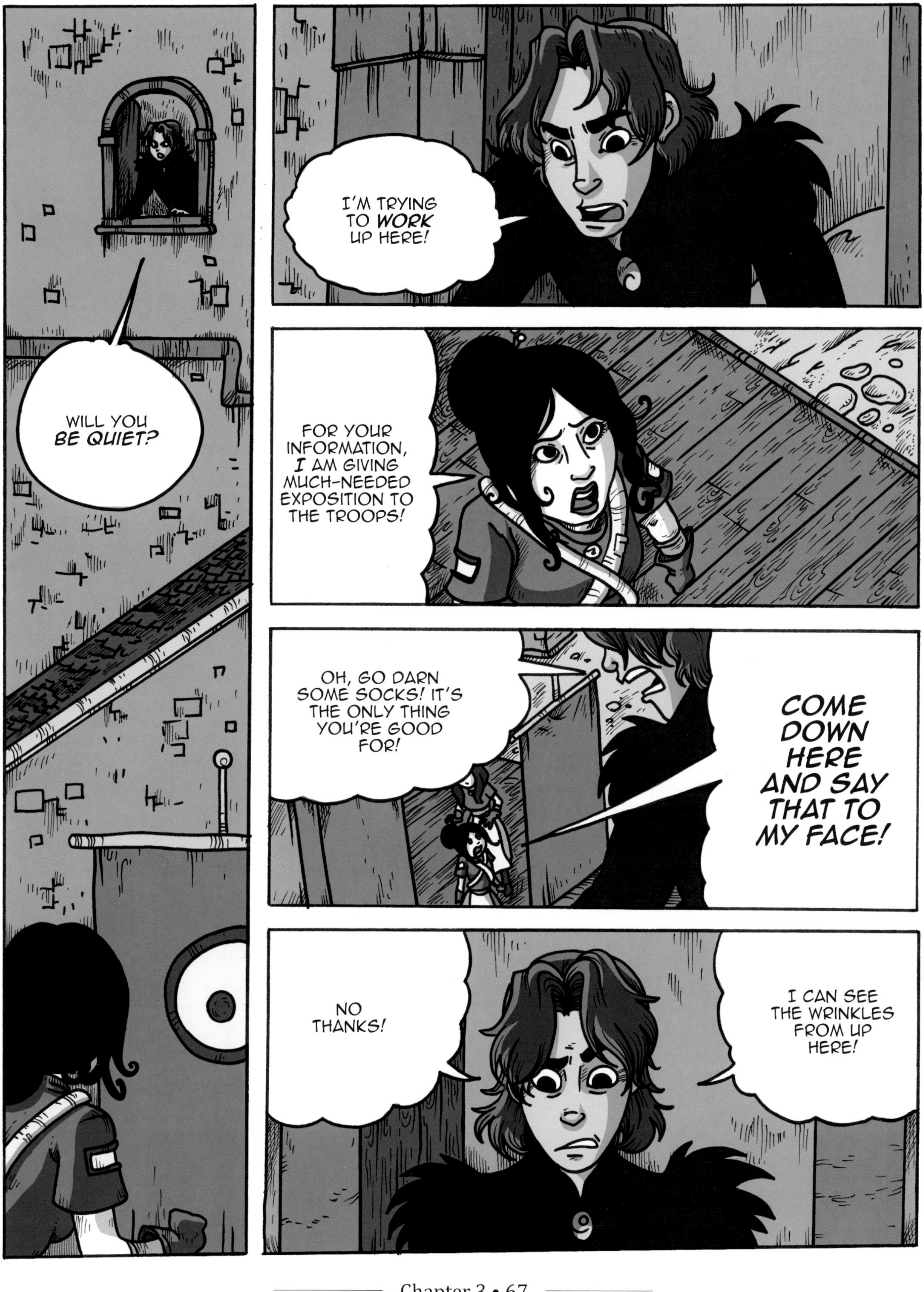
WILL YOU BE QUIET?
I'M TRYING TO WORK UP HERE!
FOR YOUR INFORMATION, I AM GIVING MUCH-NEEDED EXPOSITION TO THE TROOPS!
OH, GO DARN SOME SOCKS! IT'S THE ONLY THING YOU'RE GOOD FOR!
COME DOWN HERE AND SAY THAT TO MY FACE!
NO THANKS!
I CAN SEE THE WRINKLES FROM UP HERE!

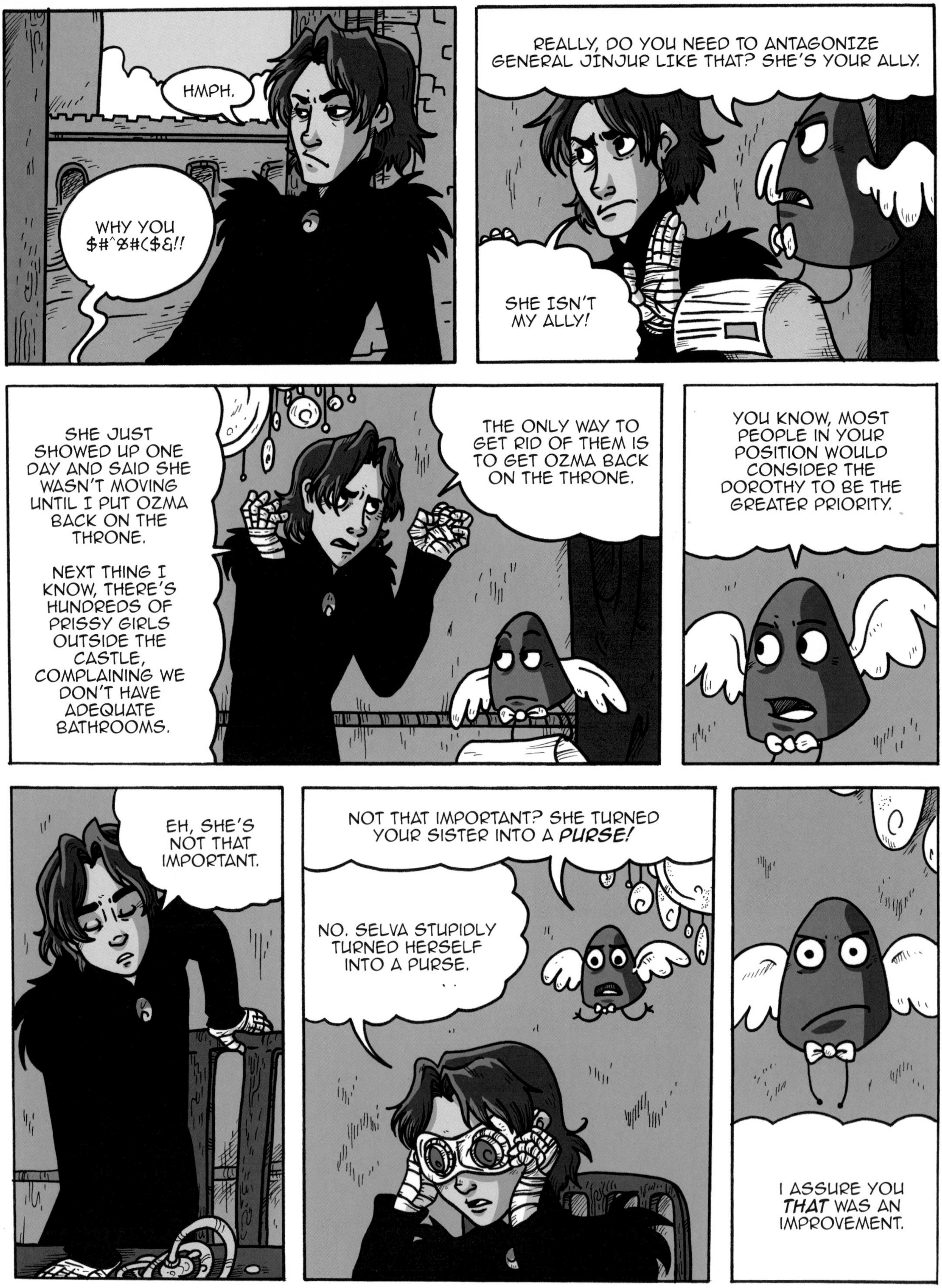
HMPH.
WHY YOU $#^&#($&!!
REALLY, DO YOU NEED TO ANTAGONIZE GENERAL JINJUR LIKE THAT? SHE'S YOUR ALLY.
SHE ISN'T MY ALLY!
SHE JUST SHOWED UP ONE DAY AND SAID SHE WASN'T MOVING UNTIL I PUT OZMA BACK ON THE THRONE.
NEXT THING I KNOW, THERE'S HUNDREDS OF PRISSY GIRLS OUTSIDE THE CASTLE, COMPLAINING WE DON'T HAVE ADEQUATE BATHROOMS.
THE ONLY WAY TO GET RID OF THEM IS TO GET OZMA BACK ON THE THRONE.
YOU KNOW, MOST PEOPLE IN YOUR POSITION WOULD CONSIDER THE DOROTHY TO BE THE GREATER PRIORITY.
EH, SHE'S NOT THAT IMPORTANT.
NOT THAT IMPORTANT? SHE TURNED YOUR SISTER INTO A *PURSE!*
NO. SELVA STUPIDLY TURNED HERSELF INTO A PURSE.
I ASSURE YOU *THAT* WAS AN IMPROVEMENT.

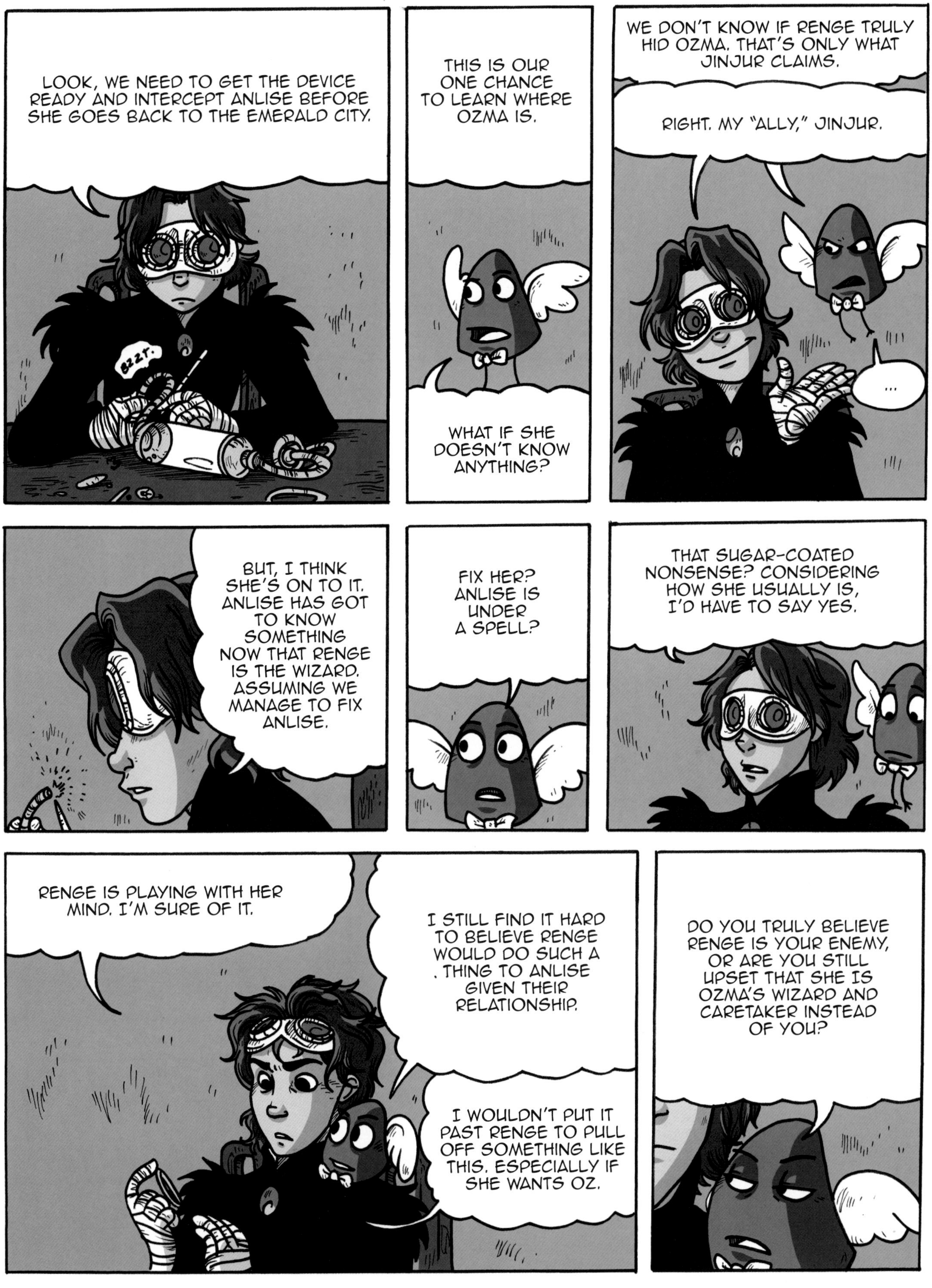
LOOK, WE NEED TO GET THE DEVICE READY AND INTERCEPT ANLISE BEFORE SHE GOES BACK TO THE EMERALD CITY.
BZZT.
THIS IS OUR ONE CHANCE TO LEARN WHERE OZMA IS.
WHAT IF SHE DOESN'T KNOW ANYTHING?
WE DON'T KNOW IF RENGE TRULY HID OZMA. THAT'S ONLY WHAT JINJUR CLAIMS.
RIGHT. MY "ALLY," JINJUR.
...
BUT, I THINK SHE'S ON TO IT. ANLISE HAS GOT TO KNOW SOMETHING NOW THAT RENGE IS THE WIZARD. ASSUMING WE MANAGE TO FIX ANLISE.
FIX HER? ANLISE IS UNDER A SPELL?
THAT SUGAR-COATED NONSENSE? CONSIDERING HOW SHE USUALLY IS, I'D HAVE TO SAY YES.
RENGE IS PLAYING WITH HER MIND. I'M SURE OF IT.
I STILL FIND IT HARD TO BELIEVE RENGE WOULD DO SUCH A THING TO ANLISE GIVEN THEIR RELATIONSHIP.
I WOULDN'T PUT IT PAST RENGE TO PULL OFF SOMETHING LIKE THIS. ESPECIALLY IF SHE WANTS OZ.
DO YOU TRULY BELIEVE RENGE IS YOUR ENEMY, OR ARE YOU STILL UPSET THAT SHE IS OZMA'S WIZARD AND CARETAKER INSTEAD OF YOU?

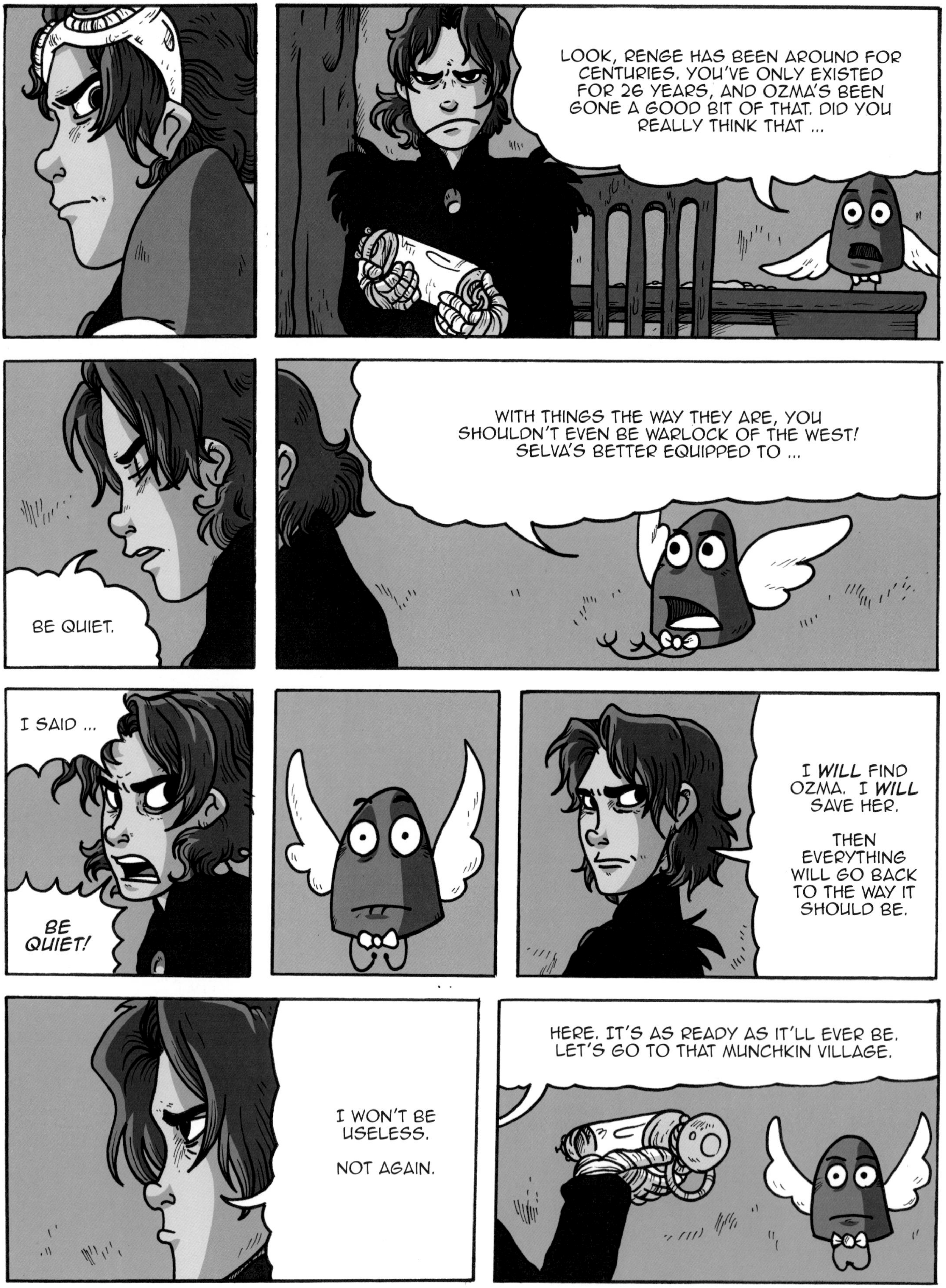
LOOK, RENGE HAS BEEN AROUND FOR CENTURIES. YOU'VE ONLY EXISTED FOR 26 YEARS, AND OZMA'S BEEN GONE A GOOD BIT OF THAT. DID YOU REALLY THINK THAT ...
BE QUIET.
WITH THINGS THE WAY THEY ARE, YOU SHOULDN'T EVEN BE WARLOCK OF THE WEST! SELVA'S BETTER EQUIPPED TO ...
I SAID ...
BE QUIET!
I *WILL* FIND OZMA. I *WILL* SAVE HER.
THEN EVERYTHING WILL GO BACK TO THE WAY IT SHOULD BE.
I WON'T BE USELESS.
NOT AGAIN.
HERE. IT'S AS READY AS IT'LL EVER BE. LET'S GO TO THAT MUNCHKIN VILLAGE.

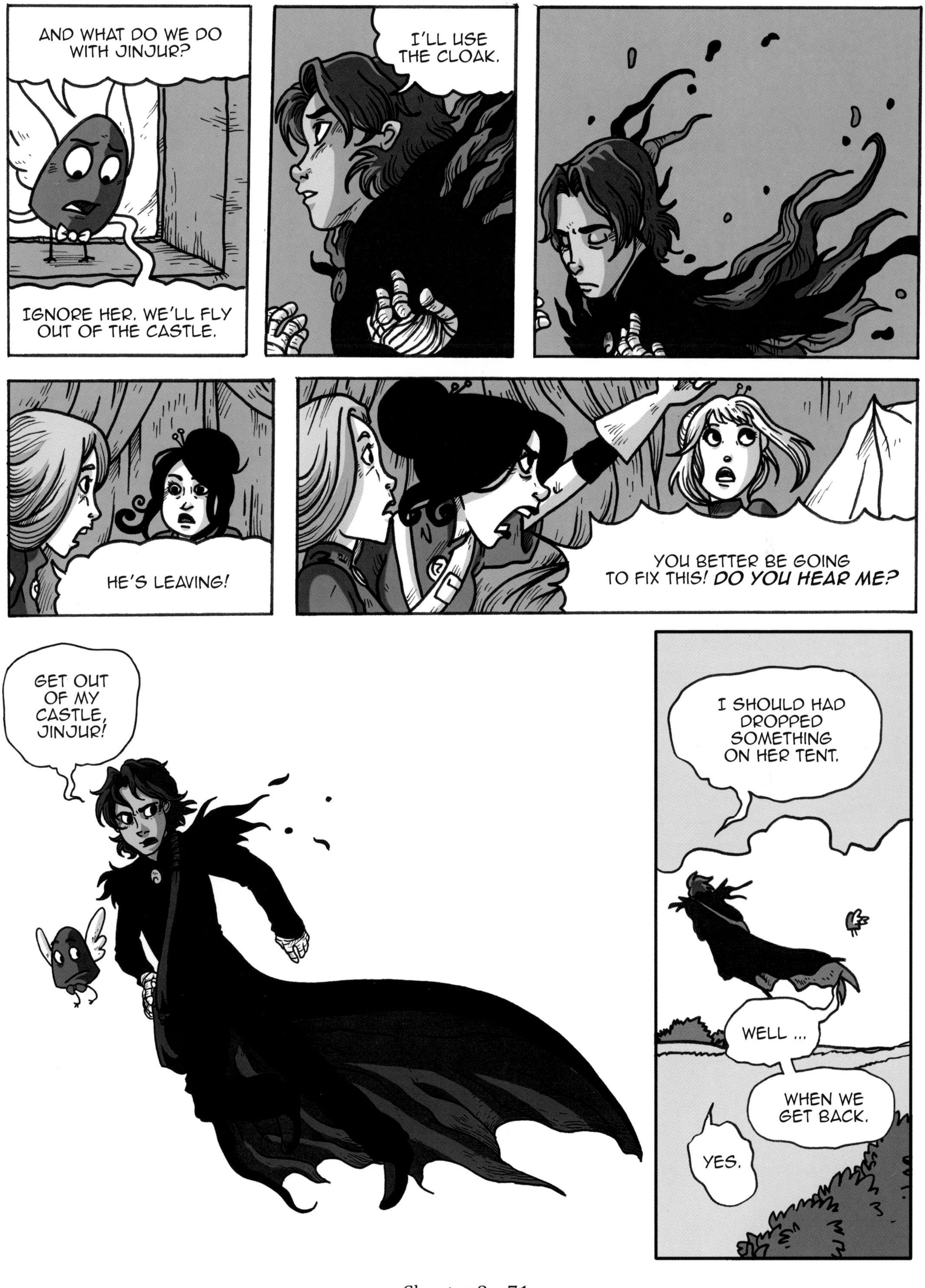
AND WHAT DO WE DO WITH JINJUR?
IGNORE HER. WE'LL FLY OUT OF THE CASTLE.
I'LL USE THE CLOAK.
HE'S LEAVING!
YOU BETTER BE GOING TO FIX THIS! DO YOU HEAR ME?
GET OUT OF MY CASTLE, JINJUR!
I SHOULD HAD DROPPED SOMETHING ON HER TENT.
WELL ...
WHEN WE GET BACK.
YES.

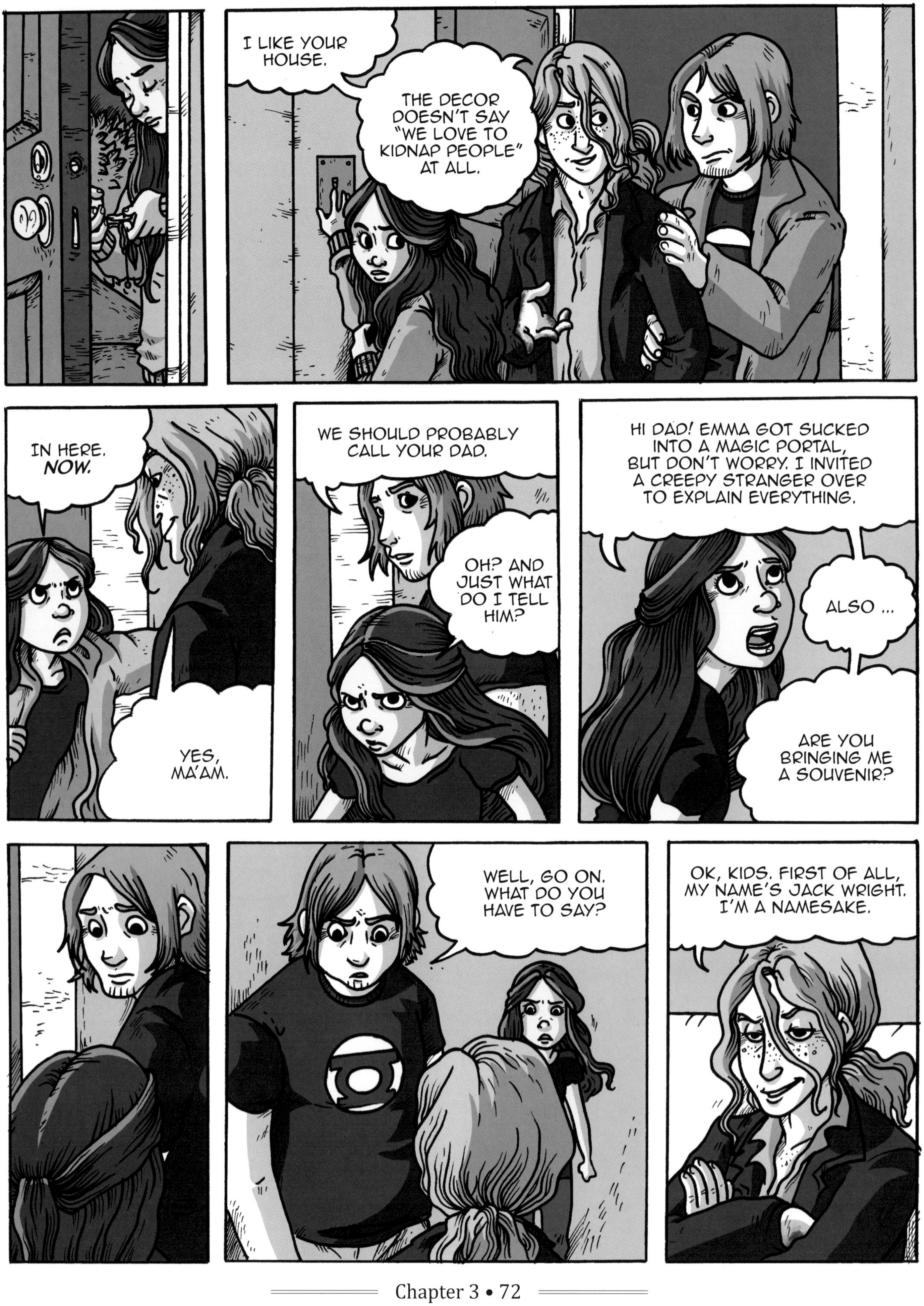
I LIKE YOUR HOUSE.
THE DECOR DOESN'T SAY "WE LOVE TO KIDNAP PEOPLE" AT ALL.
IN HERE. *NOW.*
YES, MA'AM.
WE SHOULD PROBABLY CALL YOUR DAD.
OH? AND JUST WHAT DO I TELL HIM?
HI DAD! EMMA GOT SUCKED INTO A MAGIC PORTAL, BUT DON'T WORRY. I INVITED A CREEPY STRANGER OVER TO EXPLAIN EVERYTHING.
ALSO ...
ARE YOU BRINGING ME A SOUVENIR?
WELL, GO ON. WHAT DO YOU HAVE TO SAY?
OK, KIDS. FIRST OF ALL, MY NAME'S JACK WRIGHT. I'M A NAMESAKE.

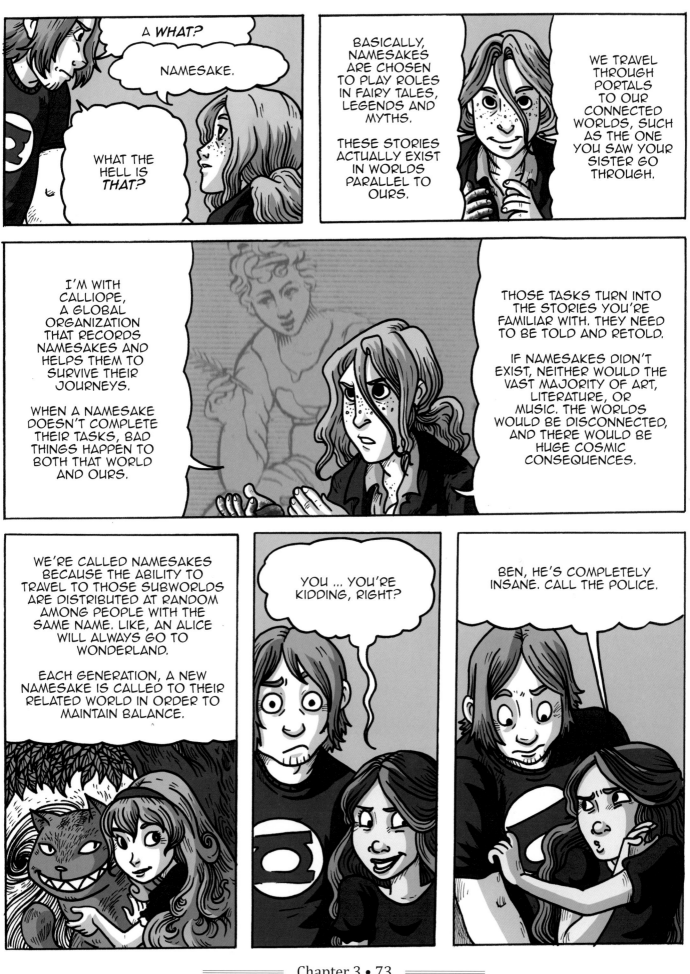

A WHAT?

NAMESAKE.

WHAT THE HELL IS *THAT?*

BASICALLY, NAMESAKES ARE CHOSEN TO PLAY ROLES IN FAIRY TALES, LEGENDS AND MYTHS.

THESE STORIES ACTUALLY EXIST IN WORLDS PARALLEL TO OURS.

WE TRAVEL THROUGH PORTALS TO OUR CONNECTED WORLDS, SUCH AS THE ONE YOU SAW YOUR SISTER GO THROUGH.

I'M WITH CALLIOPE, A GLOBAL ORGANIZATION THAT RECORDS NAMESAKES AND HELPS THEM TO SURVIVE THEIR JOURNEYS.

WHEN A NAMESAKE DOESN'T COMPLETE THEIR TASKS, BAD THINGS HAPPEN TO BOTH THAT WORLD AND OURS.

THOSE TASKS TURN INTO THE STORIES YOU'RE FAMILIAR WITH. THEY NEED TO BE TOLD AND RETOLD.

IF NAMESAKES DIDN'T EXIST, NEITHER WOULD THE VAST MAJORITY OF ART, LITERATURE, OR MUSIC. THE WORLDS WOULD BE DISCONNECTED, AND THERE WOULD BE HUGE COSMIC CONSEQUENCES.

WE'RE CALLED NAMESAKES BECAUSE THE ABILITY TO TRAVEL TO THOSE SUBWORLDS ARE DISTRIBUTED AT RANDOM AMONG PEOPLE WITH THE SAME NAME. LIKE, AN ALICE WILL ALWAYS GO TO WONDERLAND.

EACH GENERATION, A NEW NAMESAKE IS CALLED TO THEIR RELATED WORLD IN ORDER TO MAINTAIN BALANCE.

YOU ... YOU'RE KIDDING, RIGHT?

BEN, HE'S COMPLETELY INSANE. CALL THE POLICE.

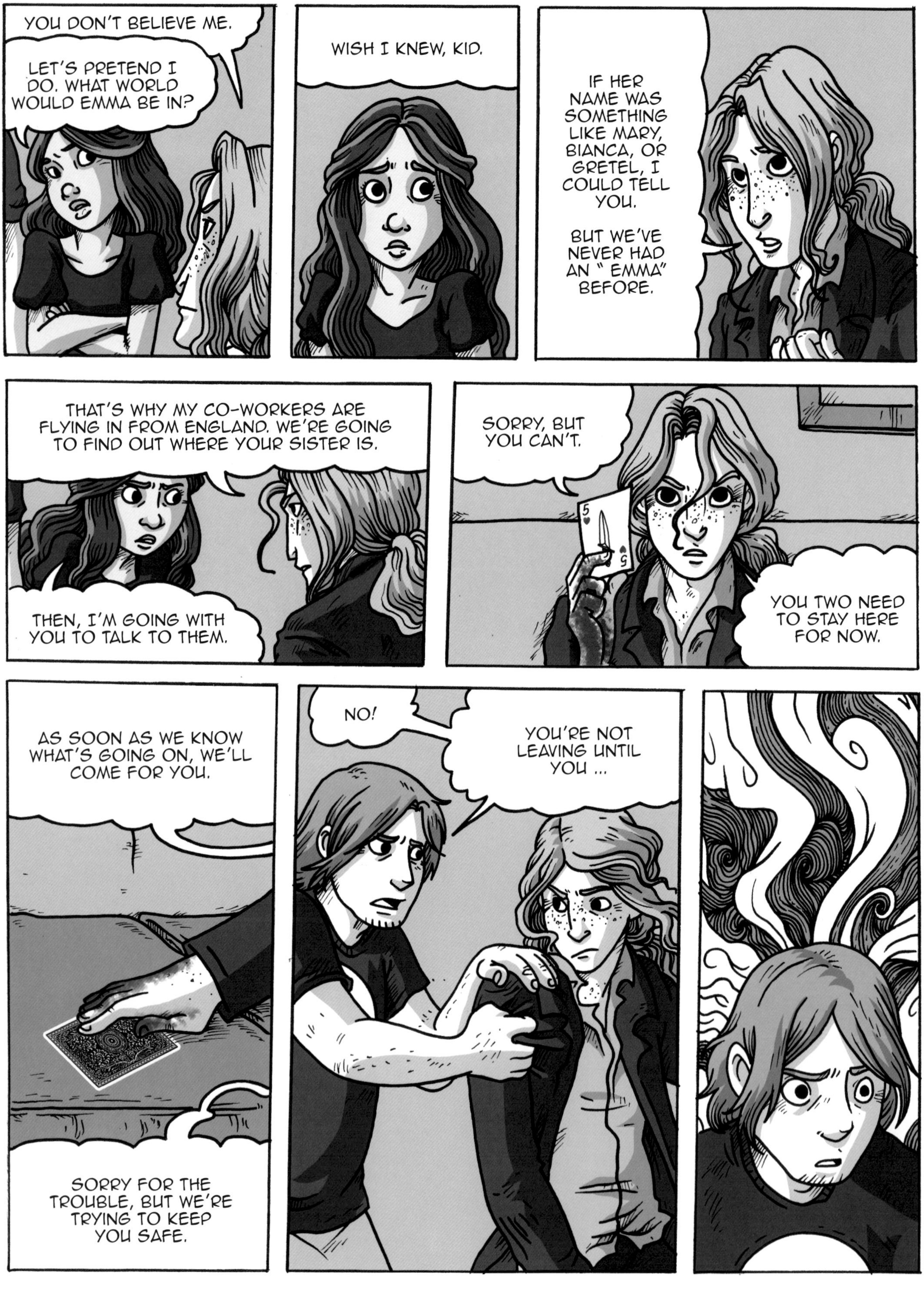

YOU DON'T BELIEVE ME.
LET'S PRETEND I DO. WHAT WORLD WOULD EMMA BE IN?
WISH I KNEW, KID.
IF HER NAME WAS SOMETHING LIKE MARY, BIANCA, OR GRETEL, I COULD TELL YOU.
BUT WE'VE NEVER HAD AN " EMMA" BEFORE.
THAT'S WHY MY CO-WORKERS ARE FLYING IN FROM ENGLAND. WE'RE GOING TO FIND OUT WHERE YOUR SISTER IS.
THEN, I'M GOING WITH YOU TO TALK TO THEM.
SORRY, BUT YOU CAN'T.
YOU TWO NEED TO STAY HERE FOR NOW.
AS SOON AS WE KNOW WHAT'S GOING ON, WE'LL COME FOR YOU.
SORRY FOR THE TROUBLE, BUT WE'RE TRYING TO KEEP YOU SAFE.
NO!
YOU'RE NOT LEAVING UNTIL YOU ...

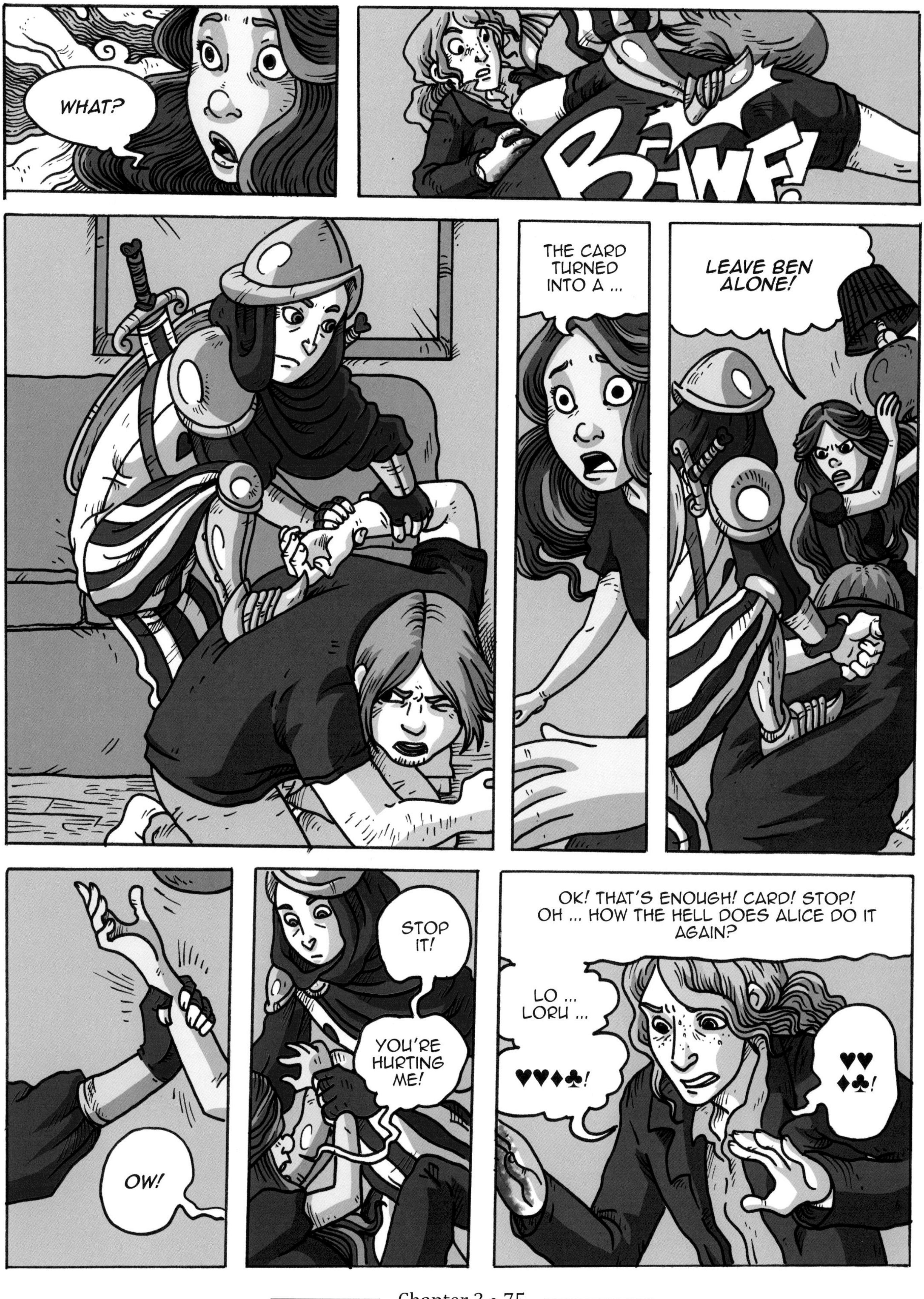
WHAT?
BENF!
THE CARD TURNED INTO A ...
LEAVE BEN ALONE!
OW!
STOP IT!
YOU'RE HURTING ME!
OK! THAT'S ENOUGH! CARD! STOP! OH ... HOW THE HELL DOES ALICE DO IT AGAIN?
LO ... LORU ...
♥♥♦♣!
♥♥ ♦♣!

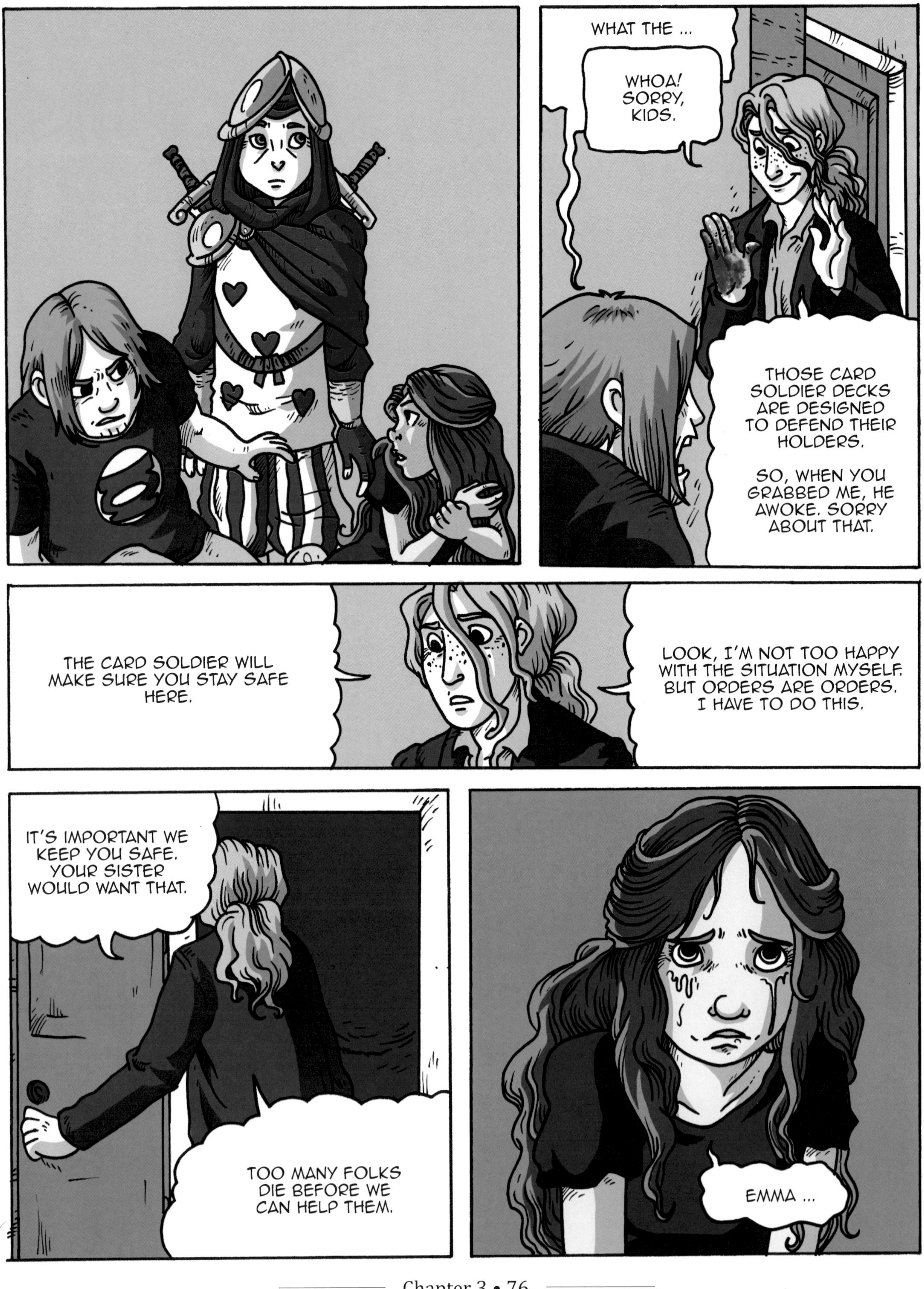
WHAT THE ...
WHOA! SORRY, KIDS.
THOSE CARD SOLDIER DECKS ARE DESIGNED TO DEFEND THEIR HOLDERS.
SO, WHEN YOU GRABBED ME, HE AWOKE. SORRY ABOUT THAT.
THE CARD SOLDIER WILL MAKE SURE YOU STAY SAFE HERE.
LOOK, I'M NOT TOO HAPPY WITH THE SITUATION MYSELF. BUT ORDERS ARE ORDERS. I HAVE TO DO THIS.
IT'S IMPORTANT WE KEEP YOU SAFE. YOUR SISTER WOULD WANT THAT.
TOO MANY FOLKS DIE BEFORE WE CAN HELP THEM.
EMMA ...

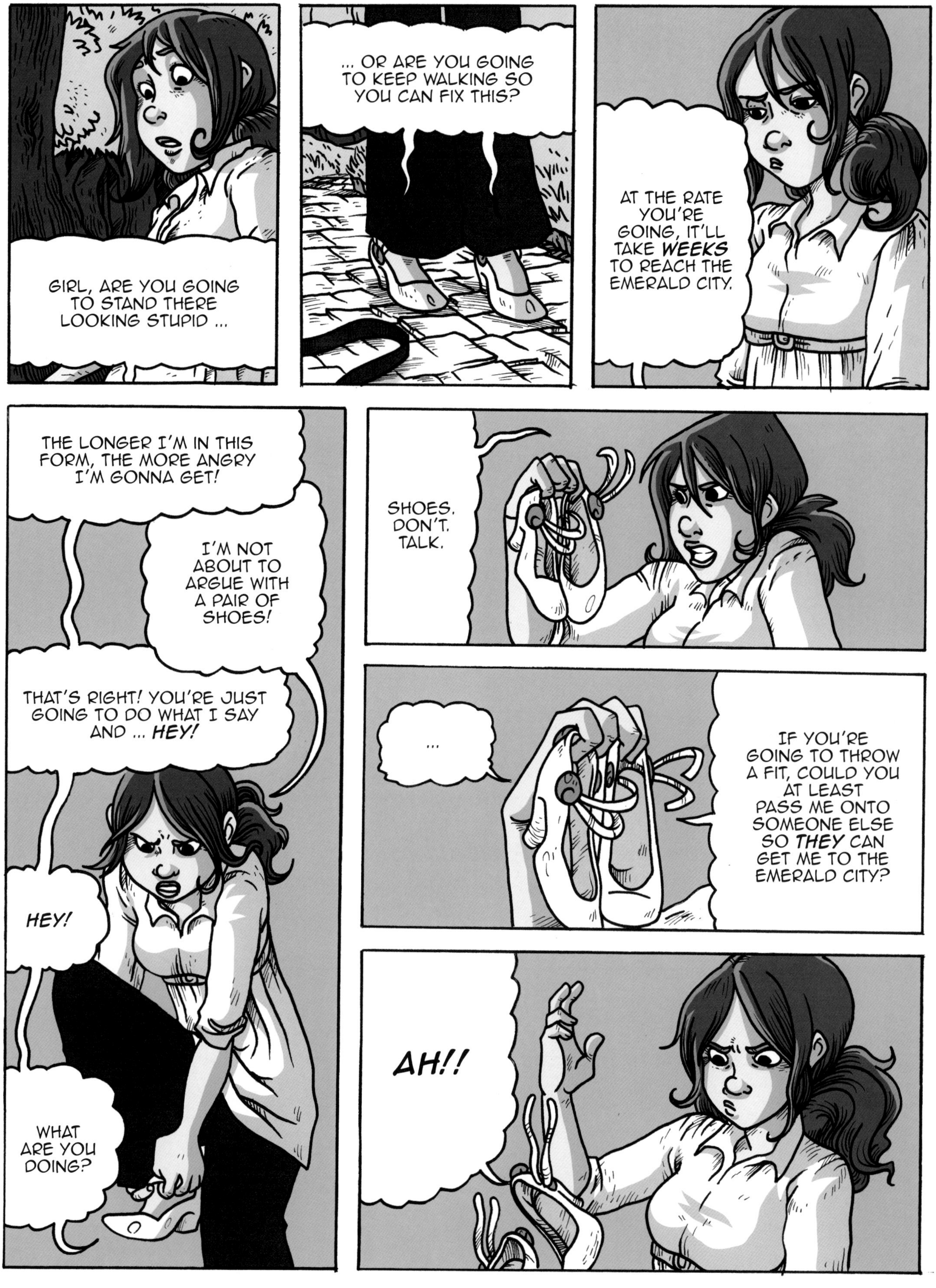

GIRL, ARE YOU GOING TO STAND THERE LOOKING STUPID ...
... OR ARE YOU GOING TO KEEP WALKING SO YOU CAN FIX THIS?
AT THE RATE YOU'RE GOING, IT'LL TAKE WEEKS TO REACH THE EMERALD CITY.
THE LONGER I'M IN THIS FORM, THE MORE ANGRY I'M GONNA GET!
I'M NOT ABOUT TO ARGUE WITH A PAIR OF SHOES!
THAT'S RIGHT! YOU'RE JUST GOING TO DO WHAT I SAY AND ... HEY!
HEY!
WHAT ARE YOU DOING?
SHOES. DON'T. TALK.
...
IF YOU'RE GOING TO THROW A FIT, COULD YOU AT LEAST PASS ME ONTO SOMEONE ELSE SO THEY CAN GET ME TO THE EMERALD CITY?
AH!!

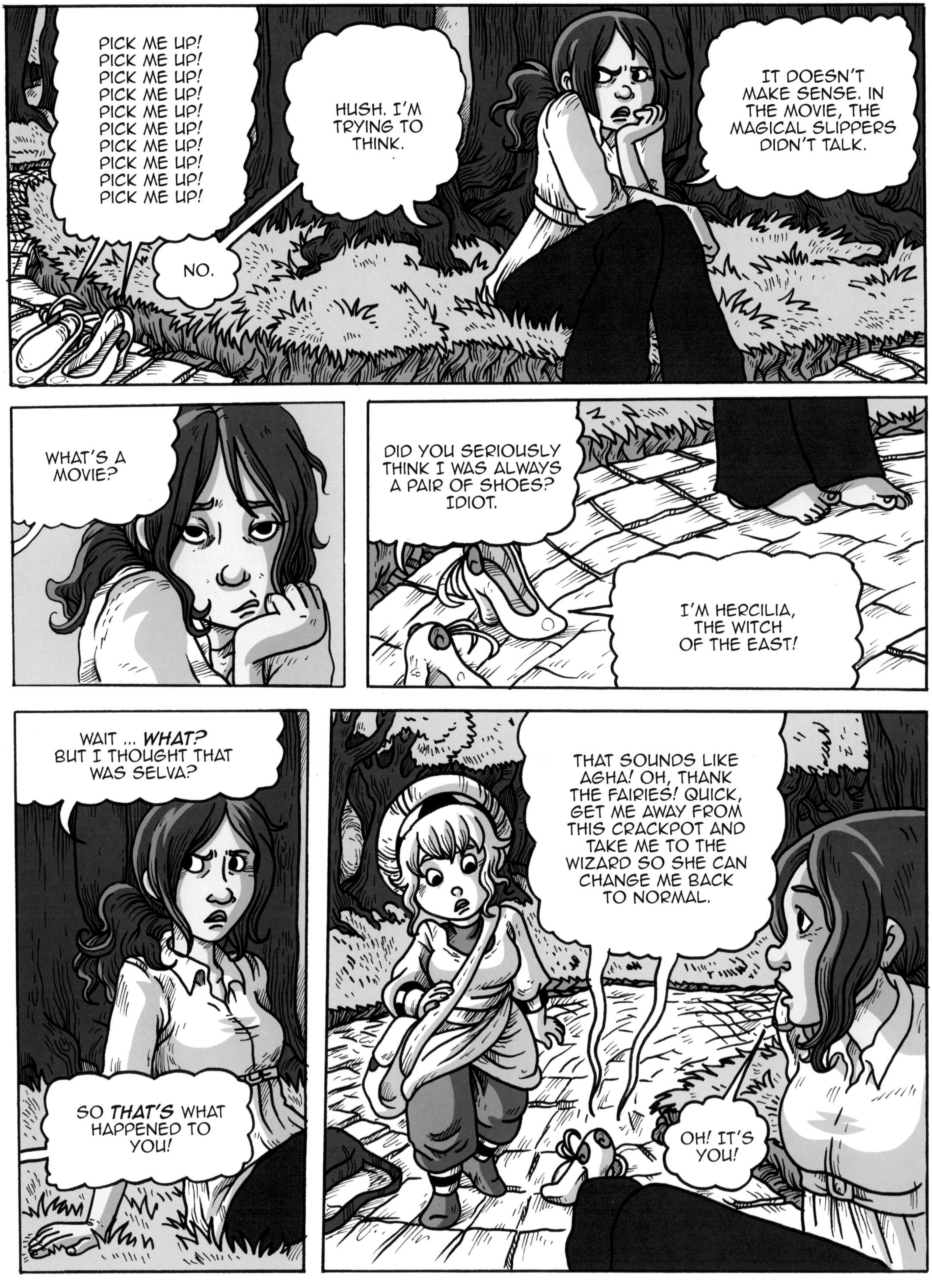
PICK ME UP! PICK ME UP! PICK ME UP! PICK ME UP! PICK ME UP! PICK ME UP! PICK ME UP! PICK ME UP! PICK ME UP! PICK ME UP!
HUSH. I'M TRYING TO THINK.
NO.
IT DOESN'T MAKE SENSE. IN THE MOVIE, THE MAGICAL SLIPPERS DIDN'T TALK.
WHAT'S A MOVIE?
DID YOU SERIOUSLY THINK I WAS ALWAYS A PAIR OF SHOES? IDIOT.
I'M HERCILIA, THE WITCH OF THE EAST!
WAIT ... *WHAT?* BUT I THOUGHT THAT WAS SELVA?
SO *THAT'S* WHAT HAPPENED TO YOU!
THAT SOUNDS LIKE AGHA! OH, THANK THE FAIRIES! QUICK, GET ME AWAY FROM THIS CRACKPOT AND TAKE ME TO THE WIZARD SO SHE CAN CHANGE ME BACK TO NORMAL.
OH! IT'S YOU!

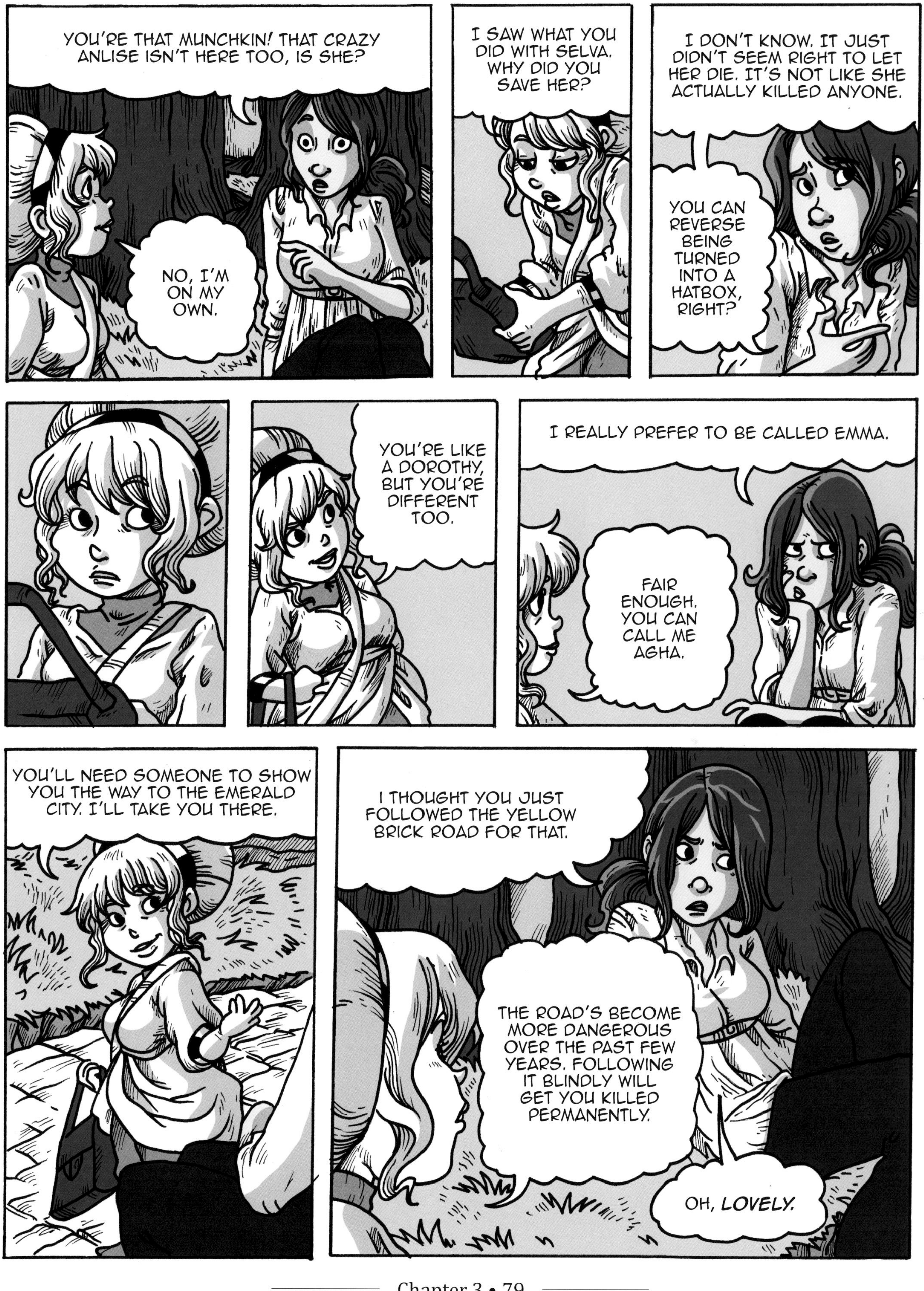
YOU'RE THAT MUNCHKIN! THAT CRAZY ANLISE ISN'T HERE TOO, IS SHE?
NO, I'M ON MY OWN.
I SAW WHAT YOU DID WITH SELVA. WHY DID YOU SAVE HER?
I DON'T KNOW. IT JUST DIDN'T SEEM RIGHT TO LET HER DIE. IT'S NOT LIKE SHE ACTUALLY KILLED ANYONE.
YOU CAN REVERSE BEING TURNED INTO A HATBOX, RIGHT?
YOU'RE LIKE A DOROTHY, BUT YOU'RE DIFFERENT TOO.
I REALLY PREFER TO BE CALLED EMMA.
FAIR ENOUGH. YOU CAN CALL ME AGHA.
YOU'LL NEED SOMEONE TO SHOW YOU THE WAY TO THE EMERALD CITY. I'LL TAKE YOU THERE.
I THOUGHT YOU JUST FOLLOWED THE YELLOW BRICK ROAD FOR THAT.
THE ROAD'S BECOME MORE DANGEROUS OVER THE PAST FEW YEARS. FOLLOWING IT BLINDLY WILL GET YOU KILLED PERMANENTLY.
OH, LOVELY.

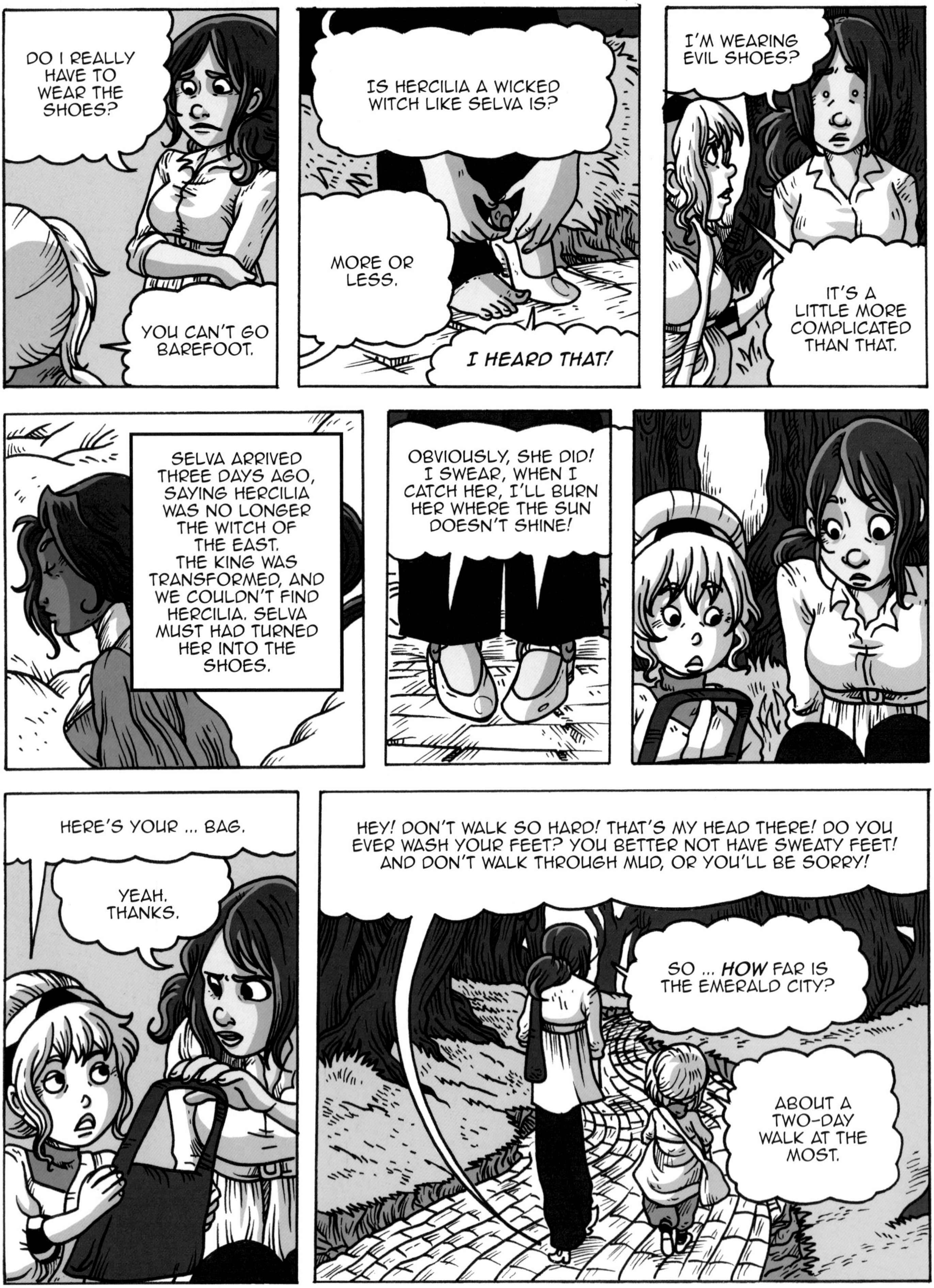
DO I REALLY HAVE TO WEAR THE SHOES?
YOU CAN'T GO BAREFOOT.
IS HERCILIA A WICKED WITCH LIKE SELVA IS?
MORE OR LESS.
I HEARD THAT!
I'M WEARING EVIL SHOES?
IT'S A LITTLE MORE COMPLICATED THAN THAT.
SELVA ARRIVED THREE DAYS AGO, SAYING HERCILIA WAS NO LONGER THE WITCH OF THE EAST. THE KING WAS TRANSFORMED, AND WE COULDN'T FIND HERCILIA. SELVA MUST HAD TURNED HER INTO THE SHOES.
OBVIOUSLY, SHE DID! I SWEAR, WHEN I CATCH HER, I'LL BURN HER WHERE THE SUN DOESN'T SHINE!
HERE'S YOUR ... BAG.
YEAH. THANKS.
HEY! DON'T WALK SO HARD! THAT'S MY HEAD THERE! DO YOU EVER WASH YOUR FEET? YOU BETTER NOT HAVE SWEATY FEET! AND DON'T WALK THROUGH MUD, OR YOU'LL BE SORRY!
SO ... HOW FAR IS THE EMERALD CITY?
ABOUT A TWO-DAY WALK AT THE MOST.

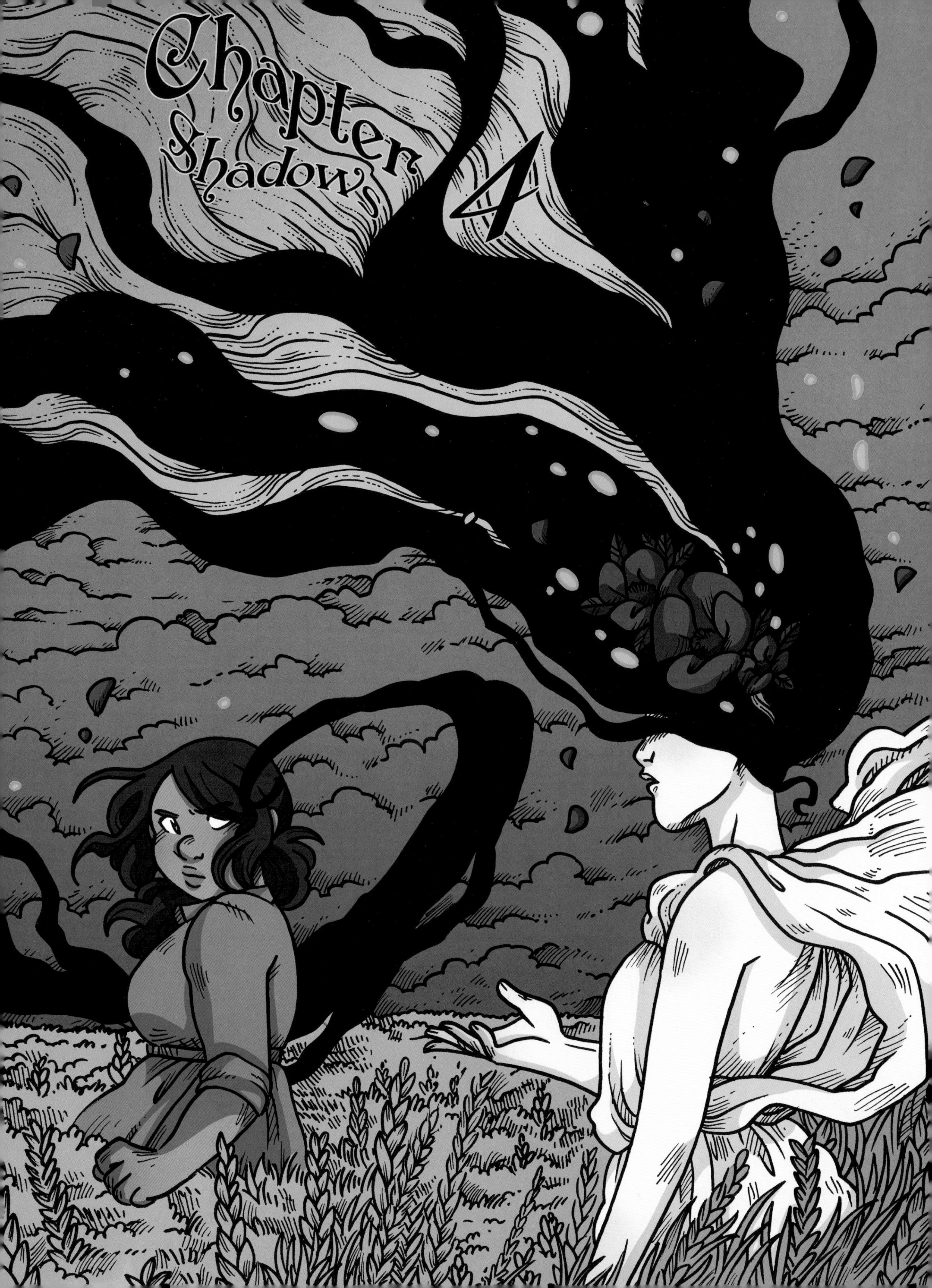
Chapter 4
Shadows

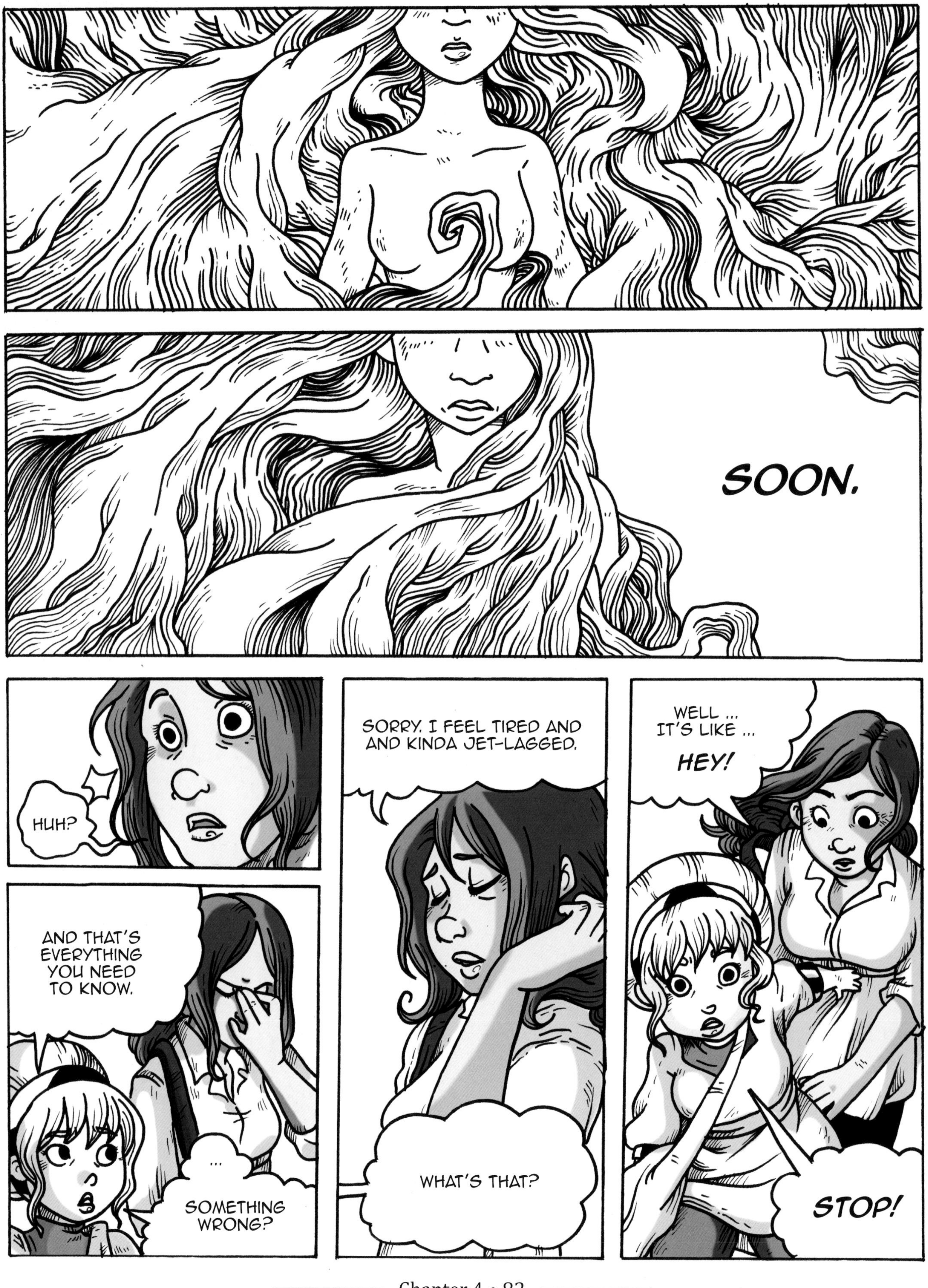
SOON.
HUH?
AND THAT'S EVERYTHING YOU NEED TO KNOW.
...
SOMETHING WRONG?
SORRY. I FEEL TIRED AND AND KINDA JET-LAGGED.
WHAT'S THAT?
WELL ... IT'S LIKE ...
HEY!
STOP!

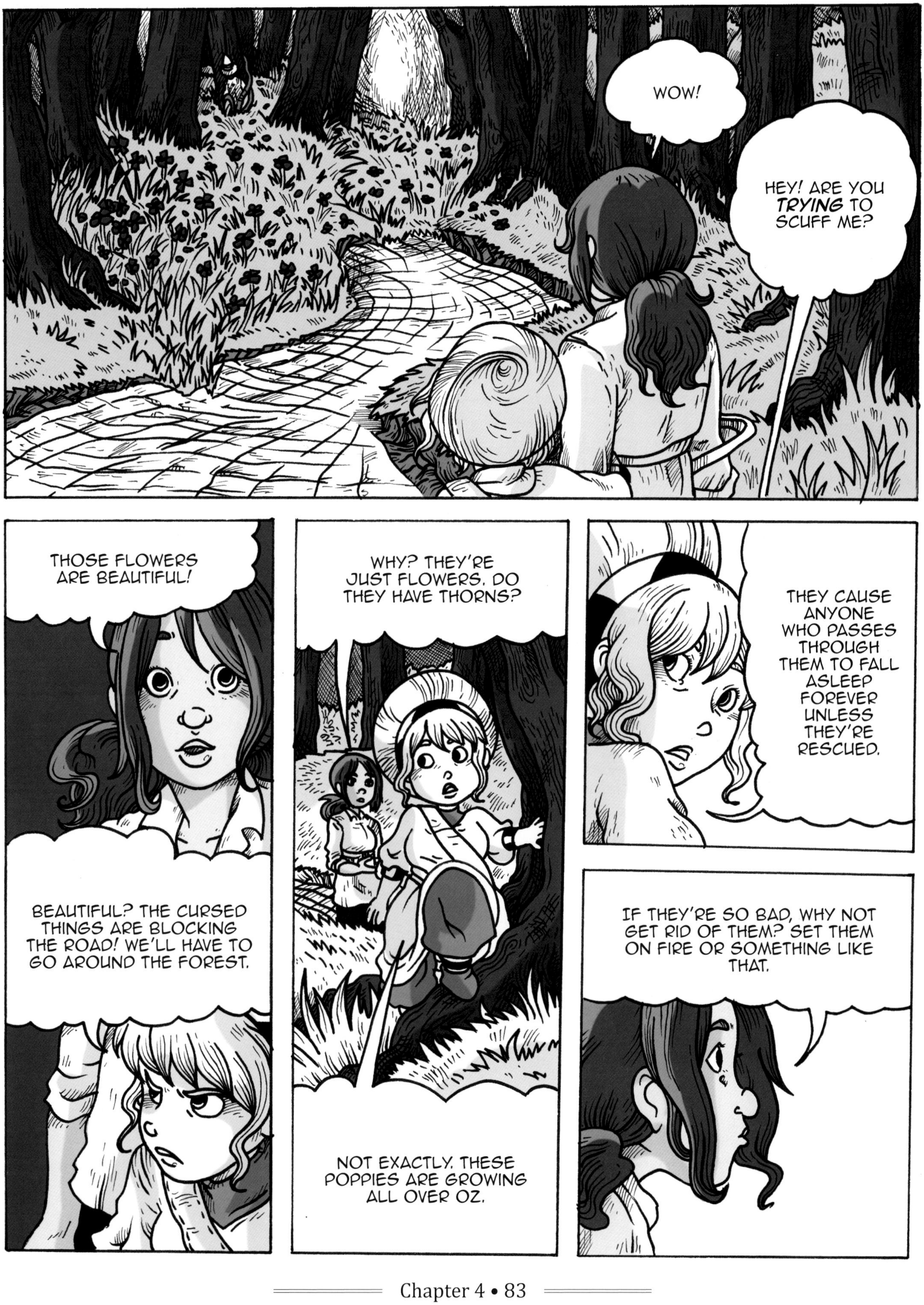
WOW!
HEY! ARE YOU *TRYING* TO SCUFF ME?
THOSE FLOWERS ARE BEAUTIFUL!
BEAUTIFUL? THE CURSED THINGS ARE BLOCKING THE ROAD! WE'LL HAVE TO GO AROUND THE FOREST.
WHY? THEY'RE JUST FLOWERS. DO THEY HAVE THORNS?
NOT EXACTLY. THESE POPPIES ARE GROWING ALL OVER OZ.
THEY CAUSE ANYONE WHO PASSES THROUGH THEM TO FALL ASLEEP FOREVER UNLESS THEY'RE RESCUED.
IF THEY'RE SO BAD, WHY NOT GET RID OF THEM? SET THEM ON FIRE OR SOMETHING LIKE THAT.

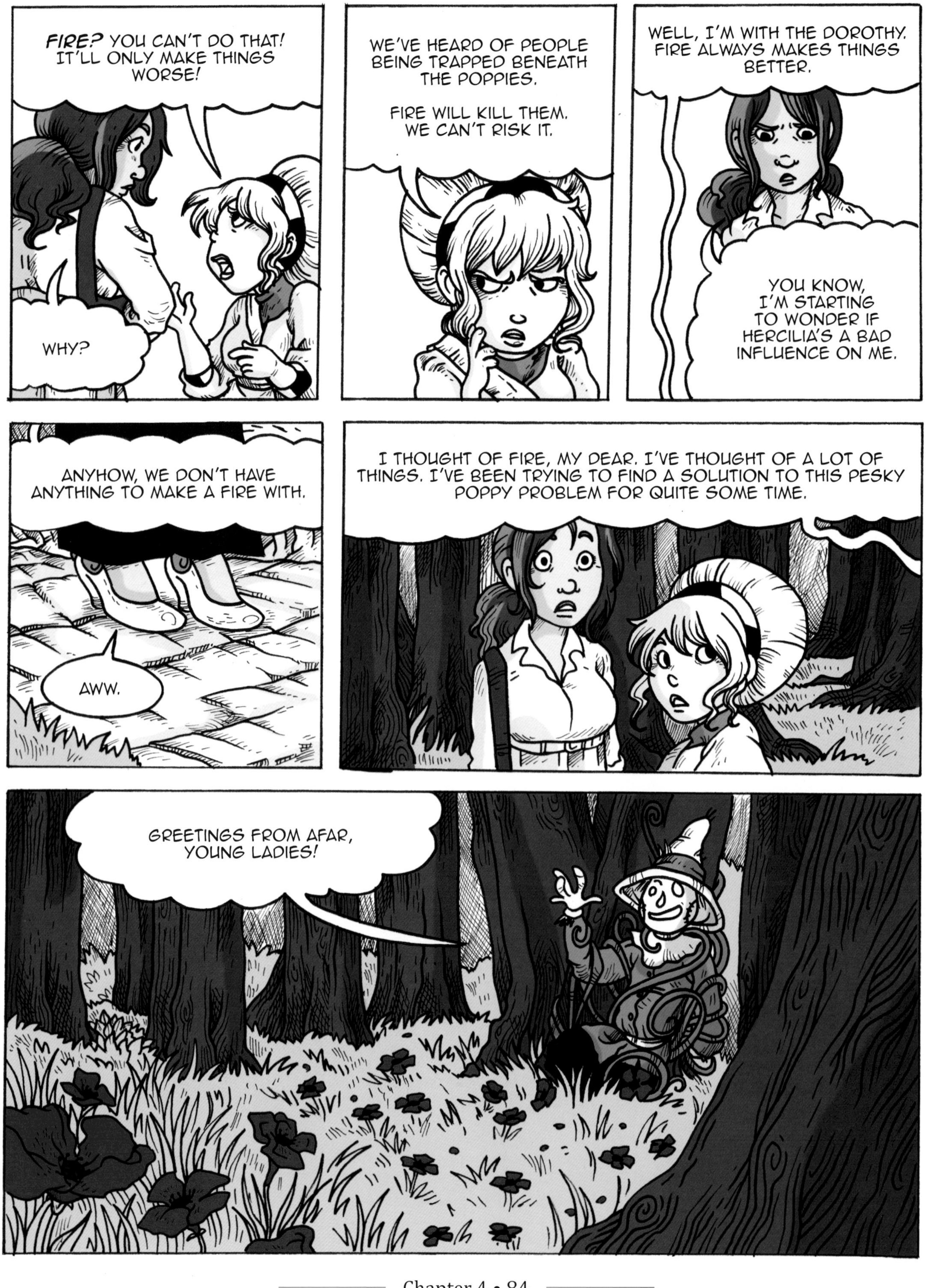

FIRE? YOU CAN'T DO THAT! IT'LL ONLY MAKE THINGS WORSE!
WHY?
WE'VE HEARD OF PEOPLE BEING TRAPPED BENEATH THE POPPIES.
FIRE WILL KILL THEM. WE CAN'T RISK IT.
WELL, I'M WITH THE DOROTHY. FIRE ALWAYS MAKES THINGS BETTER.
YOU KNOW, I'M STARTING TO WONDER IF HERCILIA'S A BAD INFLUENCE ON ME.
ANYHOW, WE DON'T HAVE ANYTHING TO MAKE A FIRE WITH.
AWW.
I THOUGHT OF FIRE, MY DEAR. I'VE THOUGHT OF A LOT OF THINGS. I'VE BEEN TRYING TO FIND A SOLUTION TO THIS PESKY POPPY PROBLEM FOR QUITE SOME TIME.
GREETINGS FROM AFAR, YOUNG LADIES!

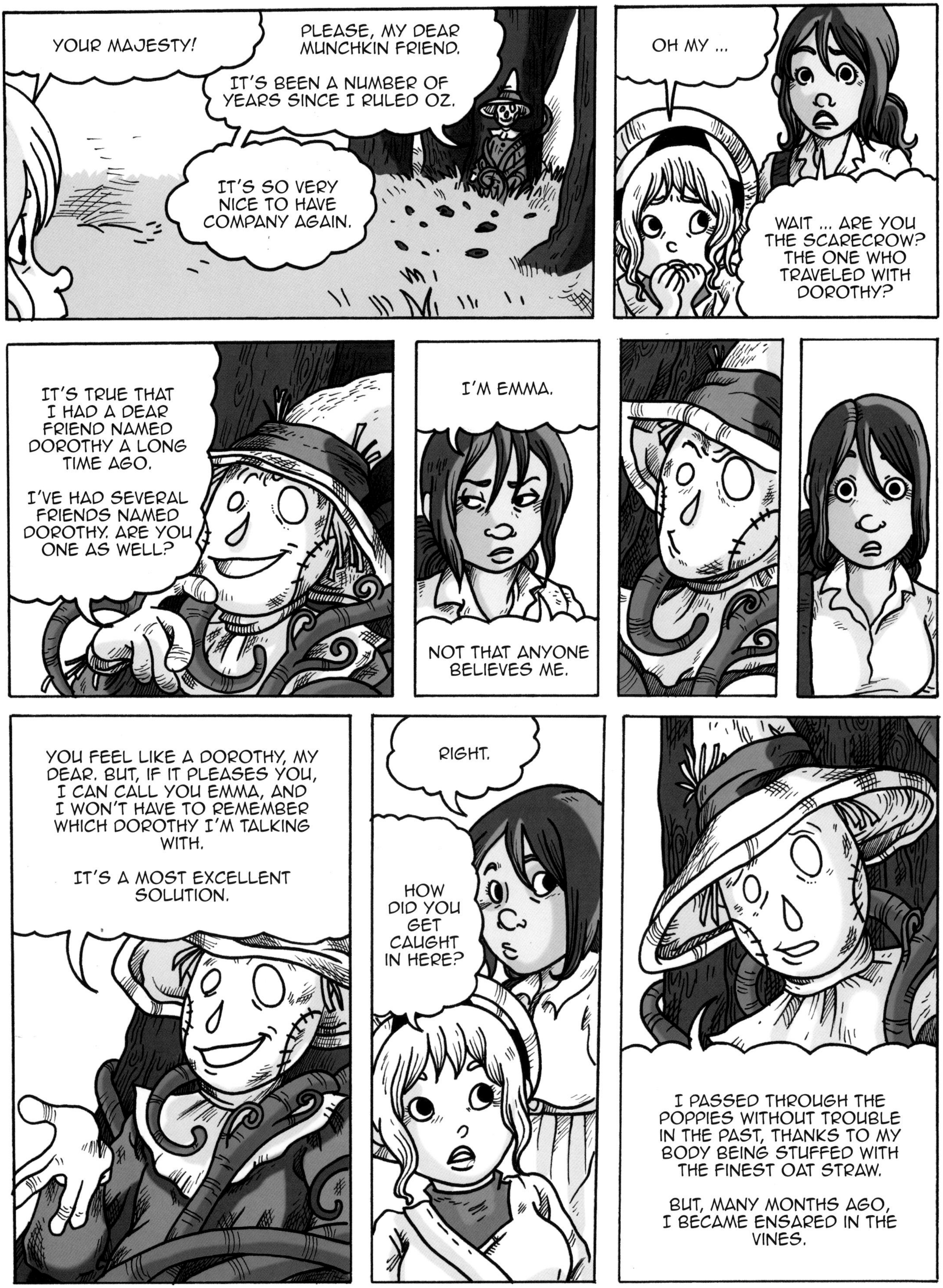
YOUR MAJESTY!
PLEASE, MY DEAR MUNCHKIN FRIEND.
IT'S BEEN A NUMBER OF YEARS SINCE I RULED OZ.
IT'S SO VERY NICE TO HAVE COMPANY AGAIN.
OH MY ...
WAIT ... ARE YOU THE SCARECROW? THE ONE WHO TRAVELED WITH DOROTHY?
IT'S TRUE THAT I HAD A DEAR FRIEND NAMED DOROTHY A LONG TIME AGO.
I'VE HAD SEVERAL FRIENDS NAMED DOROTHY. ARE YOU ONE AS WELL?
I'M EMMA.
NOT THAT ANYONE BELIEVES ME.
YOU FEEL LIKE A DOROTHY, MY DEAR. BUT, IF IT PLEASES YOU, I CAN CALL YOU EMMA, AND I WON'T HAVE TO REMEMBER WHICH DOROTHY I'M TALKING WITH.
IT'S A MOST EXCELLENT SOLUTION.
RIGHT.
HOW DID YOU GET CAUGHT IN HERE?
I PASSED THROUGH THE POPPIES WITHOUT TROUBLE IN THE PAST, THANKS TO MY BODY BEING STUFFED WITH THE FINEST OAT STRAW.
BUT, MANY MONTHS AGO, I BECAME ENSARED IN THE VINES.

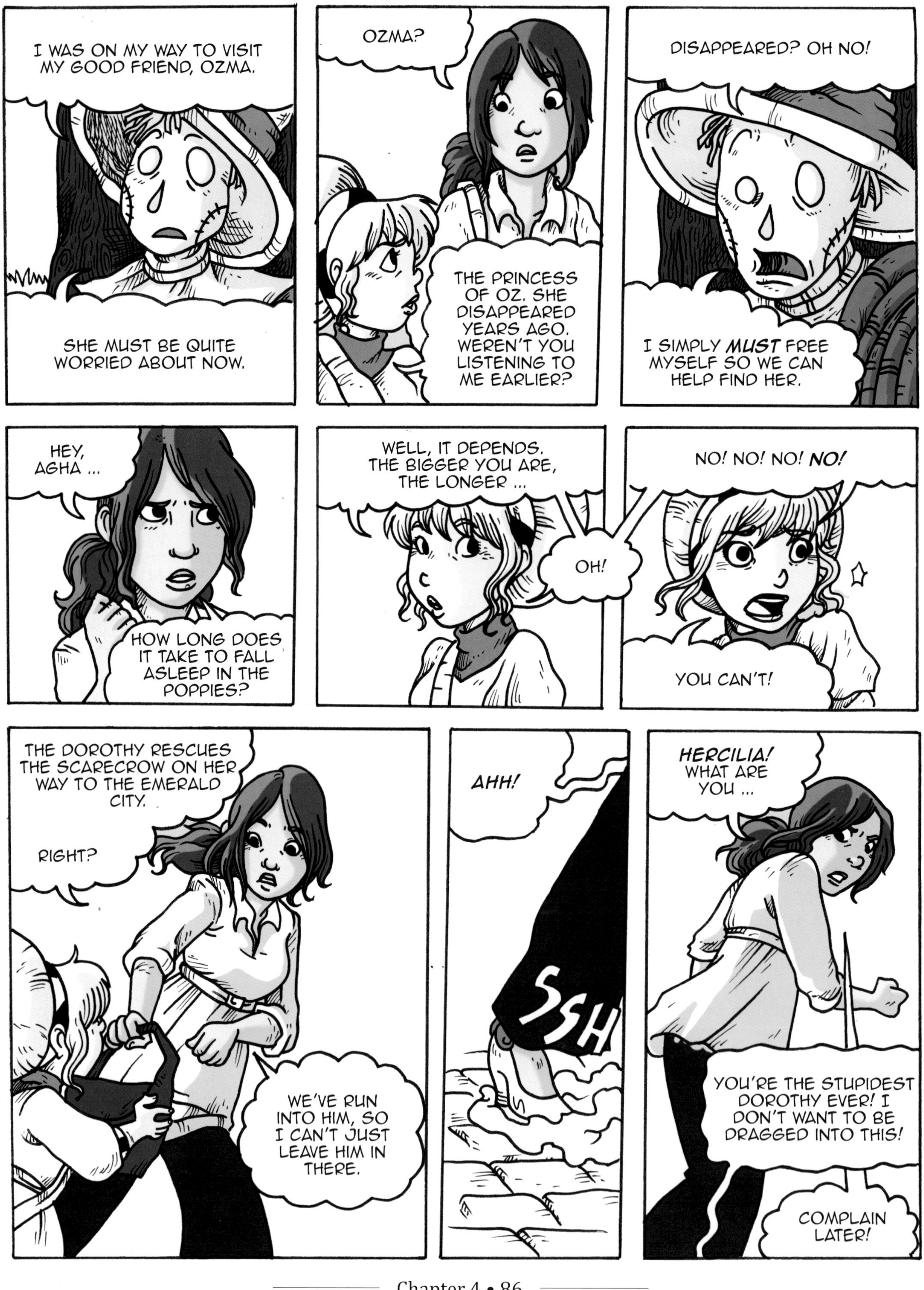
I WAS ON MY WAY TO VISIT MY GOOD FRIEND, OZMA.
SHE MUST BE QUITE WORRIED ABOUT NOW.
OZMA?
THE PRINCESS OF OZ. SHE DISAPPEARED YEARS AGO. WEREN'T YOU LISTENING TO ME EARLIER?
DISAPPEARED? OH NO!
I SIMPLY MUST FREE MYSELF SO WE CAN HELP FIND HER.
HEY, AGHA ...
HOW LONG DOES IT TAKE TO FALL ASLEEP IN THE POPPIES?
WELL, IT DEPENDS. THE BIGGER YOU ARE, THE LONGER ...
OH!
NO! NO! NO! NO!
YOU CAN'T!
THE DOROTHY RESCUES THE SCARECROW ON HER WAY TO THE EMERALD CITY.
RIGHT?
WE'VE RUN INTO HIM, SO I CAN'T JUST LEAVE HIM IN THERE.
AHH!
SSH
HERCILIA! WHAT ARE YOU ...
YOU'RE THE STUPIDEST DOROTHY EVER! I DON'T WANT TO BE DRAGGED INTO THIS!
COMPLAIN LATER!

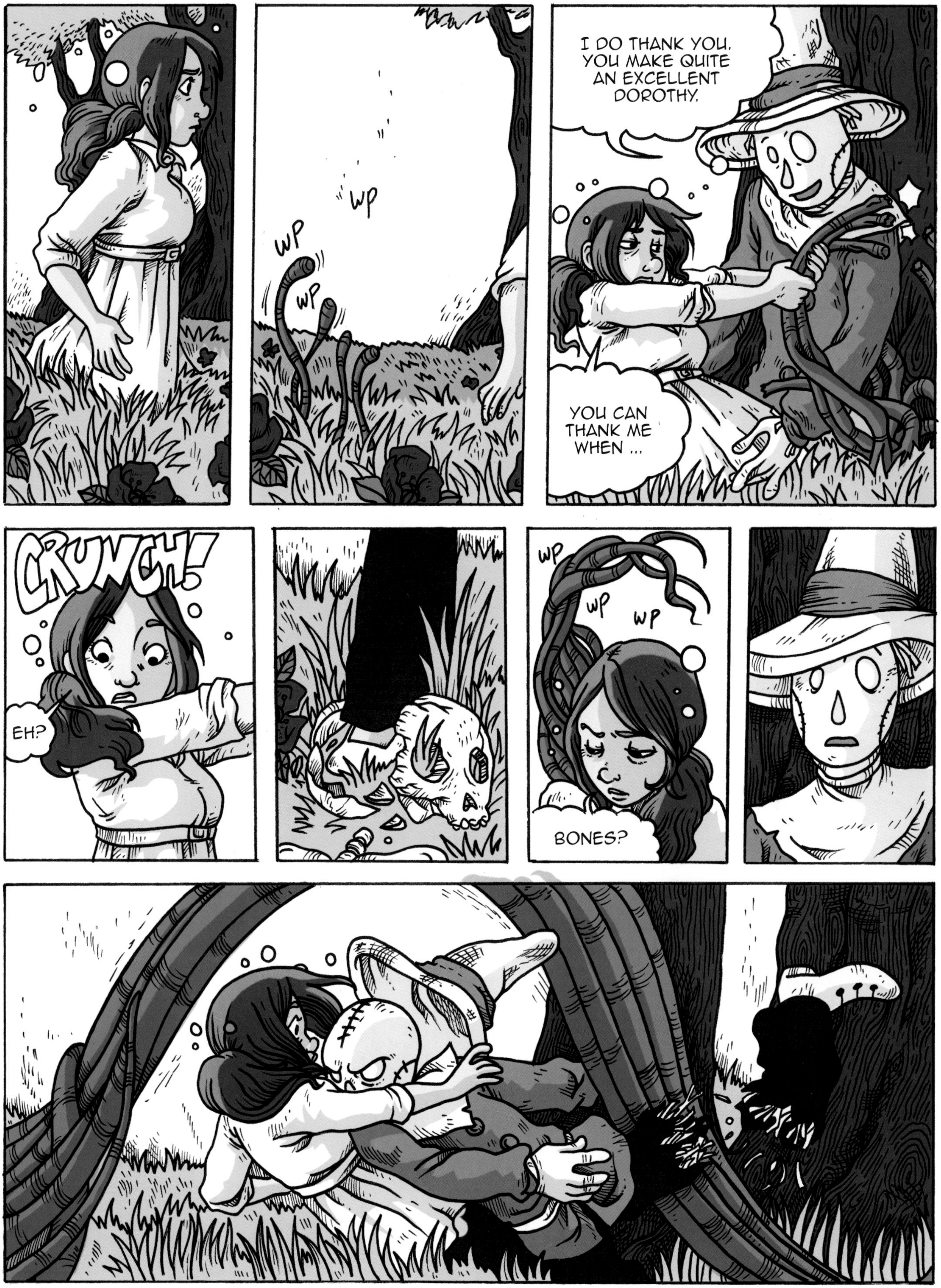
WP
WP
WP
I DO THANK YOU. YOU MAKE QUITE AN EXCELLENT DOROTHY.
YOU CAN THANK ME WHEN ...
CRUNCH!
EH?
WP
WP
WP
BONES?

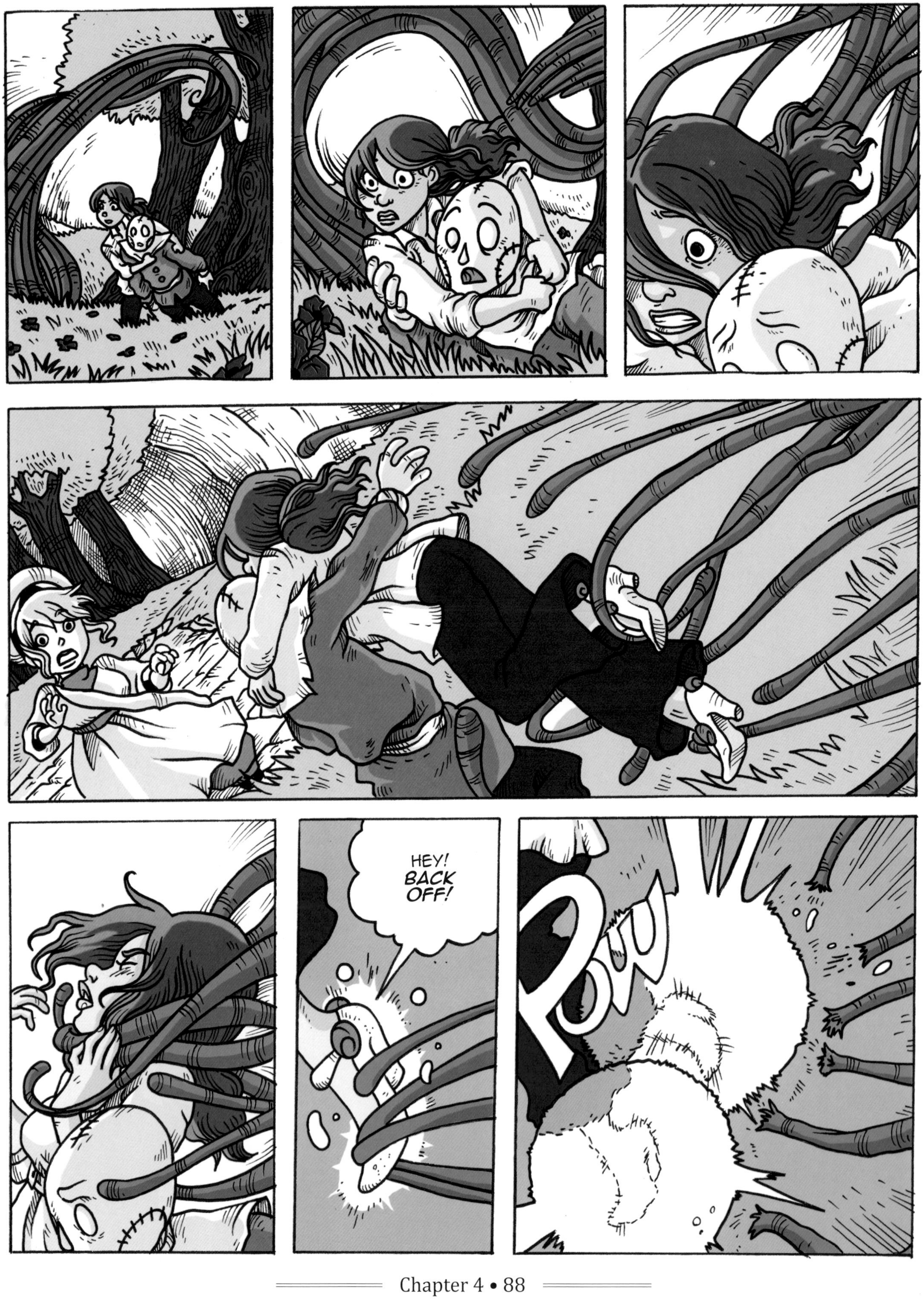
HEY! BACK OFF!
POW

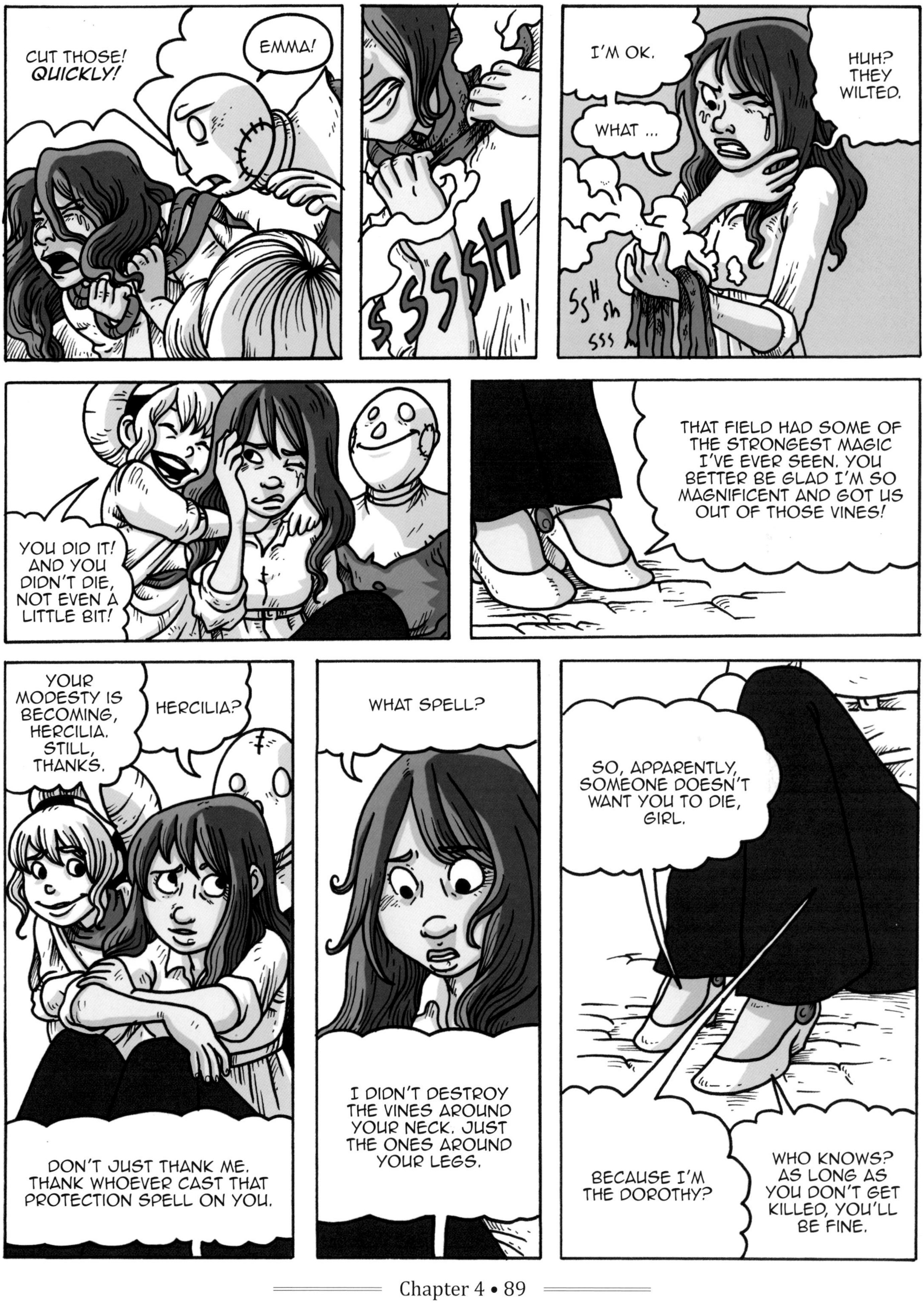

CUT THOSE! *QUICKLY!*
EMMA!
SSSSSH
I'M OK.
WHAT ...
HUH? THEY WILTED.
SSH sh sss
YOU DID IT! AND YOU DIDN'T DIE, NOT EVEN A LITTLE BIT!
THAT FIELD HAD SOME OF THE STRONGEST MAGIC I'VE EVER SEEN. YOU BETTER BE GLAD I'M SO MAGNIFICENT AND GOT US OUT OF THOSE VINES!
YOUR MODESTY IS BECOMING, HERCILIA. STILL, THANKS.
HERCILIA?
DON'T JUST THANK ME. THANK WHOEVER CAST THAT PROTECTION SPELL ON YOU.
WHAT SPELL?
I DIDN'T DESTROY THE VINES AROUND YOUR NECK. JUST THE ONES AROUND YOUR LEGS.
SO, APPARENTLY, SOMEONE DOESN'T WANT YOU TO DIE, GIRL.
BECAUSE I'M THE DOROTHY?
WHO KNOWS? AS LONG AS YOU DON'T GET KILLED, YOU'LL BE FINE.

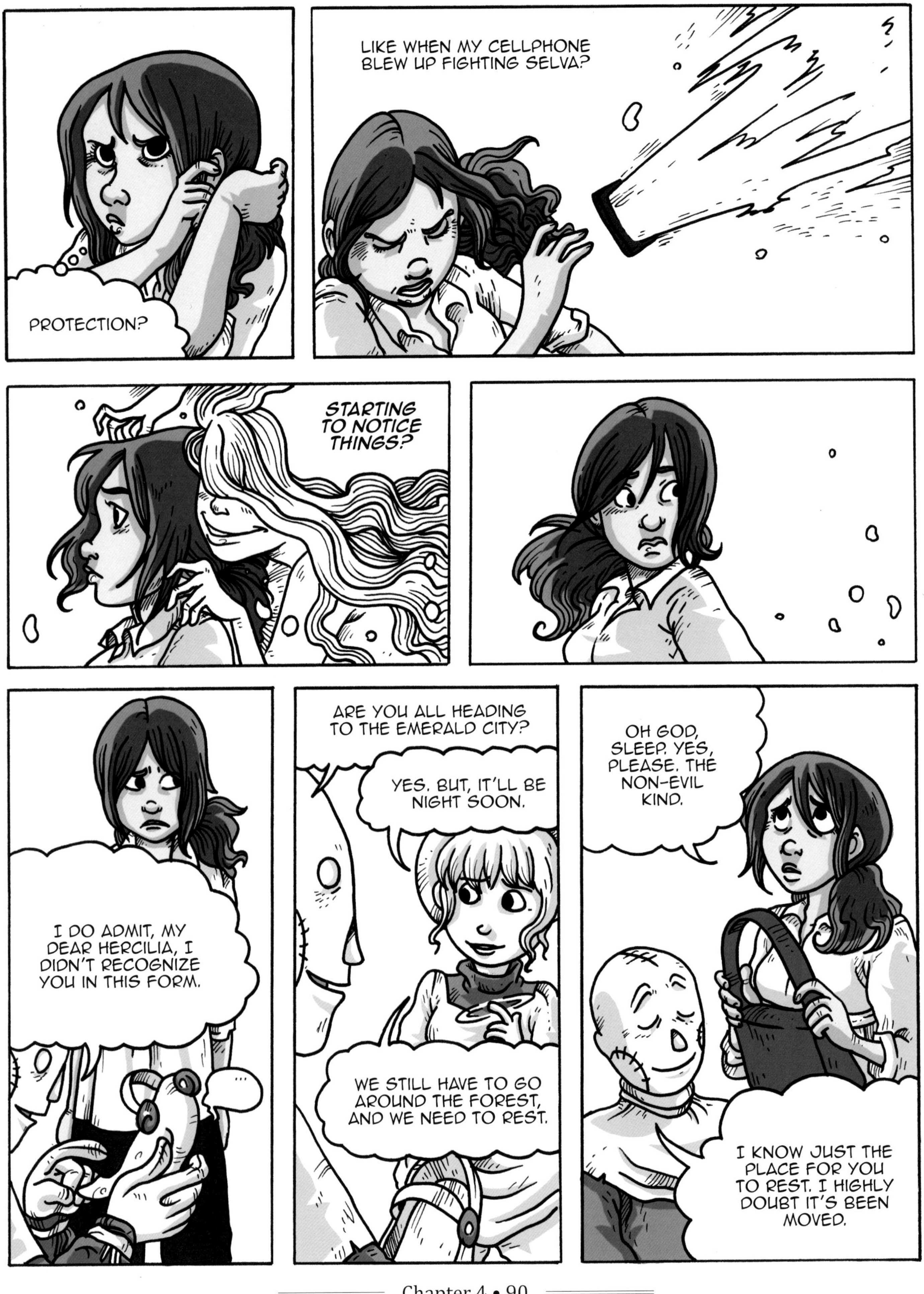
PROTECTION?
LIKE WHEN MY CELLPHONE BLEW UP FIGHTING SELVA?
STARTING TO NOTICE THINGS?
I DO ADMIT, MY DEAR HERCILIA, I DIDN'T RECOGNIZE YOU IN THIS FORM.
...
ARE YOU ALL HEADING TO THE EMERALD CITY?
YES. BUT, IT'LL BE NIGHT SOON.
WE STILL HAVE TO GO AROUND THE FOREST, AND WE NEED TO REST.
OH GOD, SLEEP. YES, PLEASE. THE NON-EVIL KIND.
I KNOW JUST THE PLACE FOR YOU TO REST. I HIGHLY DOUBT IT'S BEEN MOVED.

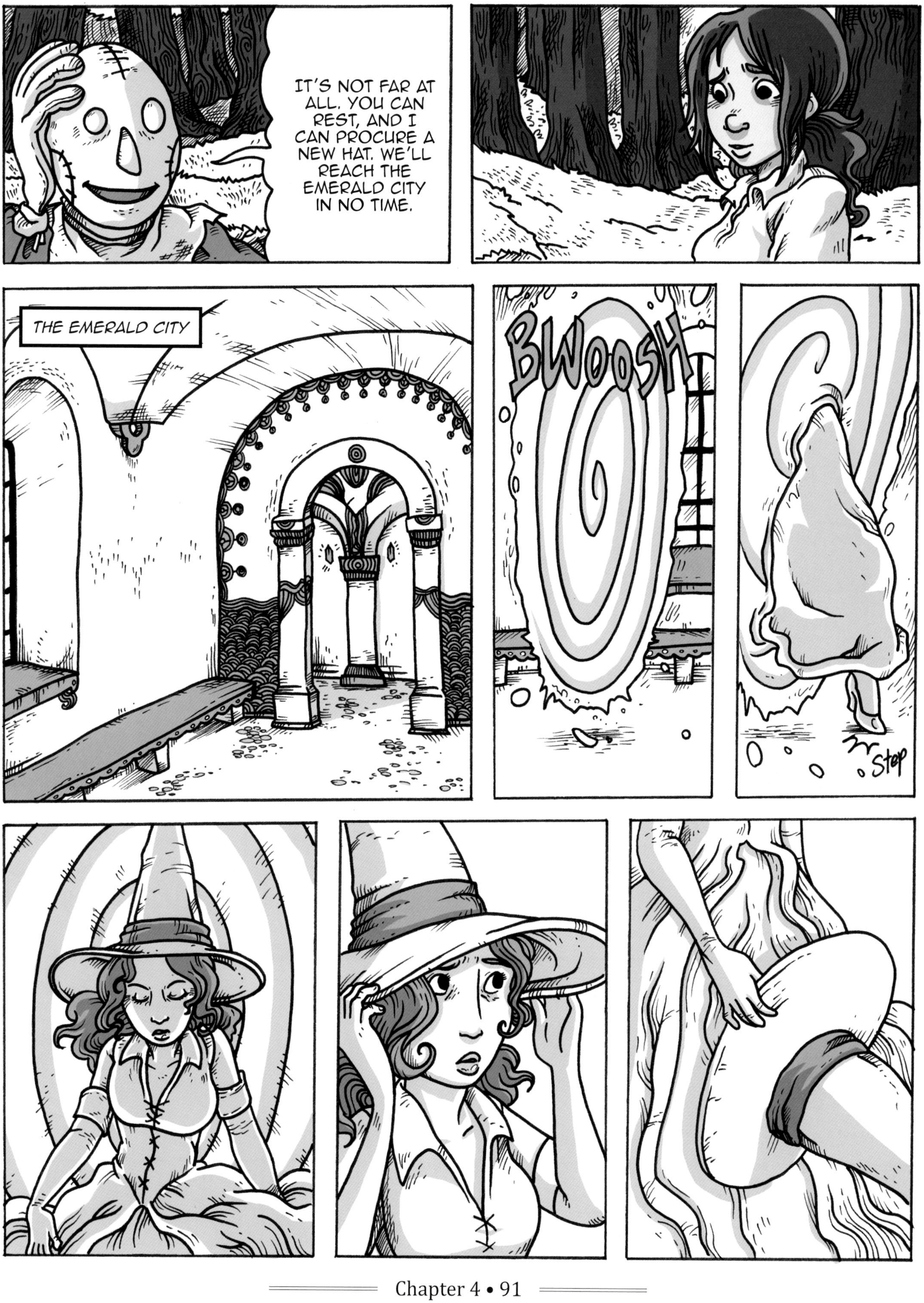
IT'S NOT FAR AT ALL. YOU CAN REST, AND I CAN PROCURE A NEW HAT. WE'LL REACH THE EMERALD CITY IN NO TIME.
THE EMERALD CITY
BWOOSH
Step

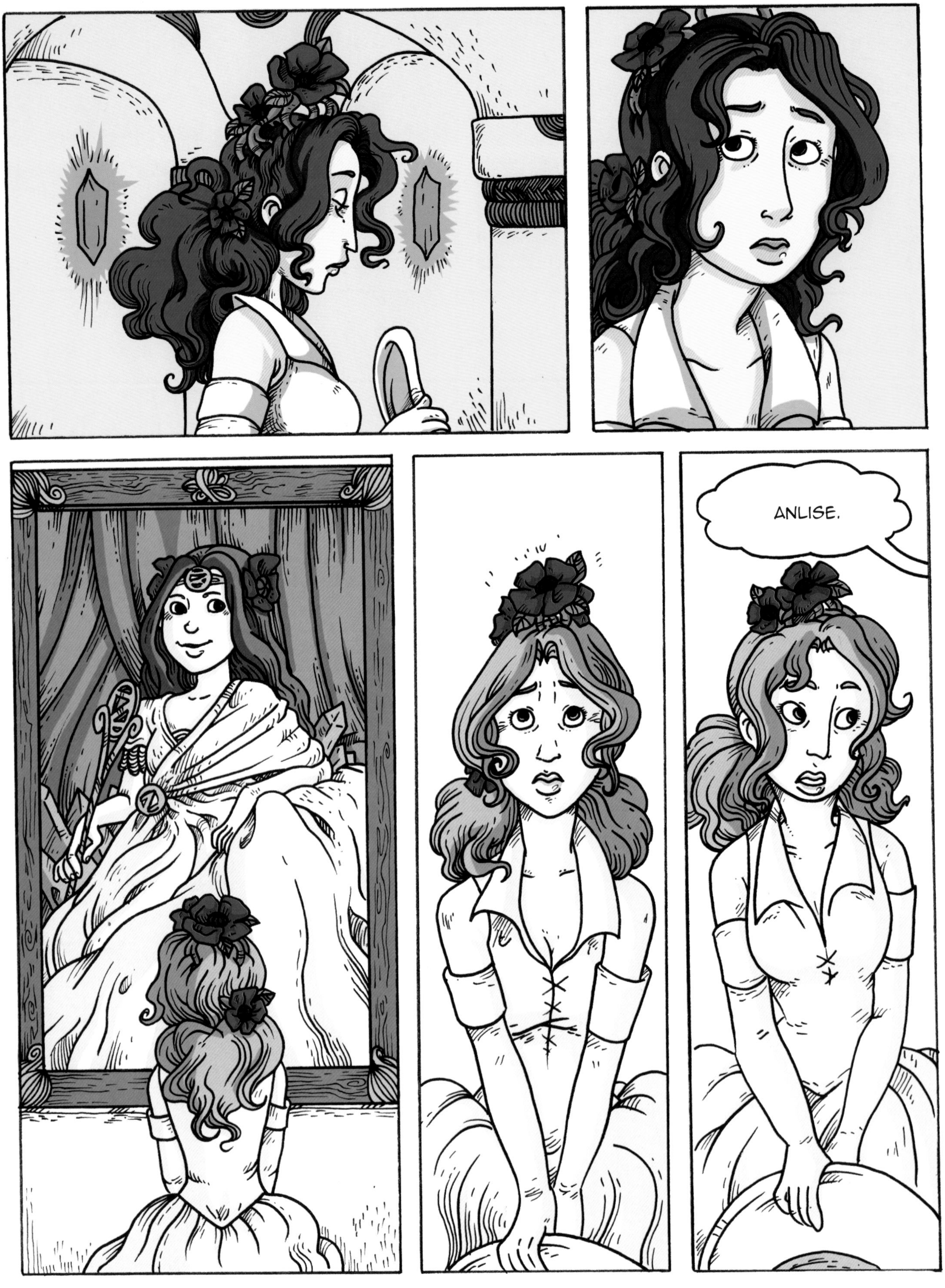
ANLISE.

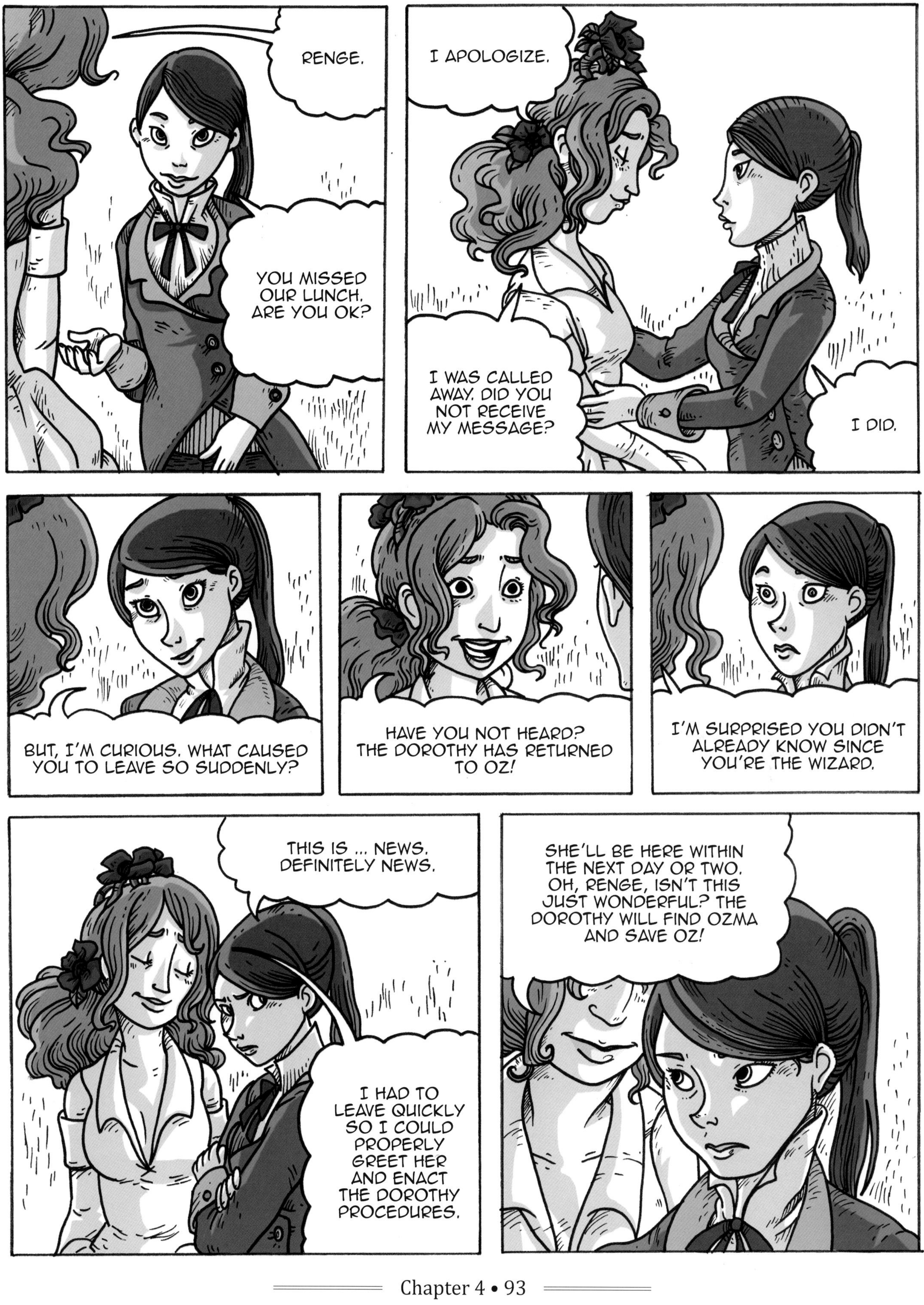
RENGE.
YOU MISSED OUR LUNCH. ARE YOU OK?
I APOLOGIZE.
I WAS CALLED AWAY. DID YOU NOT RECEIVE MY MESSAGE?
I DID.
BUT, I'M CURIOUS. WHAT CAUSED YOU TO LEAVE SO SUDDENLY?
HAVE YOU NOT HEARD? THE DOROTHY HAS RETURNED TO OZ!
I'M SURPRISED YOU DIDN'T ALREADY KNOW SINCE YOU'RE THE WIZARD.
THIS IS ... NEWS. DEFINITELY NEWS.
I HAD TO LEAVE QUICKLY SO I COULD PROPERLY GREET HER AND ENACT THE DOROTHY PROCEDURES.
SHE'LL BE HERE WITHIN THE NEXT DAY OR TWO. OH, RENGE, ISN'T THIS JUST WONDERFUL? THE DOROTHY WILL FIND OZMA AND SAVE OZ!

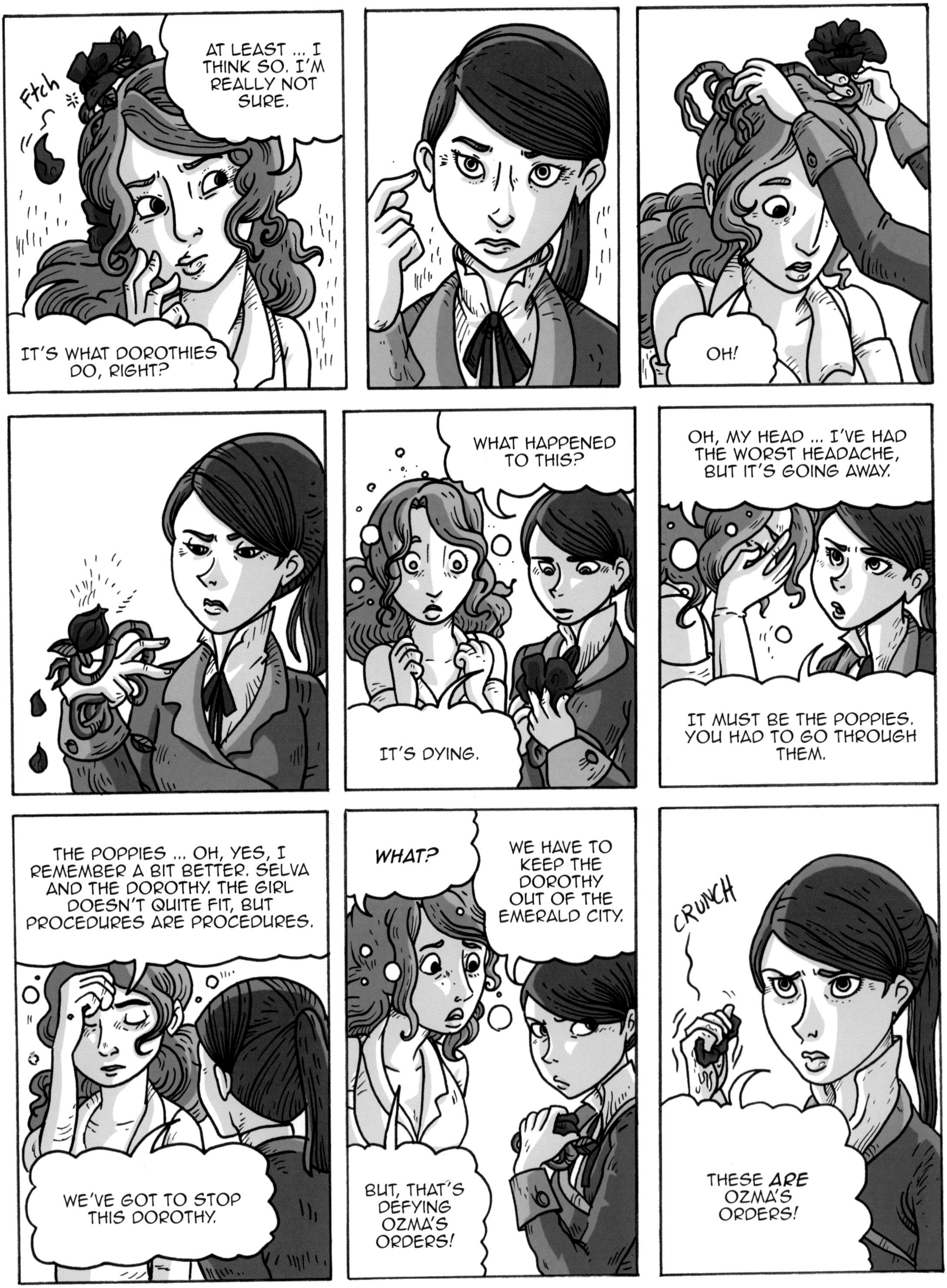
AT LEAST ... I THINK SO. I'M REALLY NOT SURE.
FTCH
IT'S WHAT DOROTHIES DO, RIGHT?
OH!
WHAT HAPPENED TO THIS?
IT'S DYING.
OH, MY HEAD ... I'VE HAD THE WORST HEADACHE, BUT IT'S GOING AWAY.
IT MUST BE THE POPPIES. YOU HAD TO GO THROUGH THEM.
THE POPPIES ... OH, YES, I REMEMBER A BIT BETTER. SELVA AND THE DOROTHY. THE GIRL DOESN'T QUITE FIT, BUT PROCEDURES ARE PROCEDURES.
WE'VE GOT TO STOP THIS DOROTHY.
WHAT?
WE HAVE TO KEEP THE DOROTHY OUT OF THE EMERALD CITY.
BUT, THAT'S DEFYING OZMA'S ORDERS!
CRUNCH
THESE *ARE* OZMA'S ORDERS!

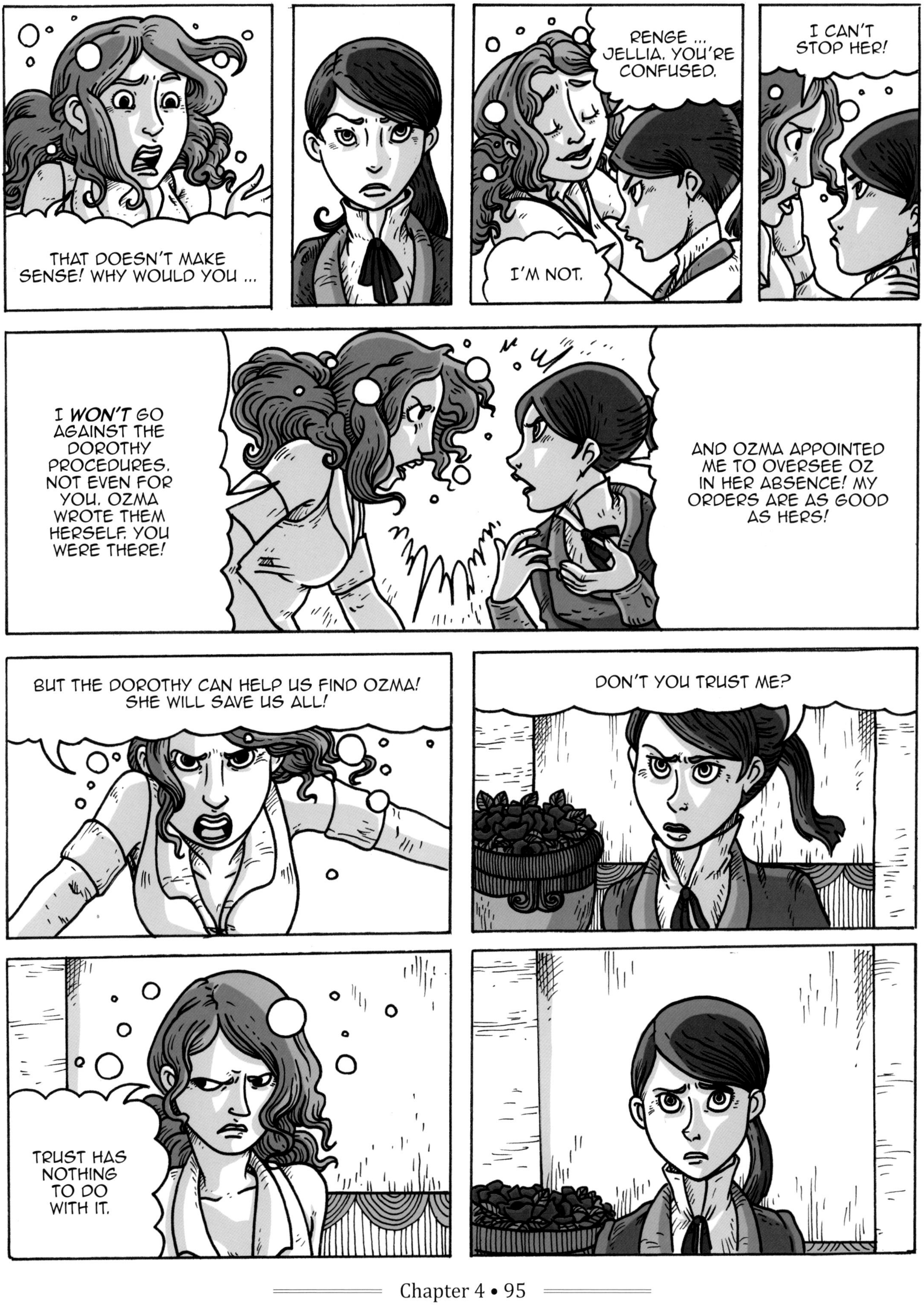
THAT DOESN'T MAKE SENSE! WHY WOULD YOU ...
RENGE ... JELLIA, YOU'RE CONFUSED.
I'M NOT.
I CAN'T STOP HER!
I WON'T GO AGAINST THE DOROTHY PROCEDURES. NOT EVEN FOR YOU. OZMA WROTE THEM HERSELF. YOU WERE THERE!
AND OZMA APPOINTED ME TO OVERSEE OZ IN HER ABSENCE! MY ORDERS ARE AS GOOD AS HERS!
BUT THE DOROTHY CAN HELP US FIND OZMA! SHE WILL SAVE US ALL!
DON'T YOU TRUST ME?
TRUST HAS NOTHING TO DO WITH IT.

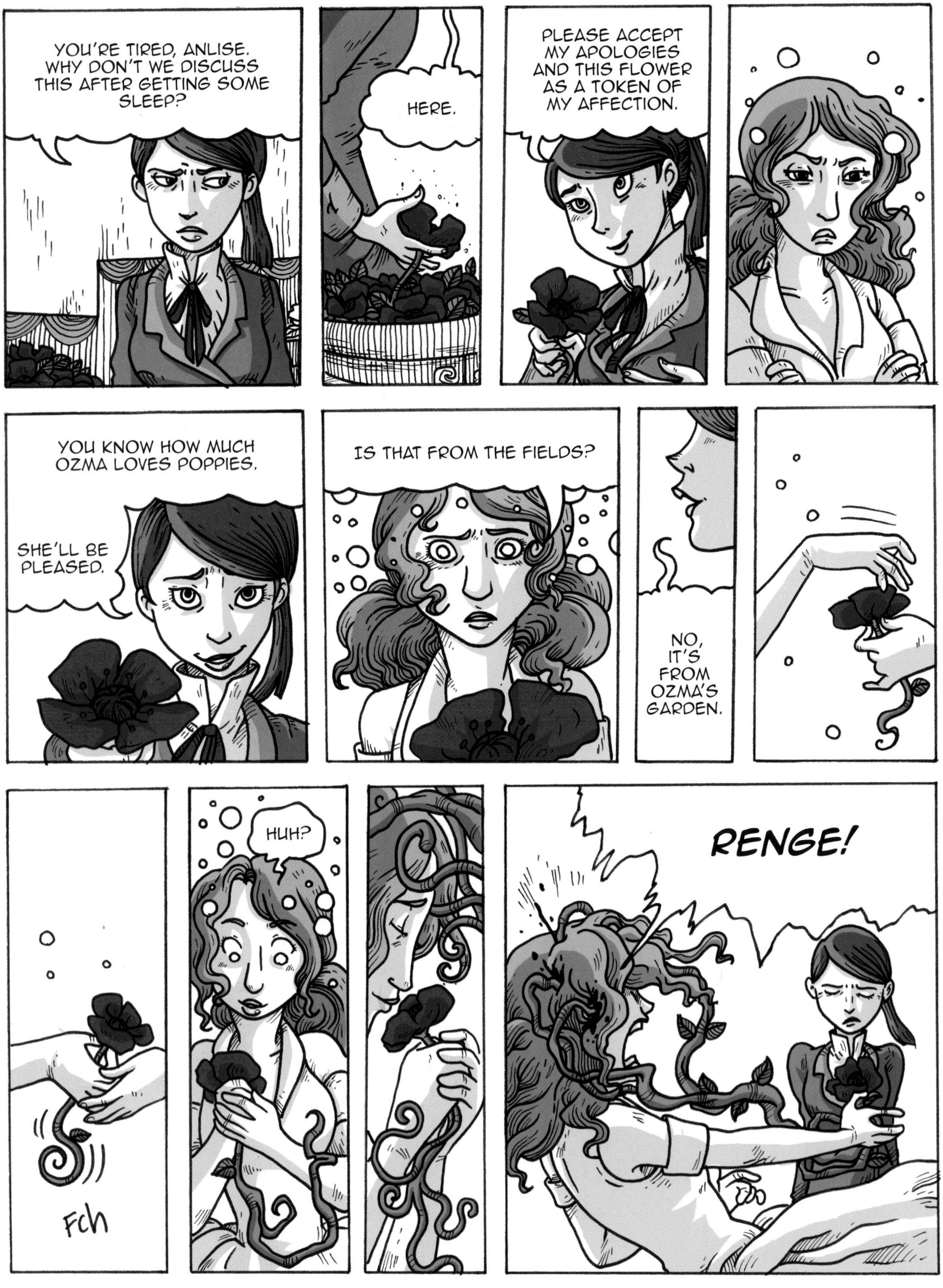

YOU'RE TIRED, ANLISE. WHY DON'T WE DISCUSS THIS AFTER GETTING SOME SLEEP?
HERE.
PLEASE ACCEPT MY APOLOGIES AND THIS FLOWER AS A TOKEN OF MY AFFECTION.
YOU KNOW HOW MUCH OZMA LOVES POPPIES.
SHE'LL BE PLEASED.
IS THAT FROM THE FIELDS?
NO, IT'S FROM OZMA'S GARDEN.
FCH
HUH?
RENGE!

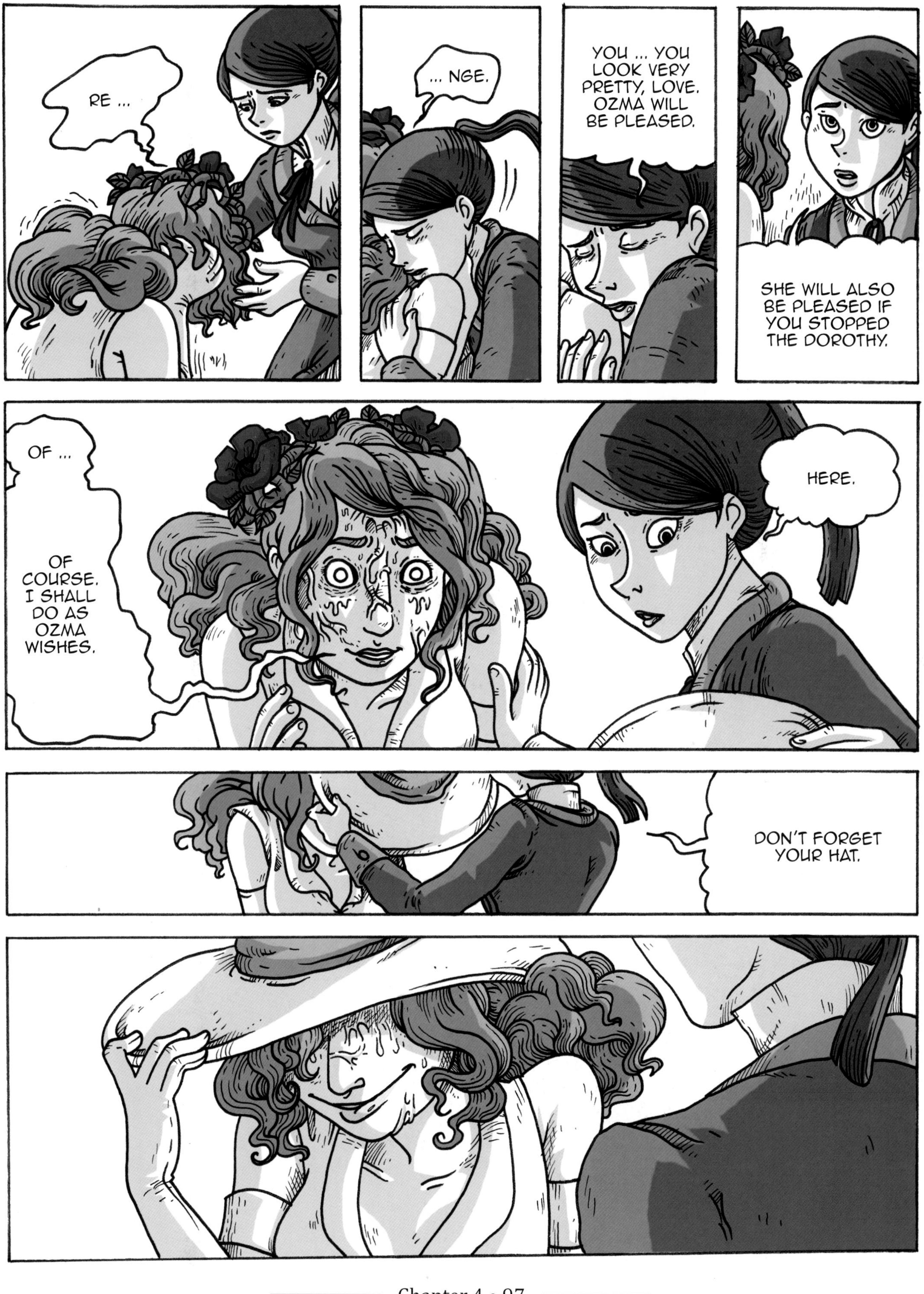
RE ...
... NGE.
YOU ... YOU LOOK VERY PRETTY, LOVE. OZMA WILL BE PLEASED.
SHE WILL ALSO BE PLEASED IF YOU STOPPED THE DOROTHY.
OF ...
OF COURSE. I SHALL DO AS OZMA WISHES.
HERE.
DON'T FORGET YOUR HAT.

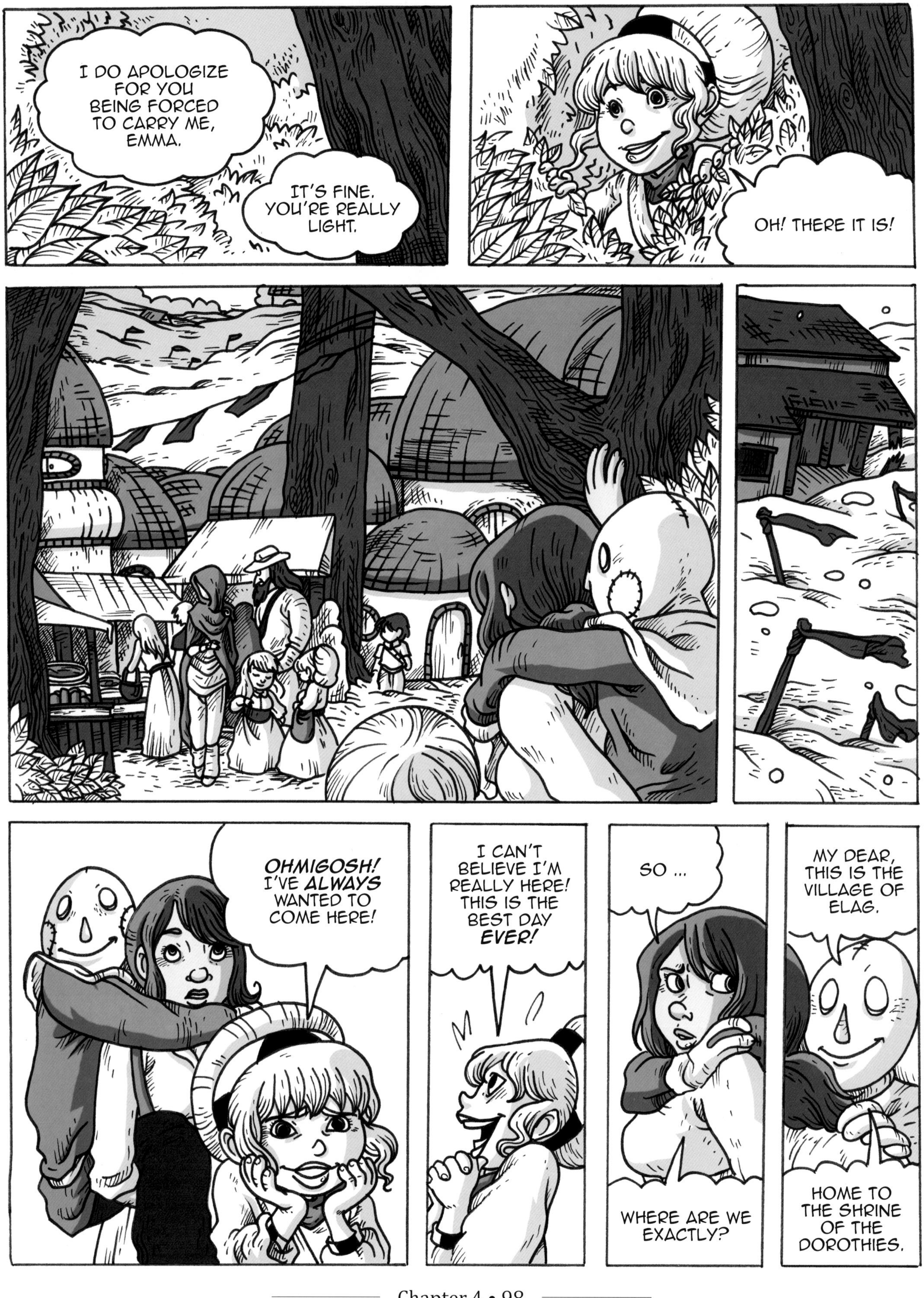
I DO APOLOGIZE FOR YOU BEING FORCED TO CARRY ME, EMMA.
IT'S FINE. YOU'RE REALLY LIGHT.
OH! THERE IT IS!
OHMIGOSH! I'VE ALWAYS WANTED TO COME HERE!
I CAN'T BELIEVE I'M REALLY HERE! THIS IS THE BEST DAY EVER!
SO ...
WHERE ARE WE EXACTLY?
MY DEAR, THIS IS THE VILLAGE OF ELAG.
HOME TO THE SHRINE OF THE DOROTHIES.

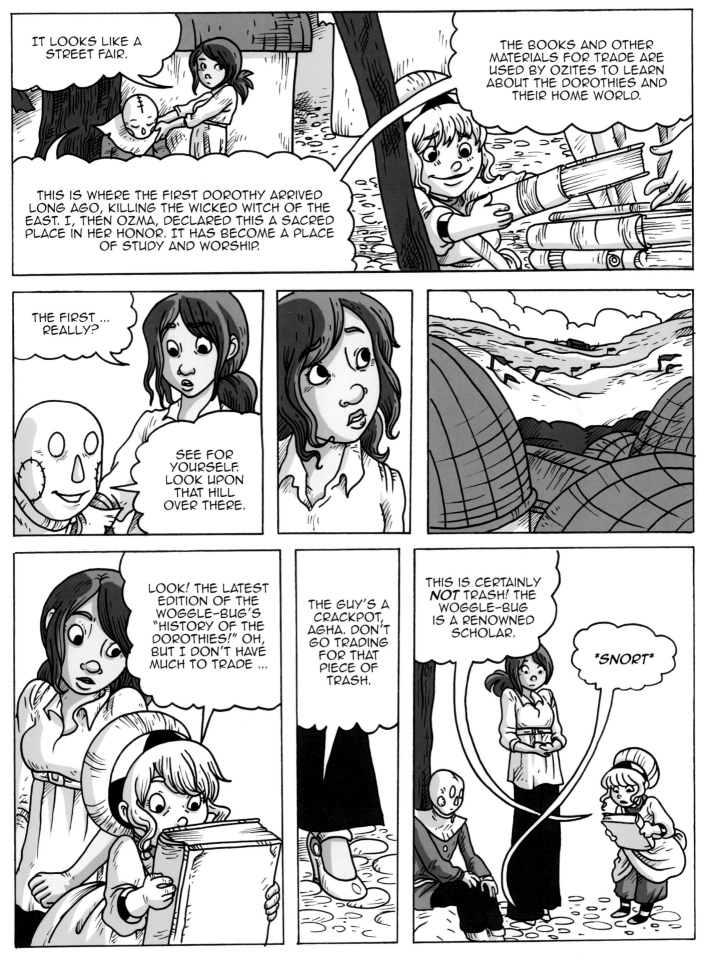

IT LOOKS LIKE A STREET FAIR.

THE BOOKS AND OTHER MATERIALS FOR TRADE ARE USED BY OZITES TO LEARN ABOUT THE DOROTHIES AND THEIR HOME WORLD.

THIS IS WHERE THE FIRST DOROTHY ARRIVED LONG AGO, KILLING THE WICKED WITCH OF THE EAST. I, THEN OZMA, DECLARED THIS A SACRED PLACE IN HER HONOR. IT HAS BECOME A PLACE OF STUDY AND WORSHIP.

THE FIRST ... REALLY?

SEE FOR YOURSELF. LOOK UPON THAT HILL OVER THERE.

LOOK! THE LATEST EDITION OF THE WOGGLE-BUG'S "HISTORY OF THE DOROTHIES!" OH, BUT I DON'T HAVE MUCH TO TRADE ...

THE GUY'S A CRACKPOT, AGHA. DON'T GO TRADING FOR THAT PIECE OF TRASH.

THIS IS CERTAINLY *NOT* TRASH! THE WOGGLE-BUG IS A RENOWNED SCHOLAR.

SNORT

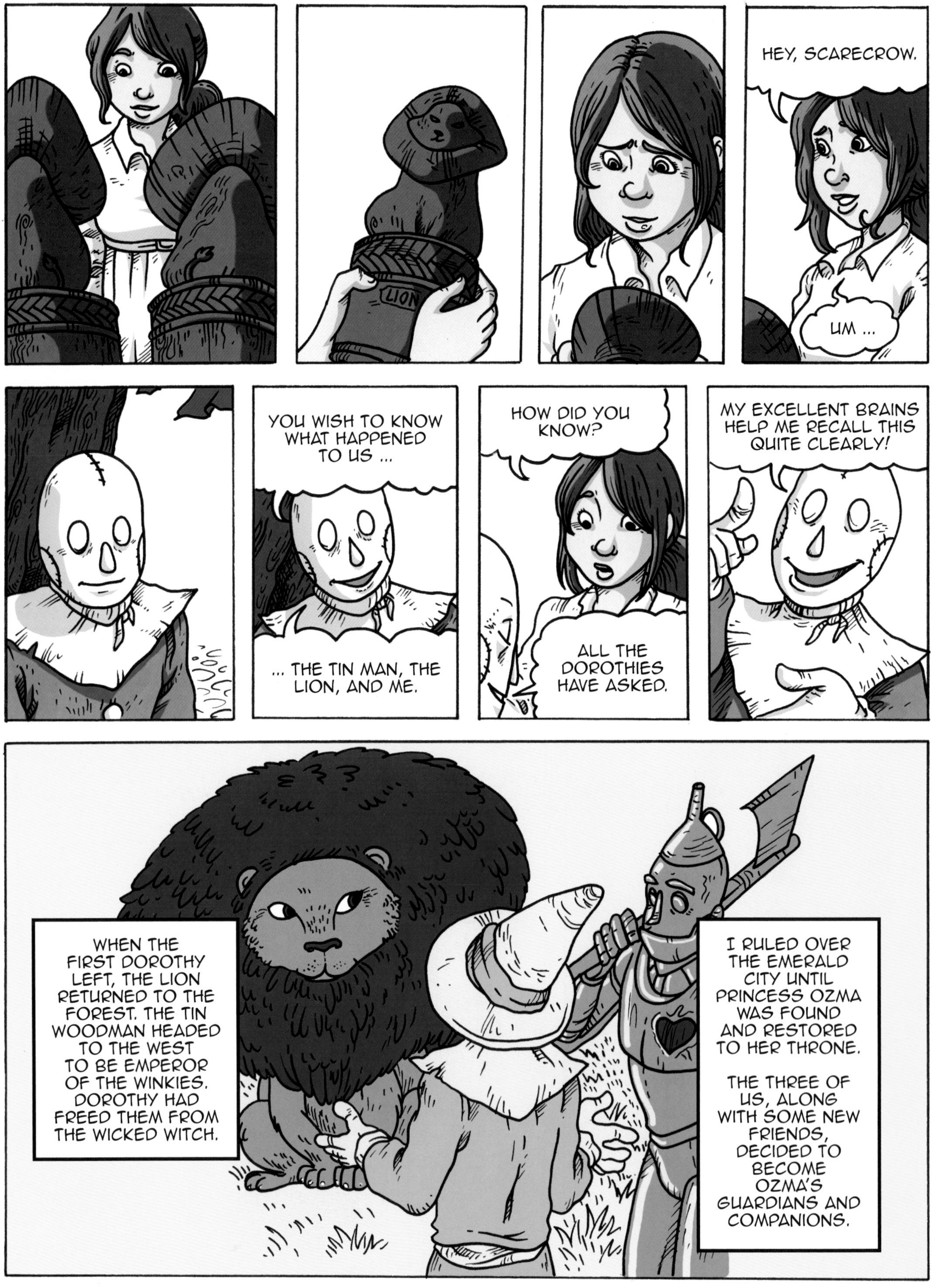
HEY, SCARECROW.
UM ...
YOU WISH TO KNOW WHAT HAPPENED TO US ...
... THE TIN MAN, THE LION, AND ME.
HOW DID YOU KNOW?
ALL THE DOROTHIES HAVE ASKED.
MY EXCELLENT BRAINS HELP ME RECALL THIS QUITE CLEARLY!
WHEN THE FIRST DOROTHY LEFT, THE LION RETURNED TO THE FOREST. THE TIN WOODMAN HEADED TO THE WEST TO BE EMPEROR OF THE WINKIES. DOROTHY HAD FREED THEM FROM THE WICKED WITCH.
I RULED OVER THE EMERALD CITY UNTIL PRINCESS OZMA WAS FOUND AND RESTORED TO HER THRONE.
THE THREE OF US, ALONG WITH SOME NEW FRIENDS, DECIDED TO BECOME OZMA'S GUARDIANS AND COMPANIONS.

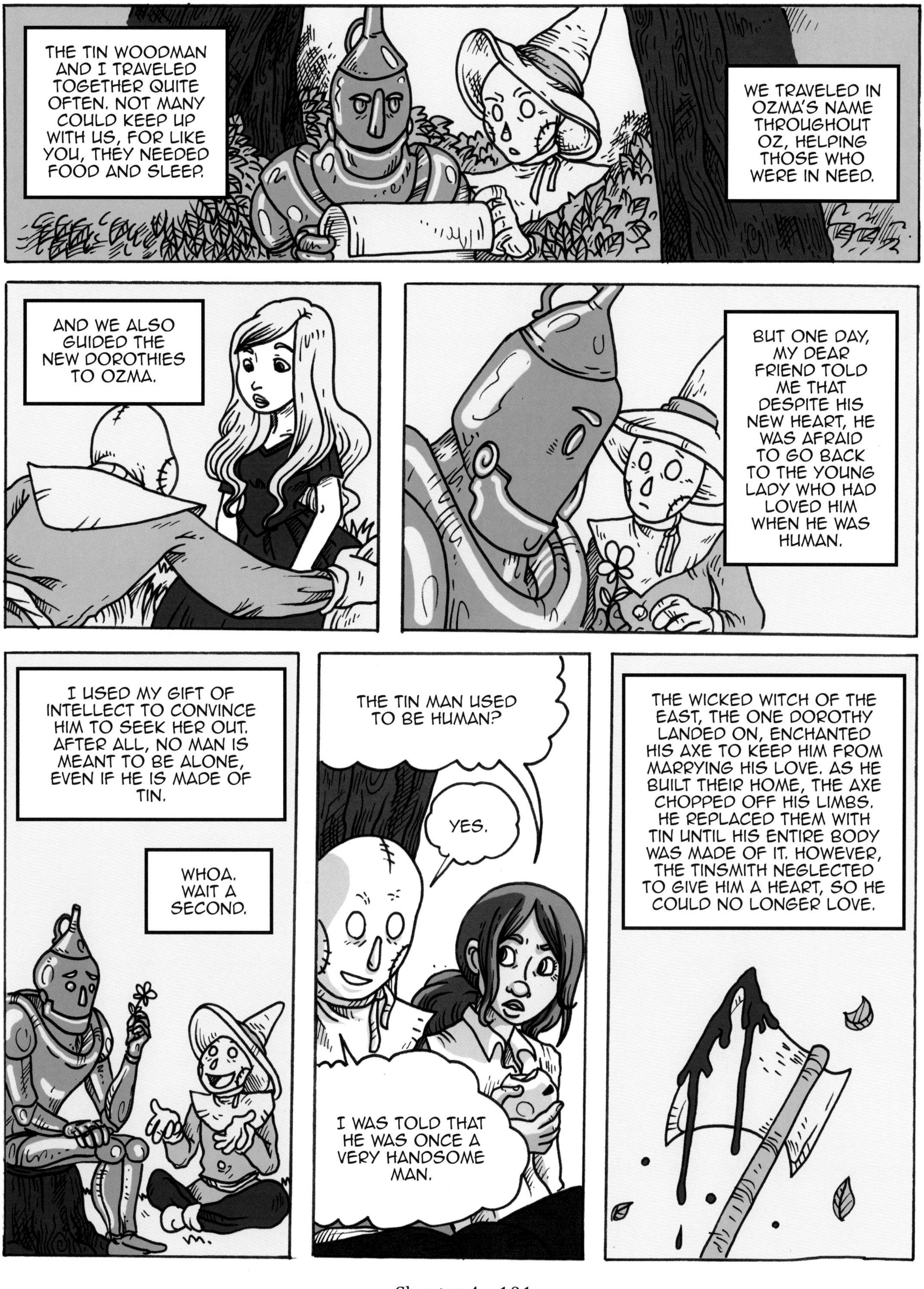
THE TIN WOODMAN AND I TRAVELED TOGETHER QUITE OFTEN. NOT MANY COULD KEEP UP WITH US, FOR LIKE YOU, THEY NEEDED FOOD AND SLEEP.
WE TRAVELED IN OZMA'S NAME THROUGHOUT OZ, HELPING THOSE WHO WERE IN NEED.
AND WE ALSO GUIDED THE NEW DOROTHIES TO OZMA.
BUT ONE DAY, MY DEAR FRIEND TOLD ME THAT DESPITE HIS NEW HEART, HE WAS AFRAID TO GO BACK TO THE YOUNG LADY WHO HAD LOVED HIM WHEN HE WAS HUMAN.
I USED MY GIFT OF INTELLECT TO CONVINCE HIM TO SEEK HER OUT. AFTER ALL, NO MAN IS MEANT TO BE ALONE, EVEN IF HE IS MADE OF TIN.
WHOA. WAIT A SECOND.
THE TIN MAN USED TO BE HUMAN?
YES.
I WAS TOLD THAT HE WAS ONCE A VERY HANDSOME MAN.
THE WICKED WITCH OF THE EAST, THE ONE DOROTHY LANDED ON, ENCHANTED HIS AXE TO KEEP HIM FROM MARRYING HIS LOVE. AS HE BUILT THEIR HOME, THE AXE CHOPPED OFF HIS LIMBS. HE REPLACED THEM WITH TIN UNTIL HIS ENTIRE BODY WAS MADE OF IT. HOWEVER, THE TINSMITH NEGLECTED TO GIVE HIM A HEART, SO HE COULD NO LONGER LOVE.

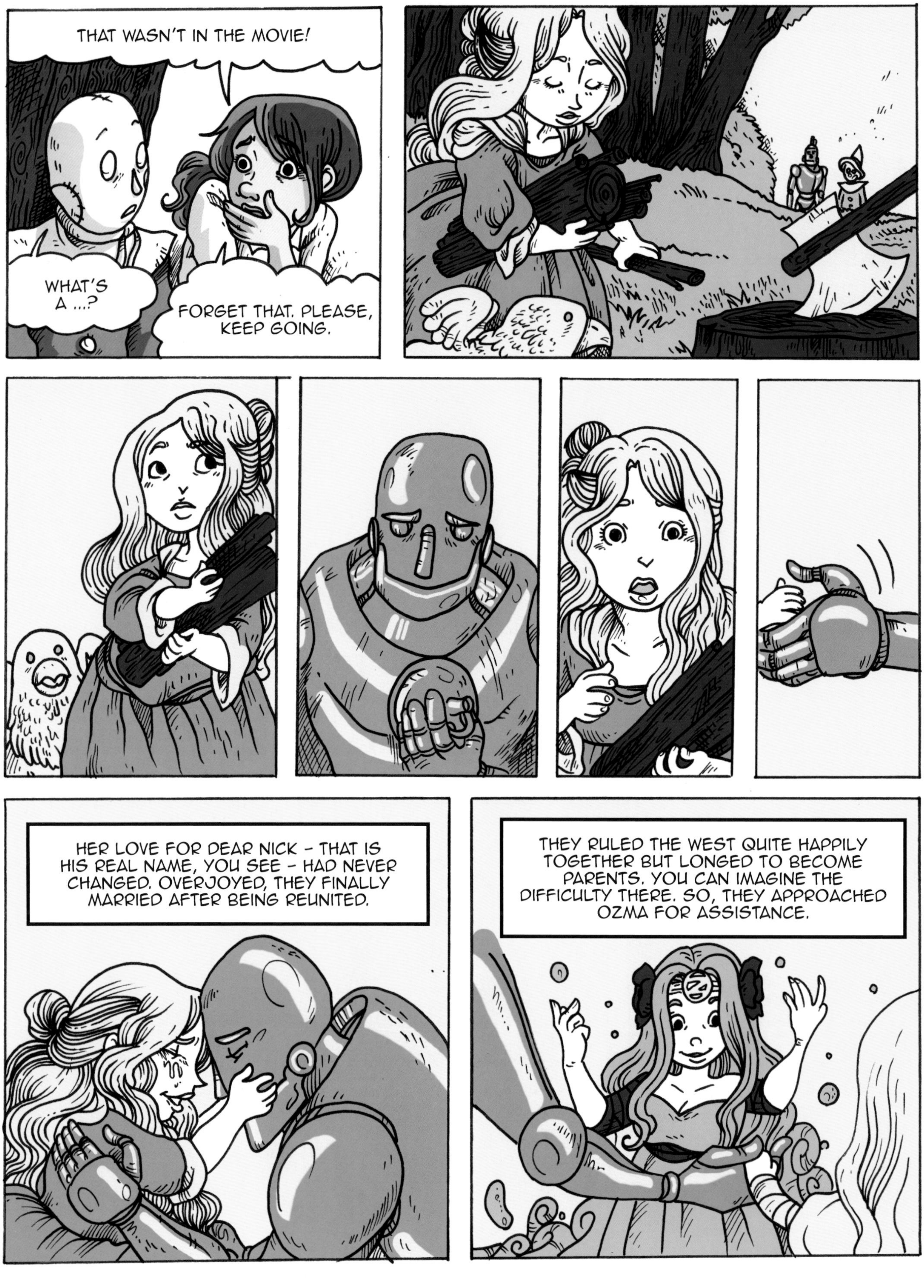
THAT WASN'T IN THE MOVIE!
WHAT'S A ...?
FORGET THAT. PLEASE, KEEP GOING.
HER LOVE FOR DEAR NICK – THAT IS HIS REAL NAME, YOU SEE – HAD NEVER CHANGED. OVERJOYED, THEY FINALLY MARRIED AFTER BEING REUNITED.
THEY RULED THE WEST QUITE HAPPILY TOGETHER BUT LONGED TO BECOME PARENTS. YOU CAN IMAGINE THE DIFFICULTY THERE. SO, THEY APPROACHED OZMA FOR ASSISTANCE.

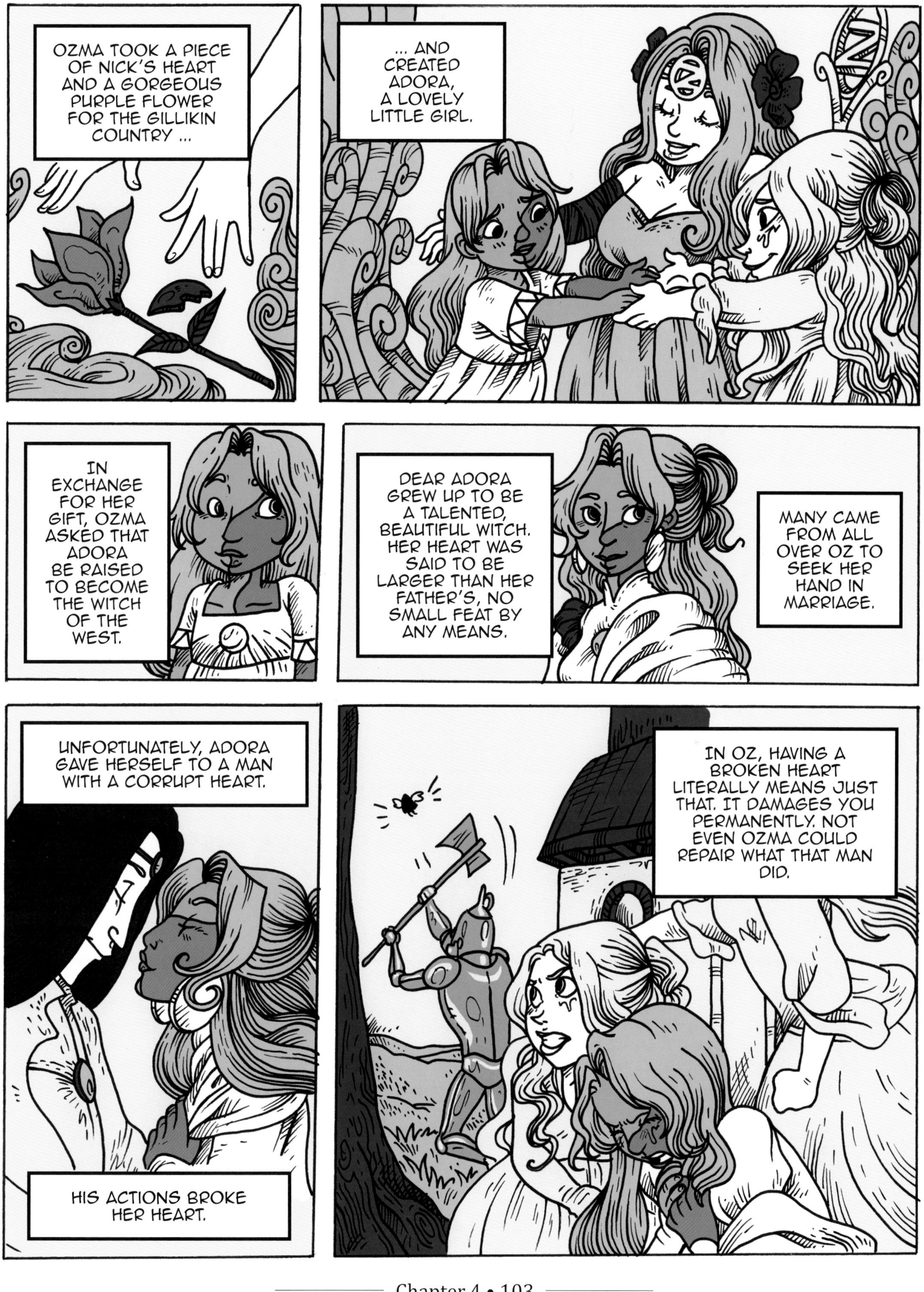

OZMA TOOK A PIECE OF NICK'S HEART AND A GORGEOUS PURPLE FLOWER FOR THE GILLIKIN COUNTRY ...
... AND CREATED ADORA, A LOVELY LITTLE GIRL.
IN EXCHANGE FOR HER GIFT, OZMA ASKED THAT ADORA BE RAISED TO BECOME THE WITCH OF THE WEST.
DEAR ADORA GREW UP TO BE A TALENTED, BEAUTIFUL WITCH. HER HEART WAS SAID TO BE LARGER THAN HER FATHER'S, NO SMALL FEAT BY ANY MEANS.
MANY CAME FROM ALL OVER OZ TO SEEK HER HAND IN MARRIAGE.
UNFORTUNATELY, ADORA GAVE HERSELF TO A MAN WITH A CORRUPT HEART.
HIS ACTIONS BROKE HER HEART.
IN OZ, HAVING A BROKEN HEART LITERALLY MEANS JUST THAT. IT DAMAGES YOU PERMANENTLY. NOT EVEN OZMA COULD REPAIR WHAT THAT MAN DID.

WITH HER DAMAGED HEART, ADORA BECAME THE FIRST AND ONLY NEUTRAL WITCH OF THE WEST.

BUT SOME GOOD COMES OUT OF EVERYTHING, EVEN THIS TRAGIC STORY.

FOR ADORA GAVE BIRTH TO TWINS, WARRICK AND SELVA. THEIR GRANDPARENTS ARE CURRENTLY RAISING THEM AND ASKED ME TO BE THEIR UNCLE.

I'M QUITE PROUD OF THEM! IT'S BEEN A NUMBER OF YEARS SINCE I'VE SEEN THEM. I WONDER HOW MUCH THEY'VE GROWN IN MY ABSENCE?

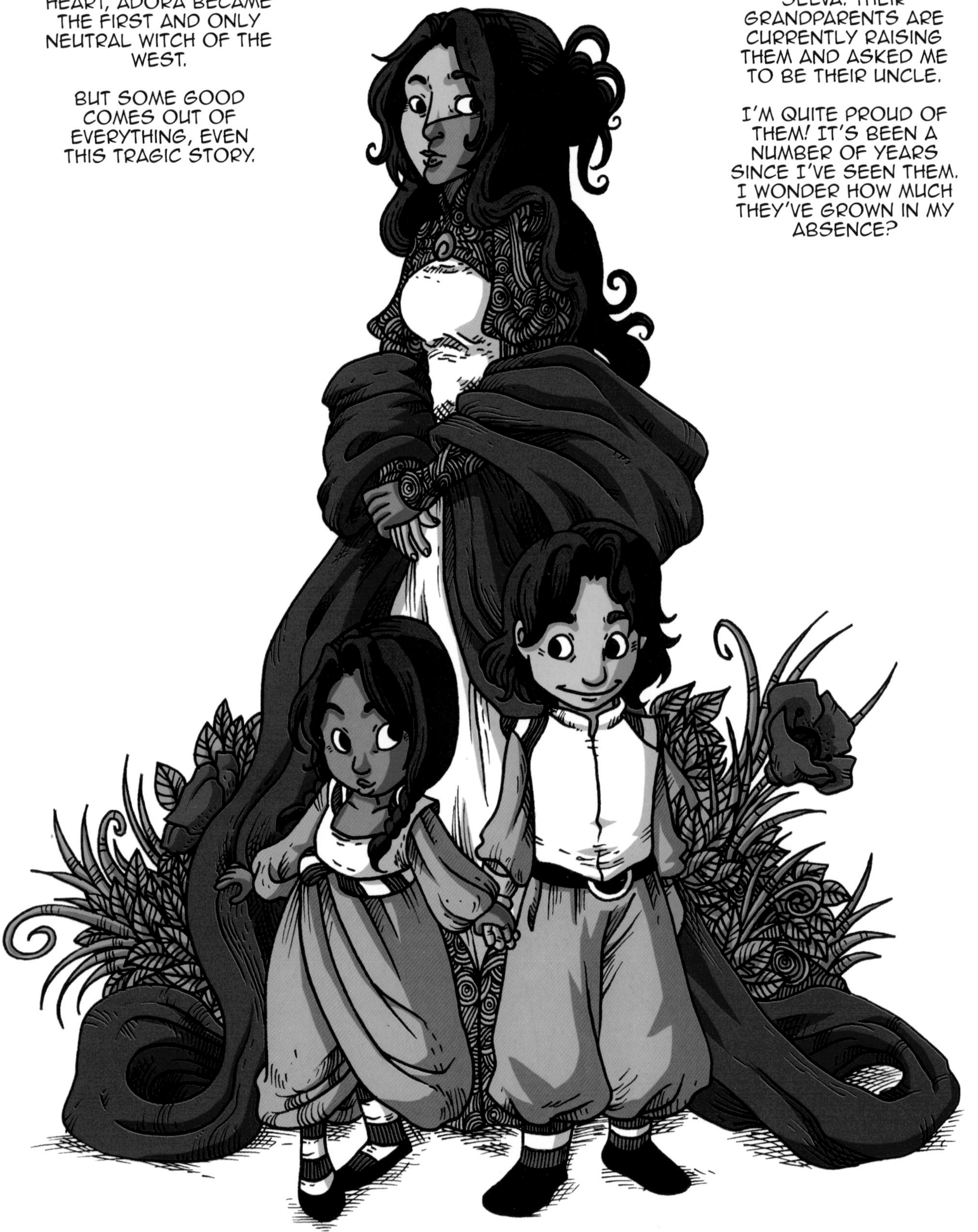

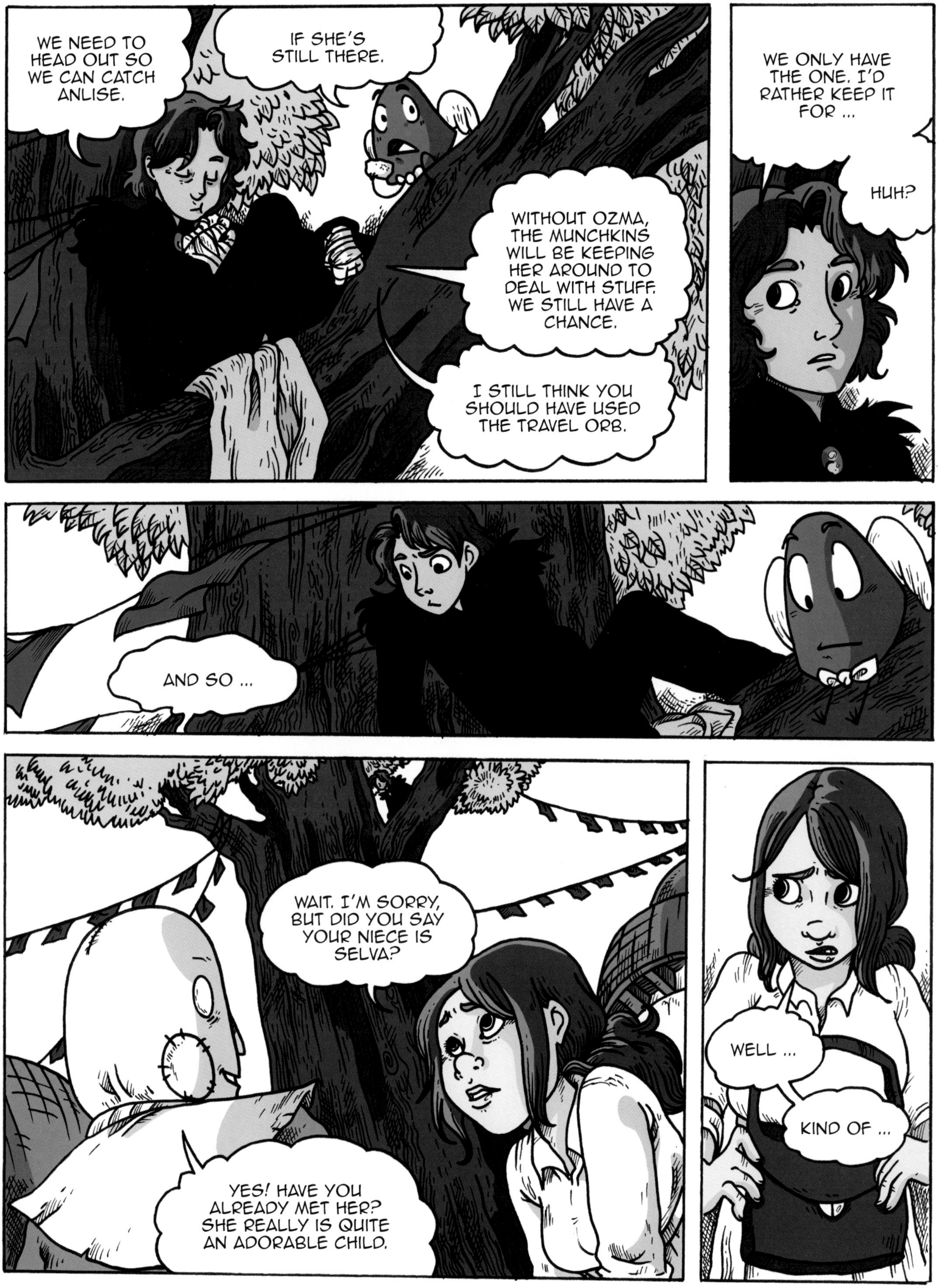
WE NEED TO HEAD OUT SO WE CAN CATCH ANLISE.
IF SHE'S STILL THERE.
WITHOUT OZMA, THE MUNCHKINS WILL BE KEEPING HER AROUND TO DEAL WITH STUFF. WE STILL HAVE A CHANCE.
I STILL THINK YOU SHOULD HAVE USED THE TRAVEL ORB.
WE ONLY HAVE THE ONE. I'D RATHER KEEP IT FOR ...
HUH?
AND SO ...
WAIT. I'M SORRY, BUT DID YOU SAY YOUR NIECE IS SELVA?
YES! HAVE YOU ALREADY MET HER? SHE REALLY IS QUITE AN ADORABLE CHILD.
WELL ...
KIND OF ...

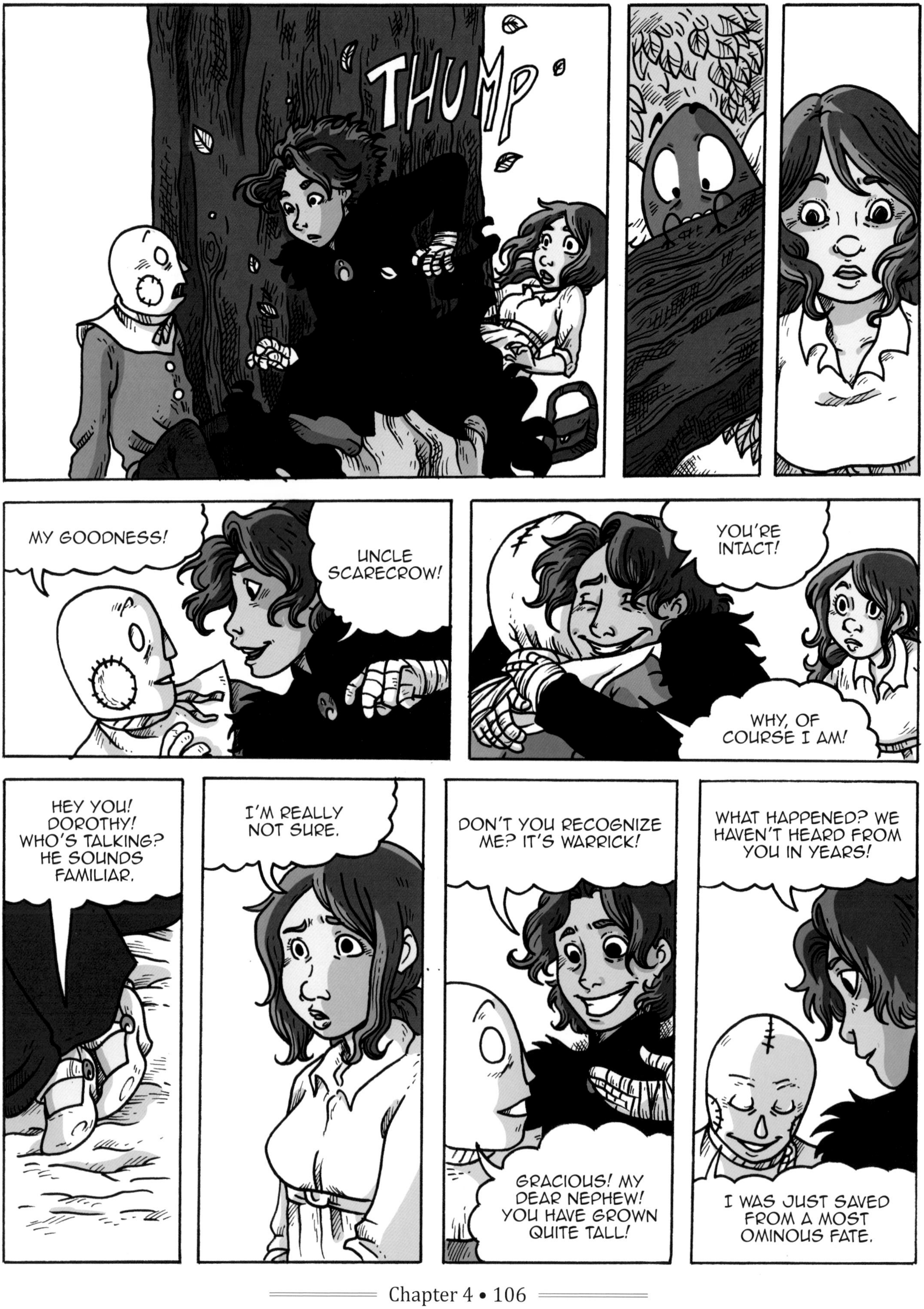
THUMP
MY GOODNESS!
UNCLE SCARECROW!
YOU'RE INTACT!
WHY, OF COURSE I AM!
HEY YOU! DOROTHY! WHO'S TALKING? HE SOUNDS FAMILIAR.
I'M REALLY NOT SURE.
DON'T YOU RECOGNIZE ME? IT'S WARRICK!
GRACIOUS! MY DEAR NEPHEW! YOU HAVE GROWN QUITE TALL!
WHAT HAPPENED? WE HAVEN'T HEARD FROM YOU IN YEARS!
I WAS JUST SAVED FROM A MOST OMINOUS FATE.

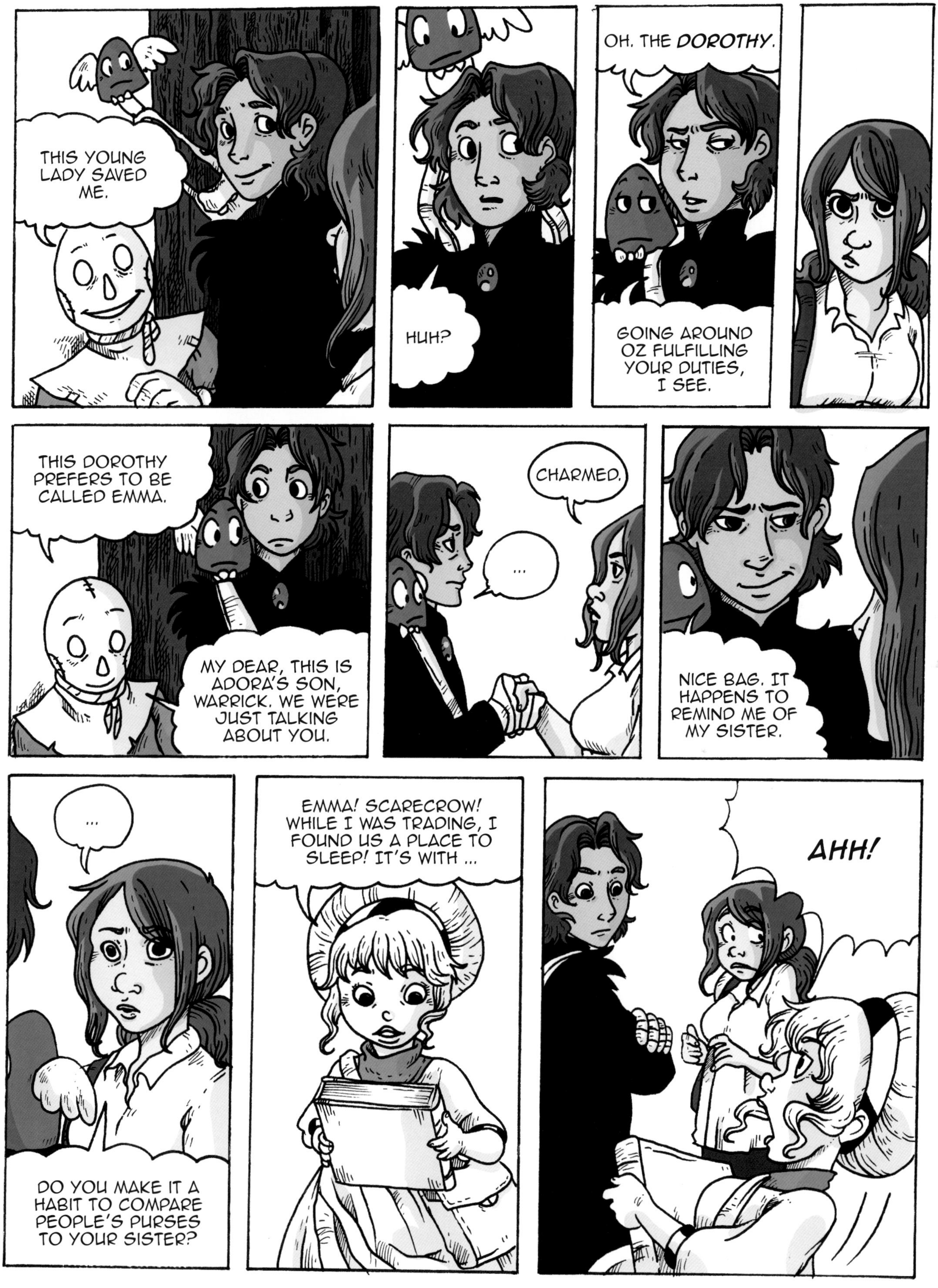

THIS YOUNG LADY SAVED ME.
HUH?
OH. THE *DOROTHY*.
GOING AROUND OZ FULFILLING YOUR DUTIES, I SEE.
THIS DOROTHY PREFERS TO BE CALLED EMMA.
MY DEAR, THIS IS ADORA'S SON, WARRICK. WE WERE JUST TALKING ABOUT YOU.
CHARMED.
...
NICE BAG. IT HAPPENS TO REMIND ME OF MY SISTER.
...
DO YOU MAKE IT A HABIT TO COMPARE PEOPLE'S PURSES TO YOUR SISTER?
EMMA! SCARECROW! WHILE I WAS TRADING, I FOUND US A PLACE TO SLEEP! IT'S WITH ...
AHH!

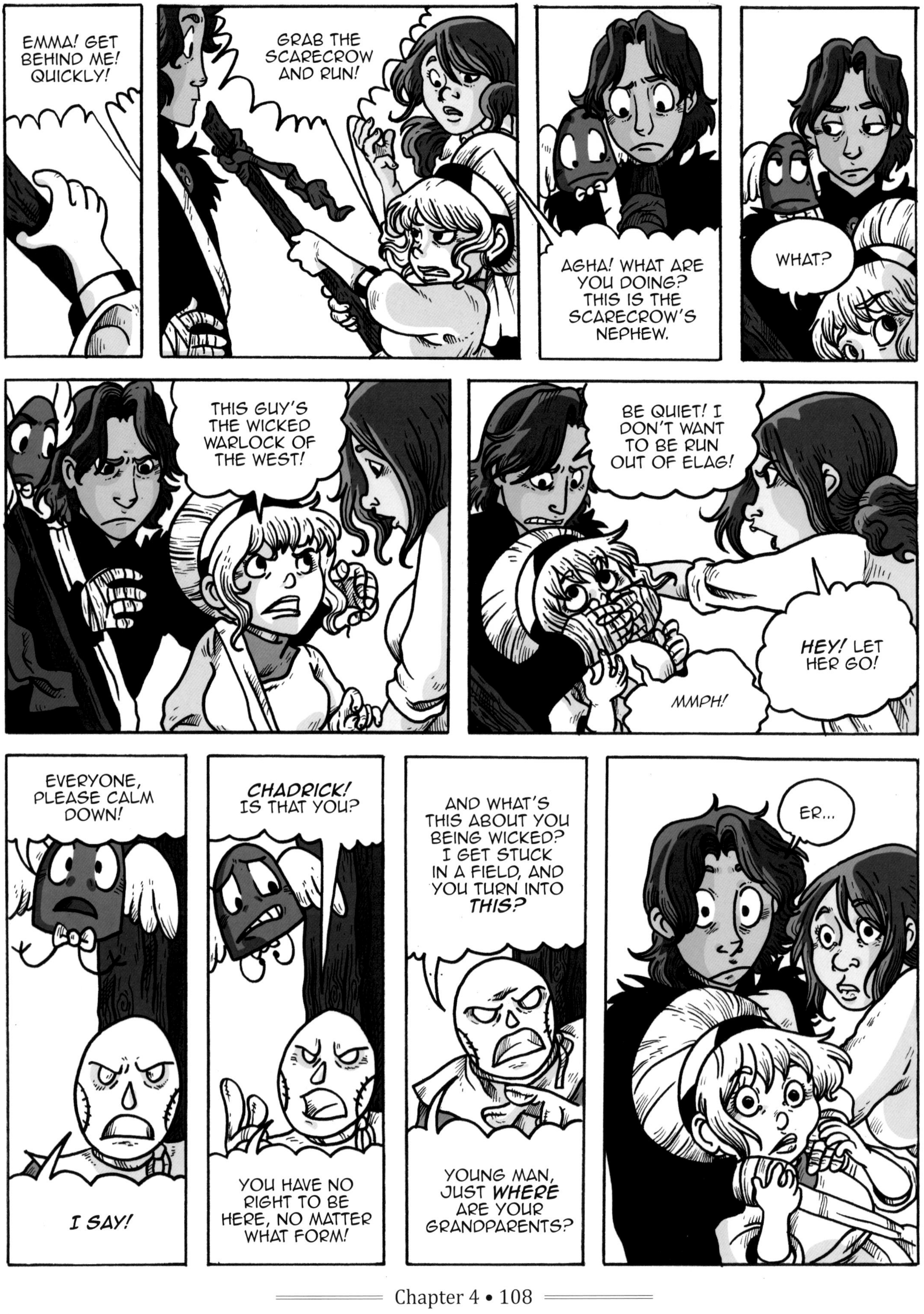
EMMA! GET BEHIND ME! QUICKLY!
GRAB THE SCARECROW AND RUN!
AGHA! WHAT ARE YOU DOING? THIS IS THE SCARECROW'S NEPHEW.
WHAT?
THIS GUY'S THE WICKED WARLOCK OF THE WEST!
BE QUIET! I DON'T WANT TO BE RUN OUT OF ELAG!
HEY! LET HER GO!
MMPH!
EVERYONE, PLEASE CALM DOWN!
I SAY!
CHADRICK! IS THAT YOU?
YOU HAVE NO RIGHT TO BE HERE, NO MATTER WHAT FORM!
AND WHAT'S THIS ABOUT YOU BEING WICKED? I GET STUCK IN A FIELD, AND YOU TURN INTO THIS?
YOUNG MAN, JUST WHERE ARE YOUR GRANDPARENTS?
ER...

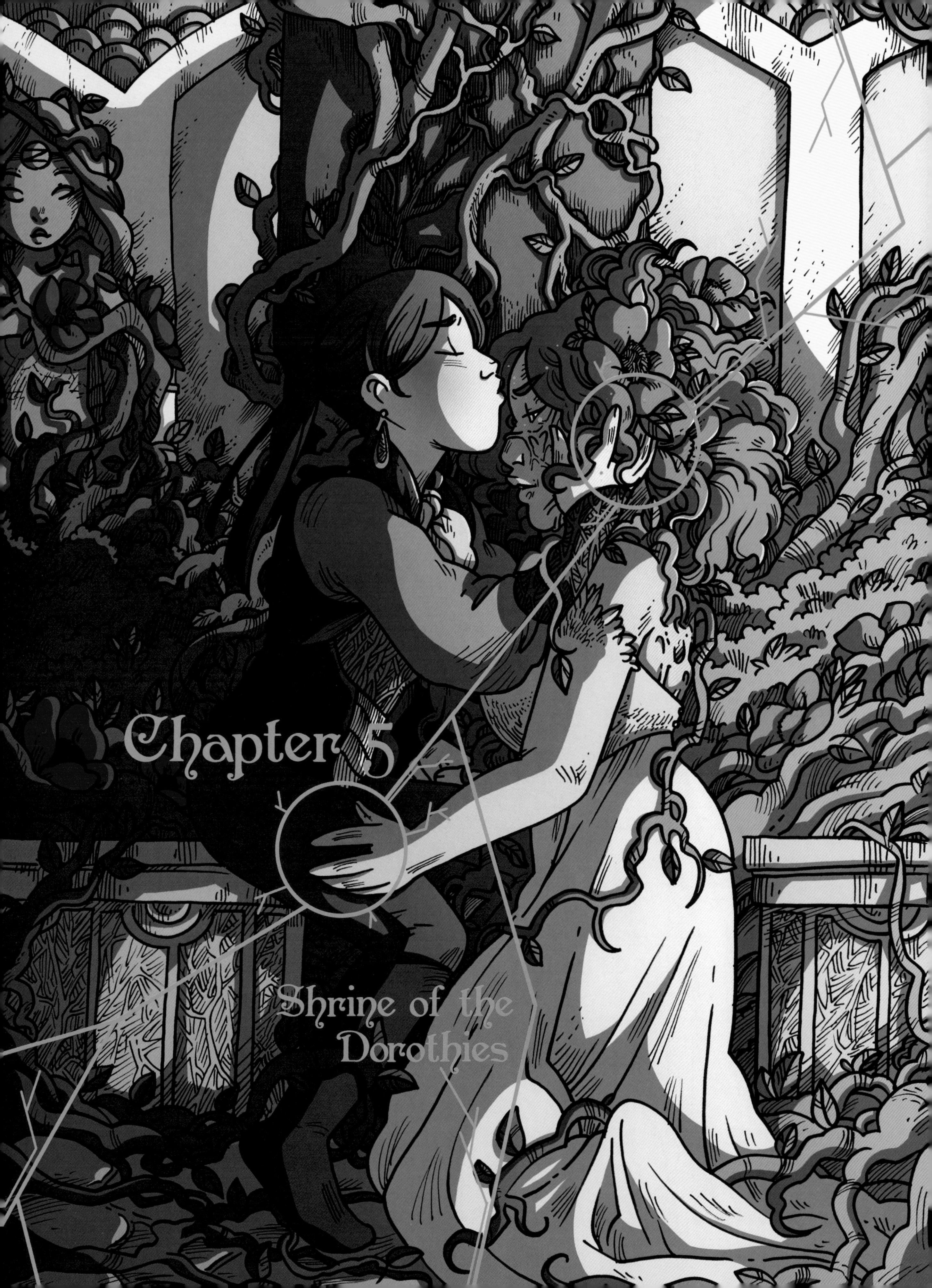
Chapter 5
Shrine of the Dorothies

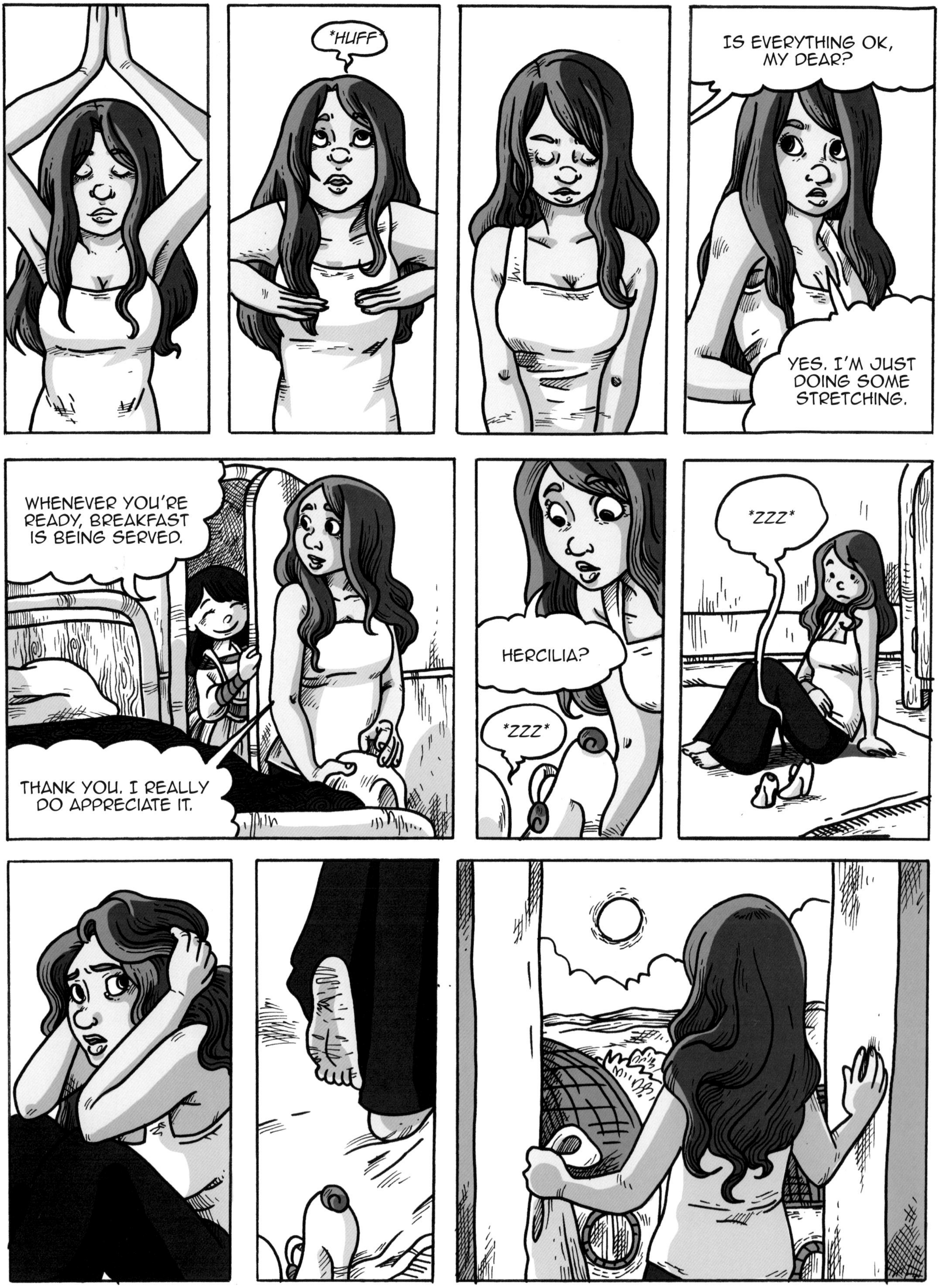
HUFF
IS EVERYTHING OK, MY DEAR?
YES. I'M JUST DOING SOME STRETCHING.
WHENEVER YOU'RE READY, BREAKFAST IS BEING SERVED.
THANK YOU. I REALLY DO APPRECIATE IT.
HERCILIA?
ZZZ
ZZZ

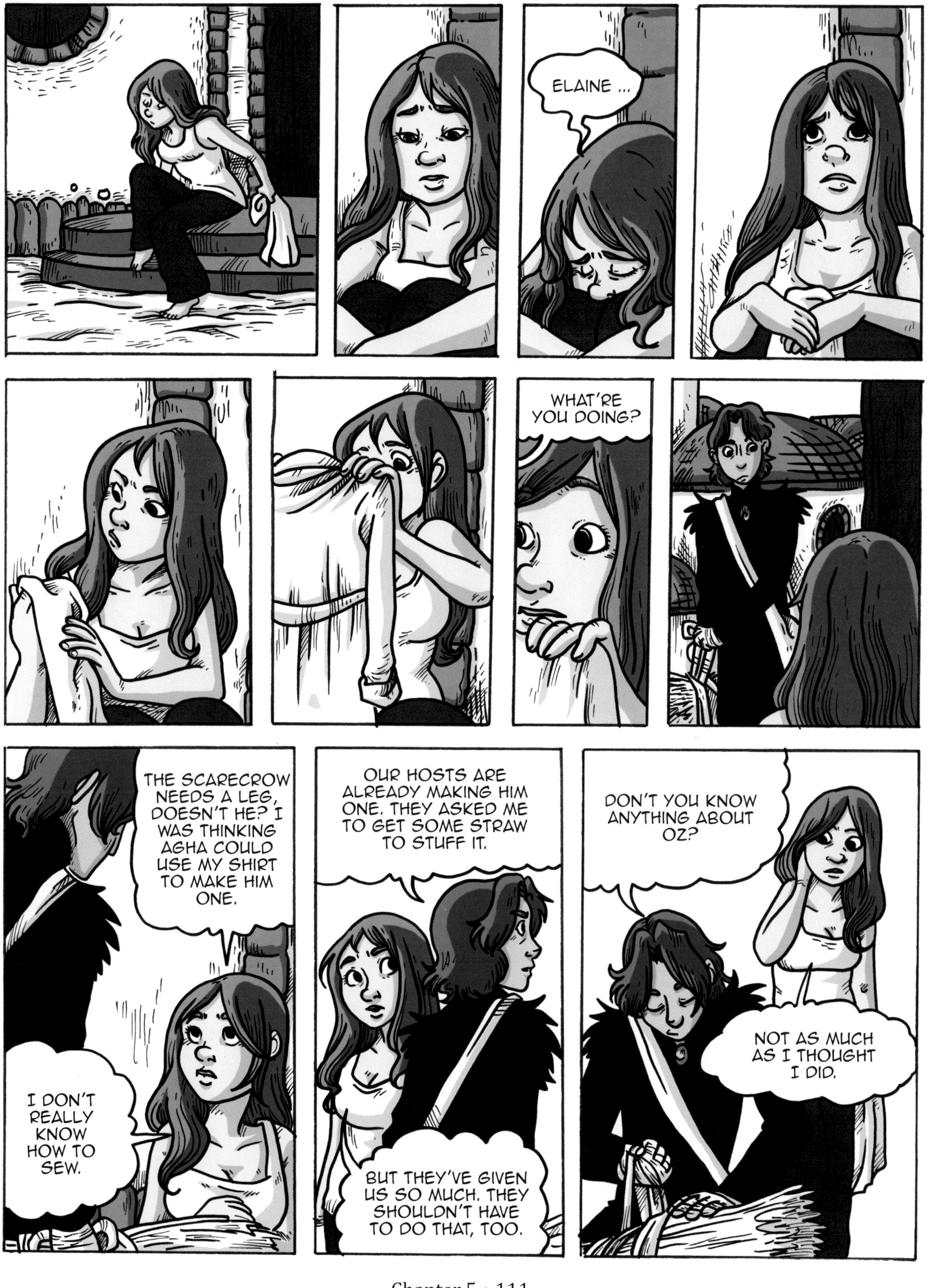
ELAINE ...
WHAT'RE YOU DOING?
THE SCARECROW NEEDS A LEG, DOESN'T HE? I WAS THINKING AGHA COULD USE MY SHIRT TO MAKE HIM ONE.
I DON'T REALLY KNOW HOW TO SEW.
OUR HOSTS ARE ALREADY MAKING HIM ONE. THEY ASKED ME TO GET SOME STRAW TO STUFF IT.
BUT THEY'VE GIVEN US SO MUCH. THEY SHOULDN'T HAVE TO DO THAT, TOO.
DON'T YOU KNOW ANYTHING ABOUT OZ?
NOT AS MUCH AS I THOUGHT I DID.

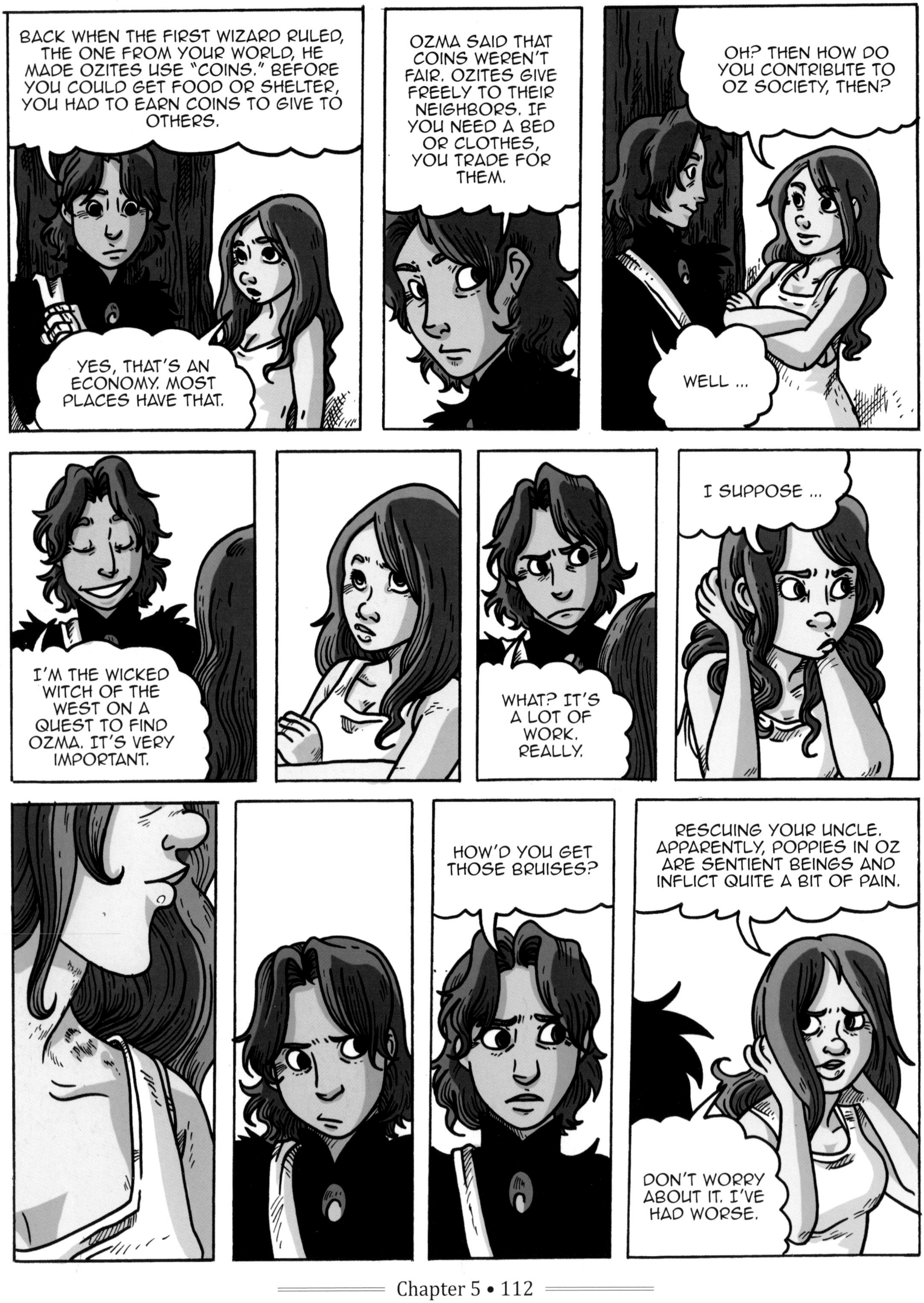
BACK WHEN THE FIRST WIZARD RULED, THE ONE FROM YOUR WORLD, HE MADE OZITES USE "COINS." BEFORE YOU COULD GET FOOD OR SHELTER, YOU HAD TO EARN COINS TO GIVE TO OTHERS.
YES, THAT'S AN ECONOMY. MOST PLACES HAVE THAT.
OZMA SAID THAT COINS WEREN'T FAIR. OZITES GIVE FREELY TO THEIR NEIGHBORS. IF YOU NEED A BED OR CLOTHES, YOU TRADE FOR THEM.
OH? THEN HOW DO YOU CONTRIBUTE TO OZ SOCIETY, THEN?
WELL ...
I'M THE WICKED WITCH OF THE WEST ON A QUEST TO FIND OZMA. IT'S VERY IMPORTANT.
WHAT? IT'S A LOT OF WORK. REALLY.
I SUPPOSE ...
HOW'D YOU GET THOSE BRUISES?
RESCUING YOUR UNCLE. APPARENTLY, POPPIES IN OZ ARE SENTIENT BEINGS AND INFLICT QUITE A BIT OF PAIN.
DON'T WORRY ABOUT IT. I'VE HAD WORSE.

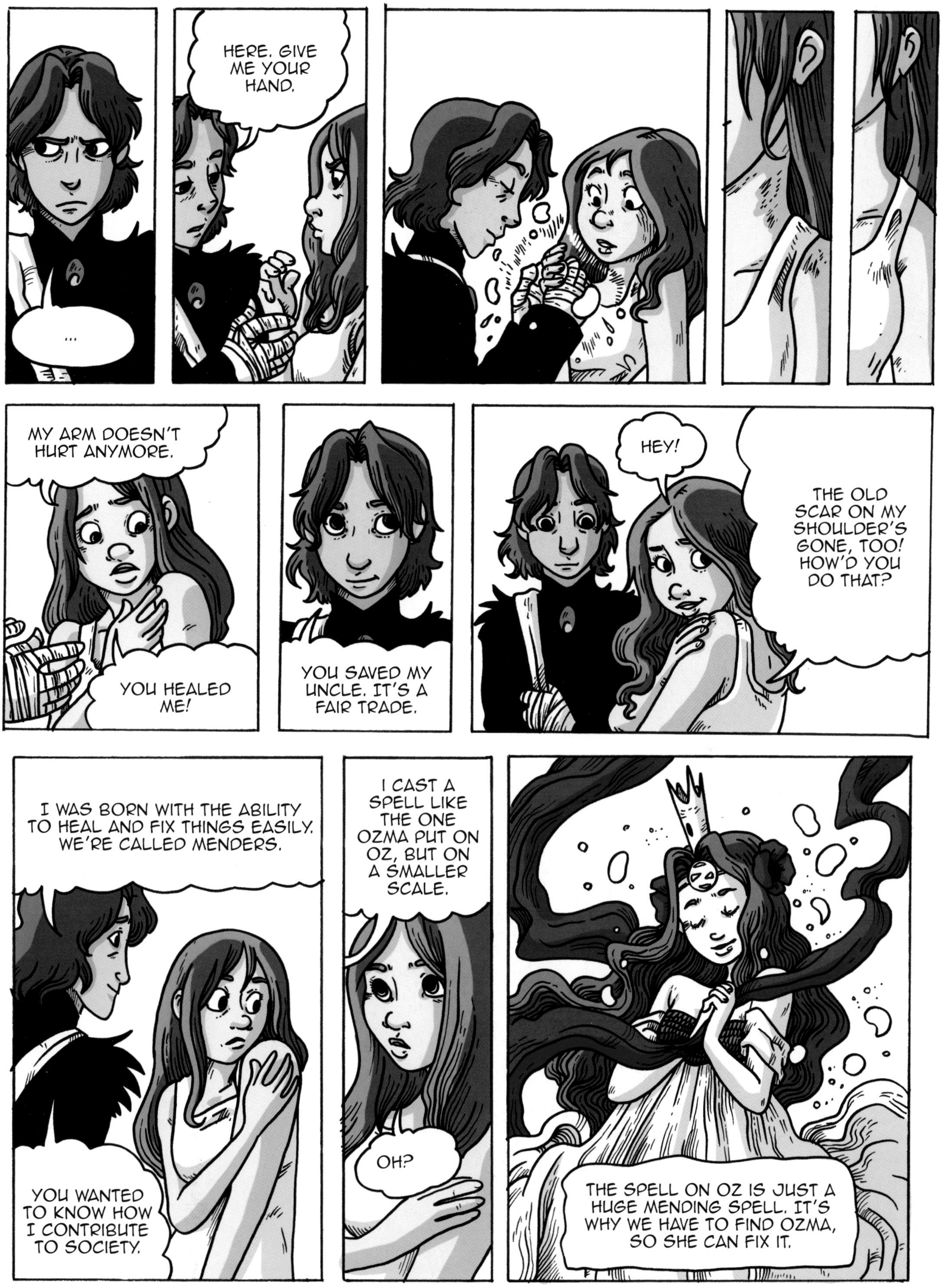
...
HERE. GIVE ME YOUR HAND.
MY ARM DOESN'T HURT ANYMORE.
YOU HEALED ME!
YOU SAVED MY UNCLE. IT'S A FAIR TRADE.
HEY!
THE OLD SCAR ON MY SHOULDER'S GONE, TOO! HOW'D YOU DO THAT?
I WAS BORN WITH THE ABILITY TO HEAL AND FIX THINGS EASILY. WE'RE CALLED MENDERS.
YOU WANTED TO KNOW HOW I CONTRIBUTE TO SOCIETY.
I CAST A SPELL LIKE THE ONE OZMA PUT ON OZ, BUT ON A SMALLER SCALE.
OH?
THE SPELL ON OZ IS JUST A HUGE MENDING SPELL. IT'S WHY WE HAVE TO FIND OZMA, SO SHE CAN FIX IT.

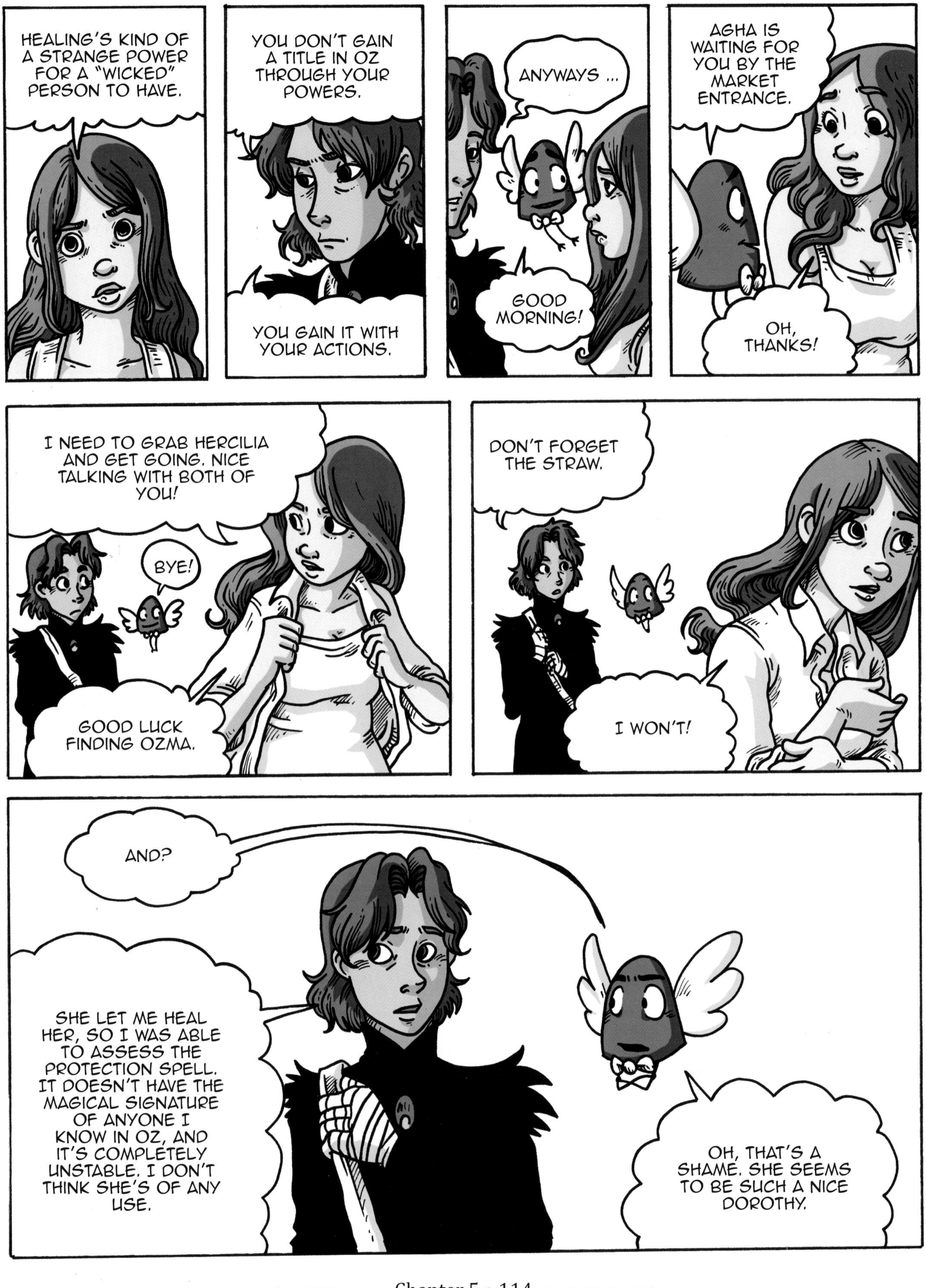
HEALING'S KIND OF A STRANGE POWER FOR A "WICKED" PERSON TO HAVE.
YOU DON'T GAIN A TITLE IN OZ THROUGH YOUR POWERS.
YOU GAIN IT WITH YOUR ACTIONS.
ANYWAYS ...
GOOD MORNING!
AGHA IS WAITING FOR YOU BY THE MARKET ENTRANCE.
OH, THANKS!
I NEED TO GRAB HERCILIA AND GET GOING. NICE TALKING WITH BOTH OF YOU!
BYE!
GOOD LUCK FINDING OZMA.
DON'T FORGET THE STRAW.
I WON'T!
AND?
SHE LET ME HEAL HER, SO I WAS ABLE TO ASSESS THE PROTECTION SPELL. IT DOESN'T HAVE THE MAGICAL SIGNATURE OF ANYONE I KNOW IN OZ, AND IT'S COMPLETELY UNSTABLE. I DON'T THINK SHE'S OF ANY USE.
OH, THAT'S A SHAME. SHE SEEMS TO BE SUCH A NICE DOROTHY.

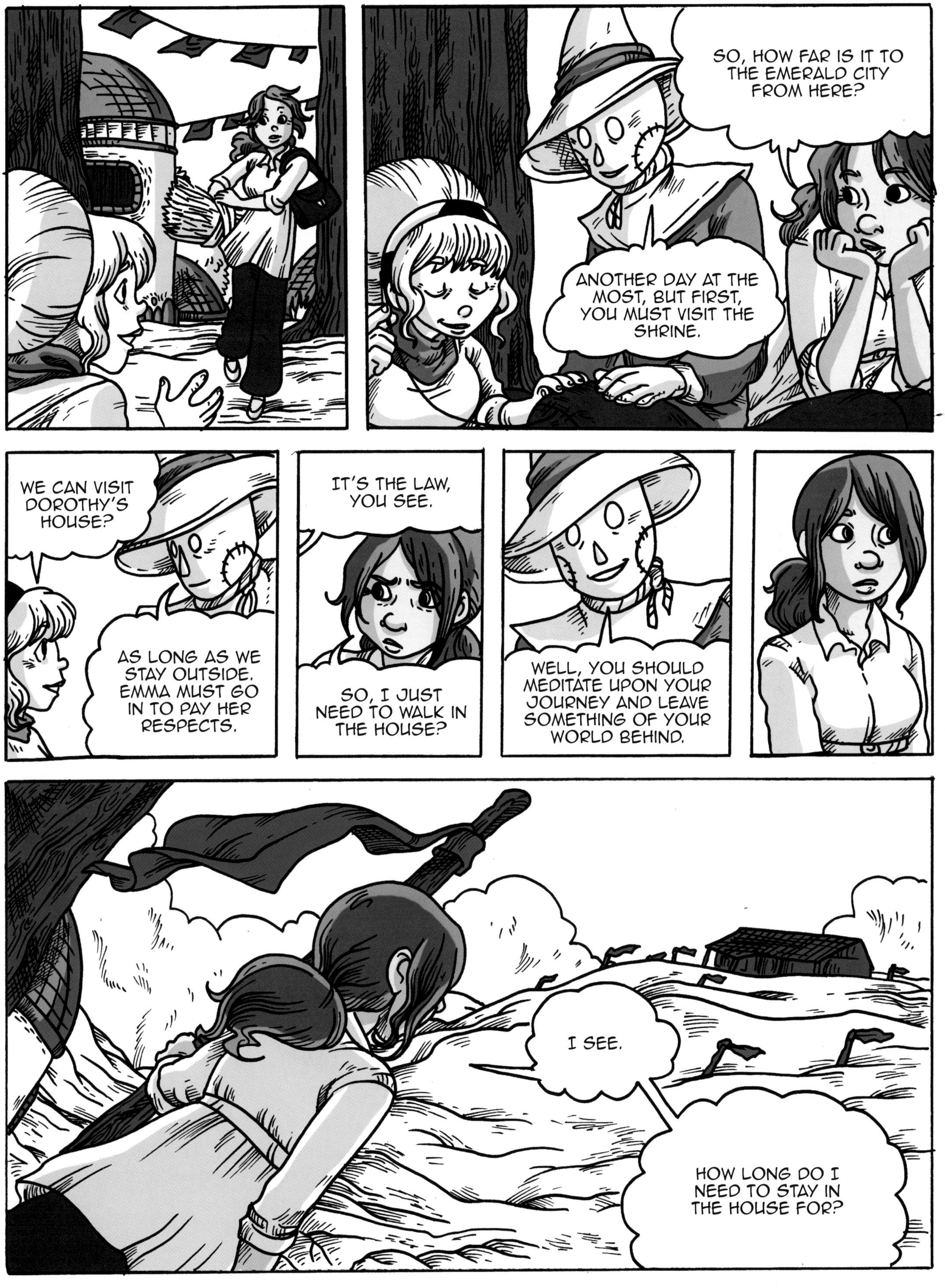
SO, HOW FAR IS IT TO THE EMERALD CITY FROM HERE?
ANOTHER DAY AT THE MOST, BUT FIRST, YOU MUST VISIT THE SHRINE.
WE CAN VISIT DOROTHY'S HOUSE?
AS LONG AS WE STAY OUTSIDE. EMMA MUST GO IN TO PAY HER RESPECTS.
IT'S THE LAW, YOU SEE.
SO, I JUST NEED TO WALK IN THE HOUSE?
WELL, YOU SHOULD MEDITATE UPON YOUR JOURNEY AND LEAVE SOMETHING OF YOUR WORLD BEHIND.
I SEE.
HOW LONG DO I NEED TO STAY IN THE HOUSE FOR?

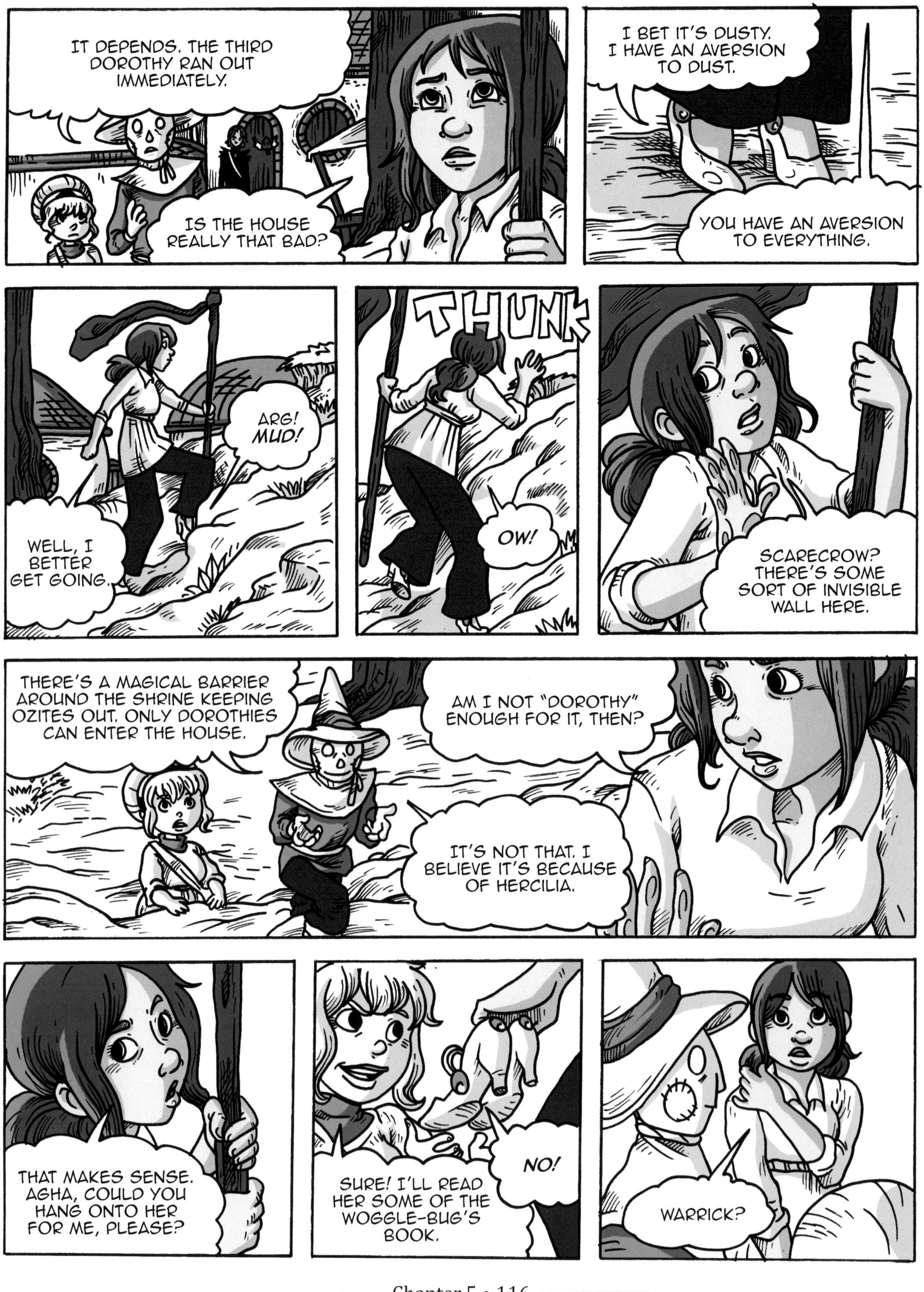
IT DEPENDS. THE THIRD DOROTHY RAN OUT IMMEDIATELY.
IS THE HOUSE REALLY THAT BAD?
I BET IT'S DUSTY. I HAVE AN AVERSION TO DUST.
YOU HAVE AN AVERSION TO EVERYTHING.
ARG! MUD!
WELL, I BETTER GET GOING.
THUNK
OW!
SCARECROW? THERE'S SOME SORT OF INVISIBLE WALL HERE.
THERE'S A MAGICAL BARRIER AROUND THE SHRINE KEEPING OZITES OUT. ONLY DOROTHIES CAN ENTER THE HOUSE.
AM I NOT "DOROTHY" ENOUGH FOR IT, THEN?
IT'S NOT THAT. I BELIEVE IT'S BECAUSE OF HERCILIA.
THAT MAKES SENSE. AGHA, COULD YOU HANG ONTO HER FOR ME, PLEASE?
SURE! I'LL READ HER SOME OF THE WOGGLE-BUG'S BOOK.
NO!
WARRICK?

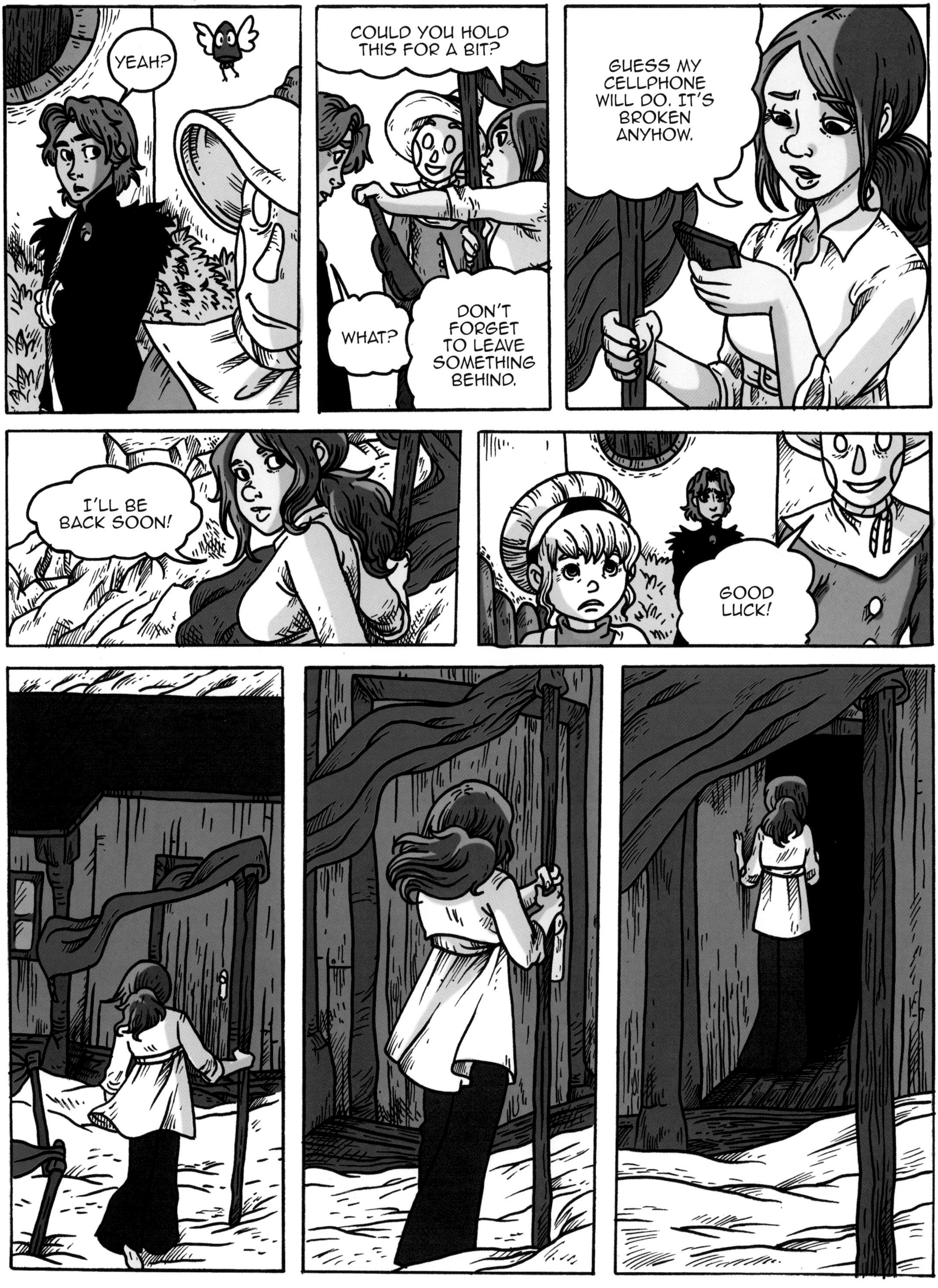
YEAH?
COULD YOU HOLD THIS FOR A BIT?
WHAT?
DON'T FORGET TO LEAVE SOMETHING BEHIND.
GUESS MY CELLPHONE WILL DO. IT'S BROKEN ANYHOW.
I'LL BE BACK SOON!
GOOD LUCK!

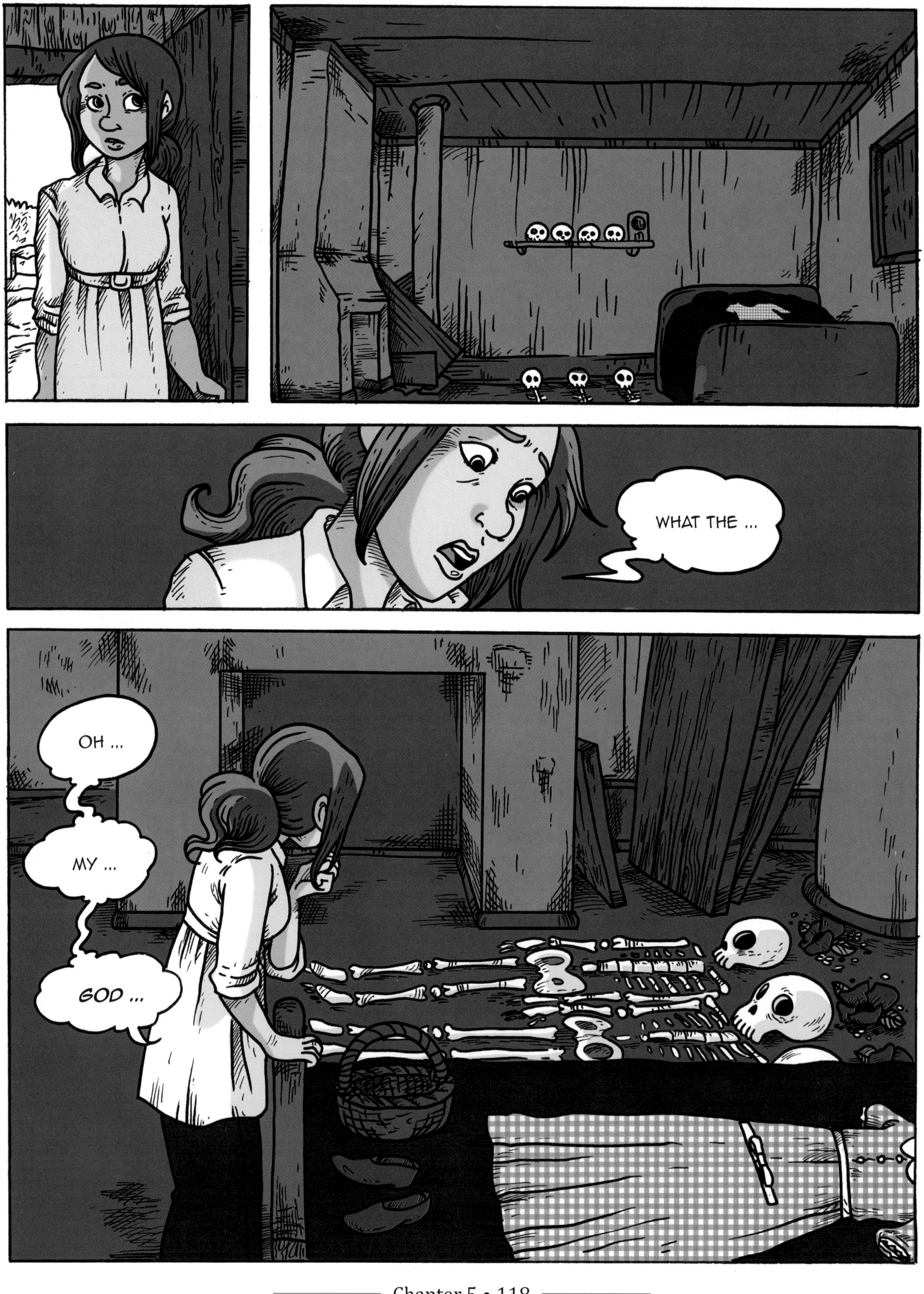
WHAT THE ...
OH ...
MY ...
GOD ...

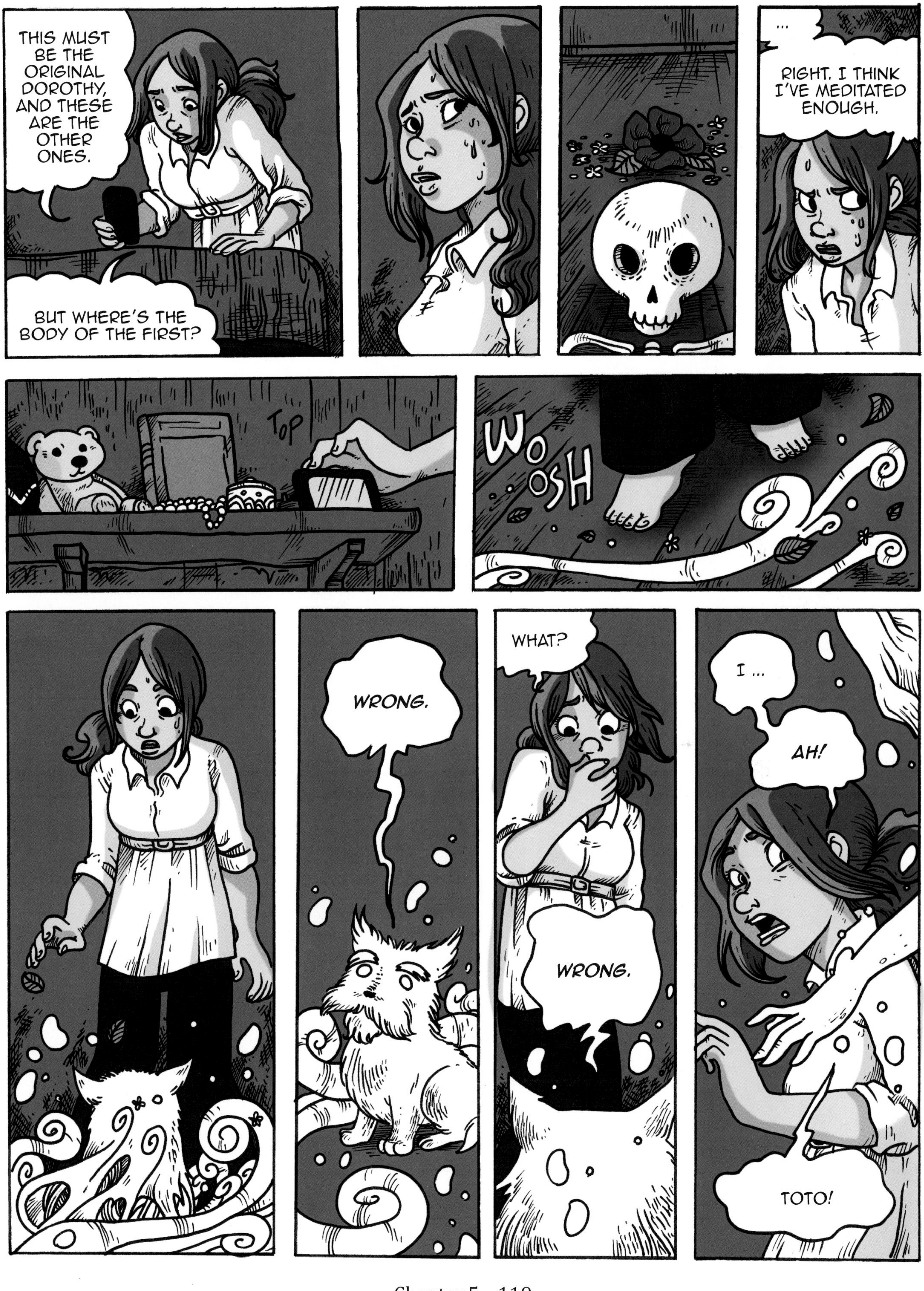

THIS MUST BE THE ORIGINAL DOROTHY, AND THESE ARE THE OTHER ONES.
BUT WHERE'S THE BODY OF THE FIRST?
...
RIGHT. I THINK I'VE MEDITATED ENOUGH.
TOP
WOOSH
WRONG.
WHAT?
WRONG.
I ...
AH!
TOTO!

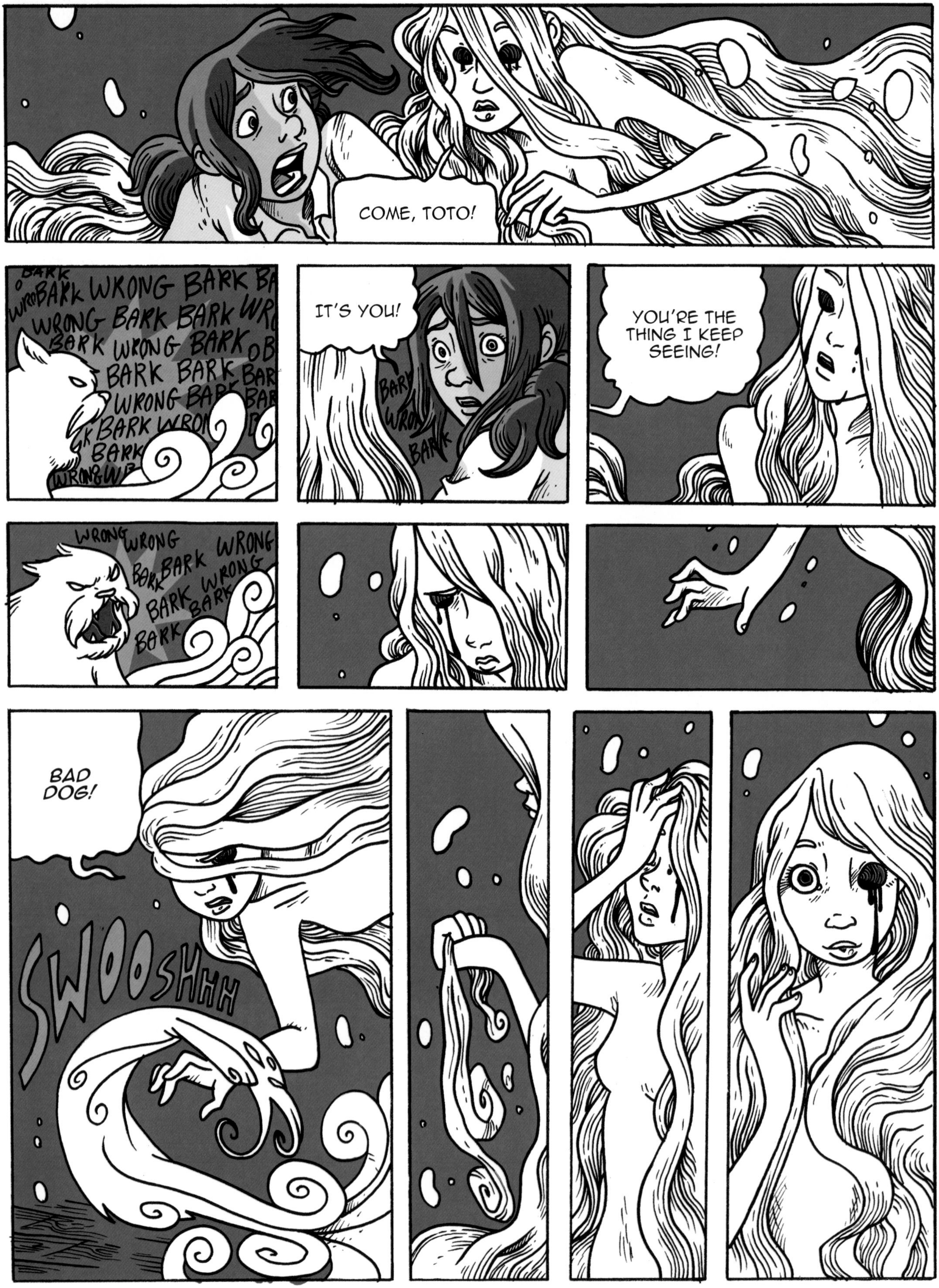
COME, TOTO!
BARK WRONG BARK
WRONG BARK BARK
BARK WRONG BARK
BARK BARK
WRONG BARK
BARK
IT'S YOU!
YOU'RE THE THING I KEEP SEEING!
WRONG WRONG
BARK BARK WRONG
BARK BARK
BARK
BAD DOG!
SWOOSHHH

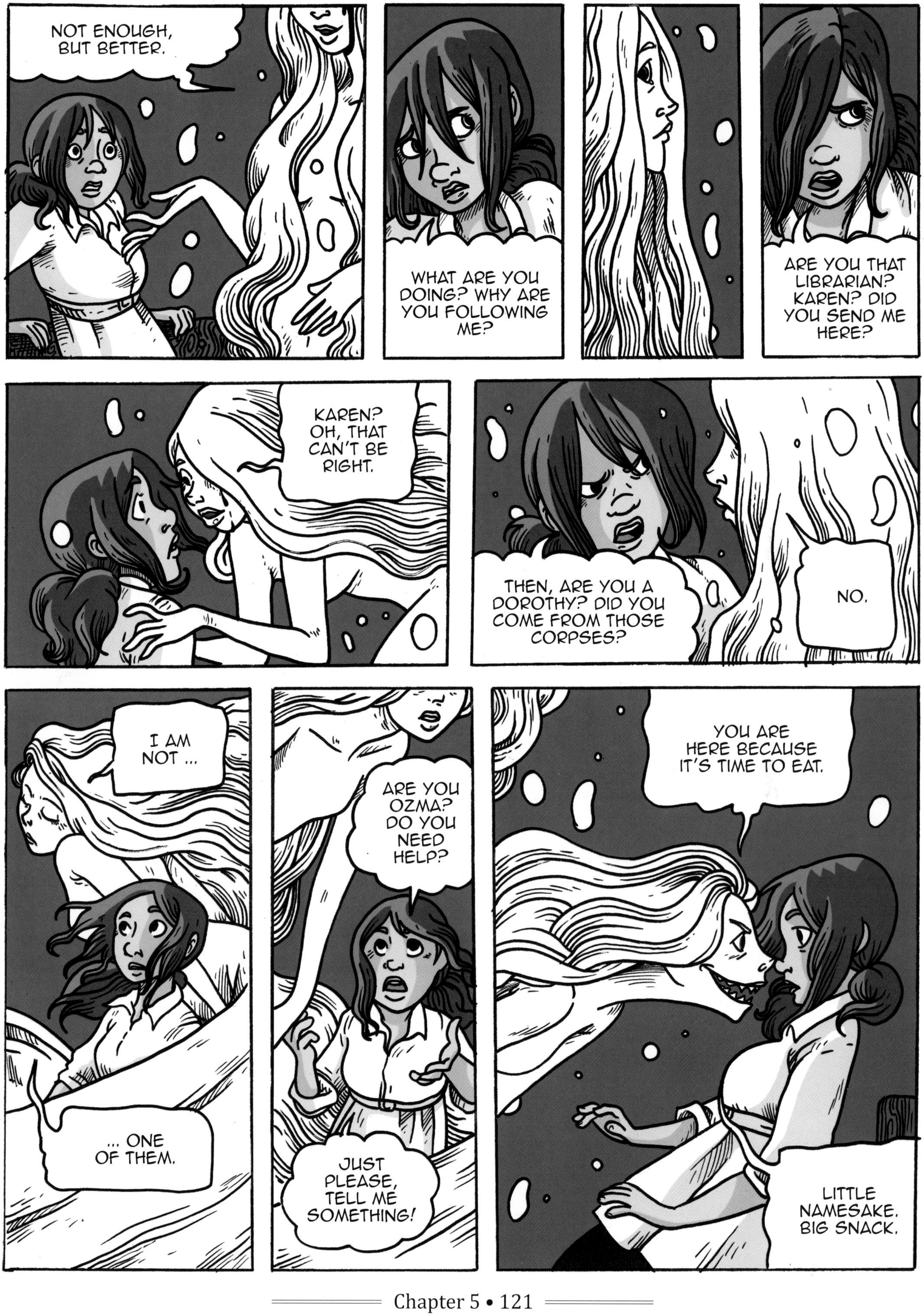
NOT ENOUGH, BUT BETTER.
WHAT ARE YOU DOING? WHY ARE YOU FOLLOWING ME?
ARE YOU THAT LIBRARIAN? KAREN? DID YOU SEND ME HERE?
KAREN? OH, THAT CAN'T BE RIGHT.
THEN, ARE YOU A DOROTHY? DID YOU COME FROM THOSE CORPSES?
NO.
I AM NOT ...
... ONE OF THEM.
ARE YOU OZMA? DO YOU NEED HELP?
JUST PLEASE, TELL ME SOMETHING!
YOU ARE HERE BECAUSE IT'S TIME TO EAT.
LITTLE NAMESAKE. BIG SNACK.

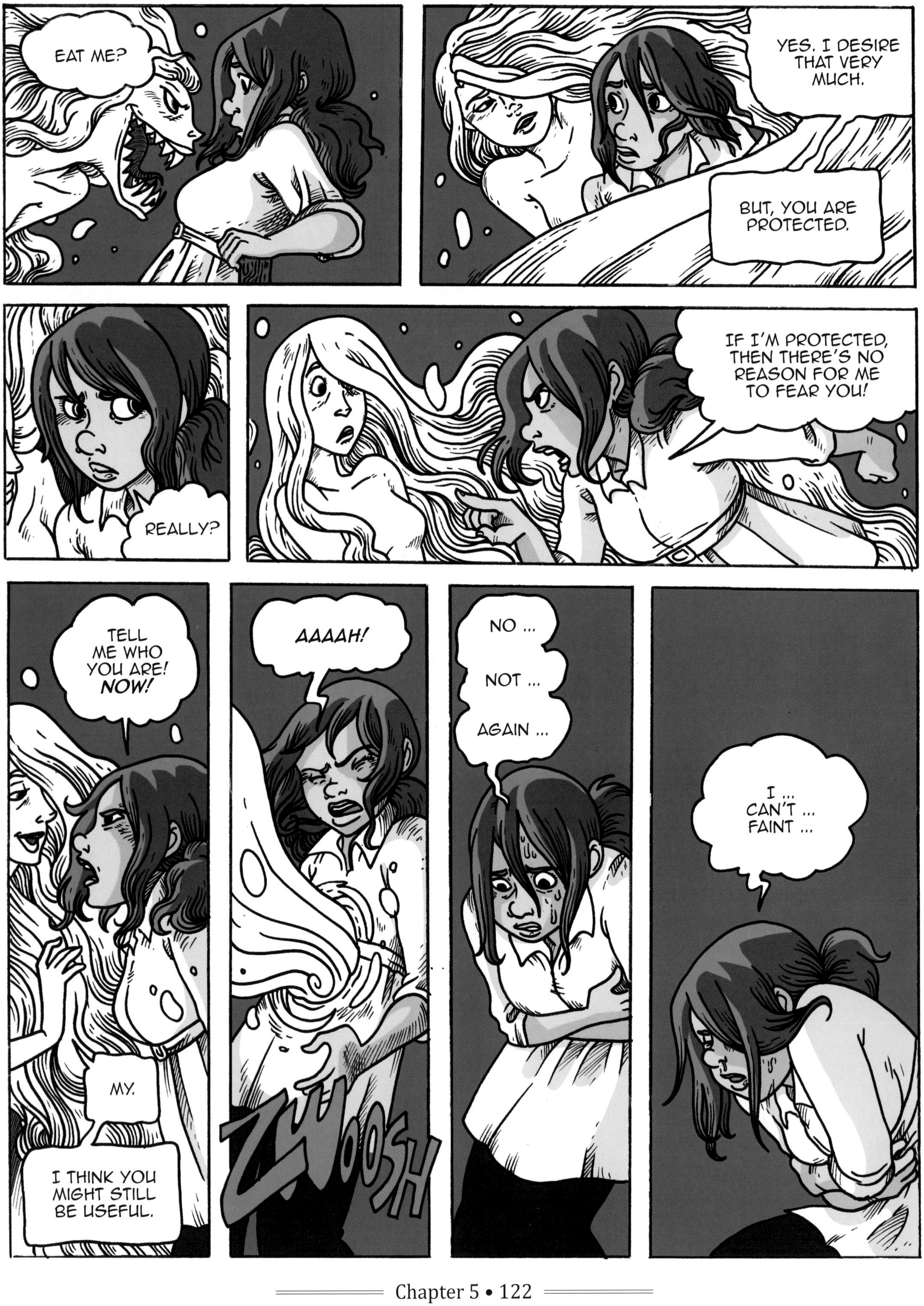
EAT ME?
YES. I DESIRE THAT VERY MUCH.
BUT, YOU ARE PROTECTED.
REALLY?
IF I'M PROTECTED, THEN THERE'S NO REASON FOR ME TO FEAR YOU!
TELL ME WHO YOU ARE! NOW!
MY.
I THINK YOU MIGHT STILL BE USEFUL.
AAAAH!
ZWOOSH
NO ...
NOT ...
AGAIN ...
I ... CAN'T ... FAINT ...

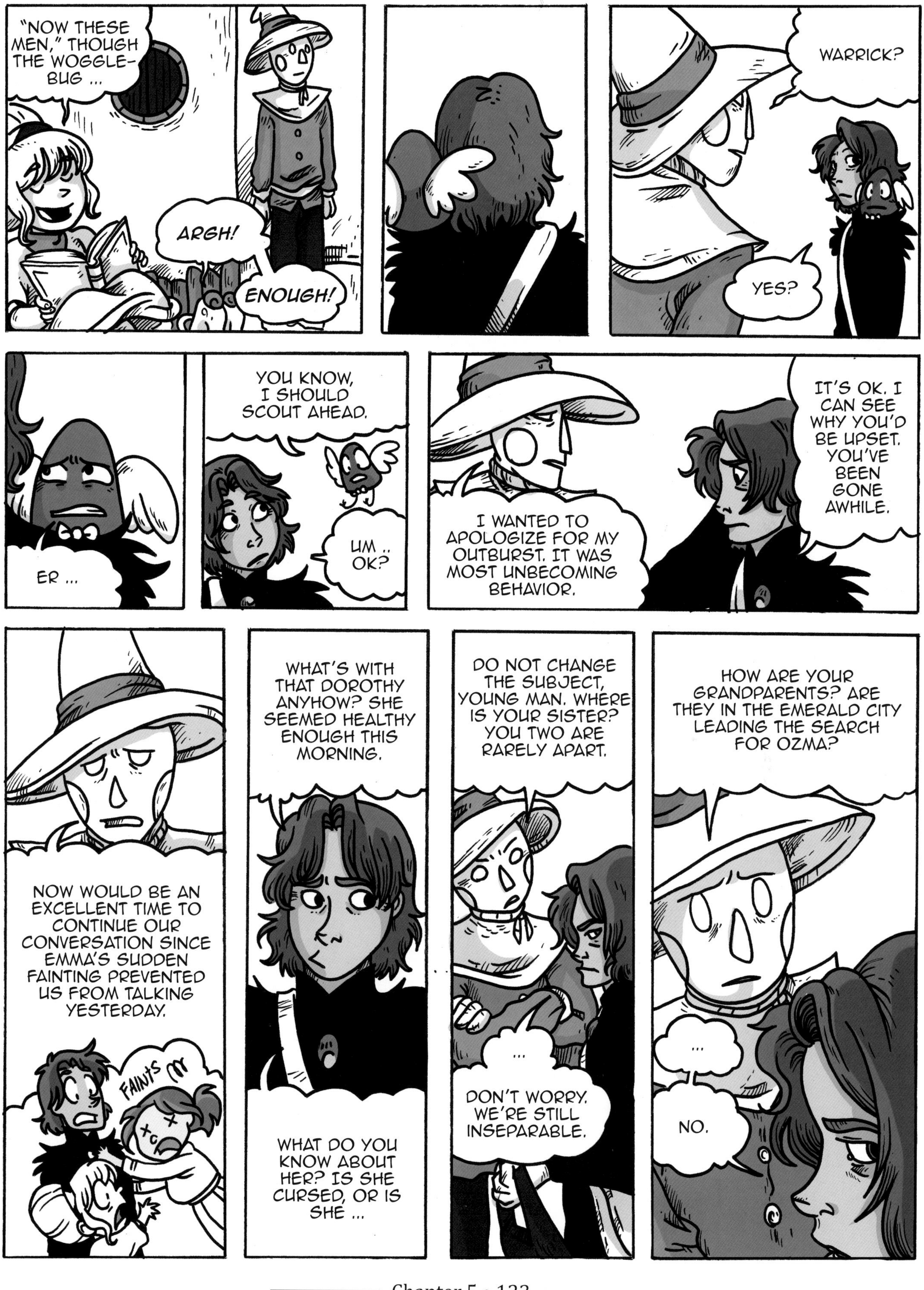
"NOW THESE MEN," THOUGH THE WOGGLE-BUG ...
ARGH!
ENOUGH!
WARRICK?
YES?
ER ...
YOU KNOW, I SHOULD SCOUT AHEAD.
UM .. OK?
I WANTED TO APOLOGIZE FOR MY OUTBURST. IT WAS MOST UNBECOMING BEHAVIOR.
IT'S OK. I CAN SEE WHY YOU'D BE UPSET. YOU'VE BEEN GONE AWHILE.
NOW WOULD BE AN EXCELLENT TIME TO CONTINUE OUR CONVERSATION SINCE EMMA'S SUDDEN FAINTING PREVENTED US FROM TALKING YESTERDAY.
FAINTS
WHAT'S WITH THAT DOROTHY ANYHOW? SHE SEEMED HEALTHY ENOUGH THIS MORNING.
WHAT DO YOU KNOW ABOUT HER? IS SHE CURSED, OR IS SHE ...
DO NOT CHANGE THE SUBJECT, YOUNG MAN. WHERE IS YOUR SISTER? YOU TWO ARE RARELY APART.
...
DON'T WORRY. WE'RE STILL INSEPARABLE.
HOW ARE YOUR GRANDPARENTS? ARE THEY IN THE EMERALD CITY LEADING THE SEARCH FOR OZMA?
...
NO.

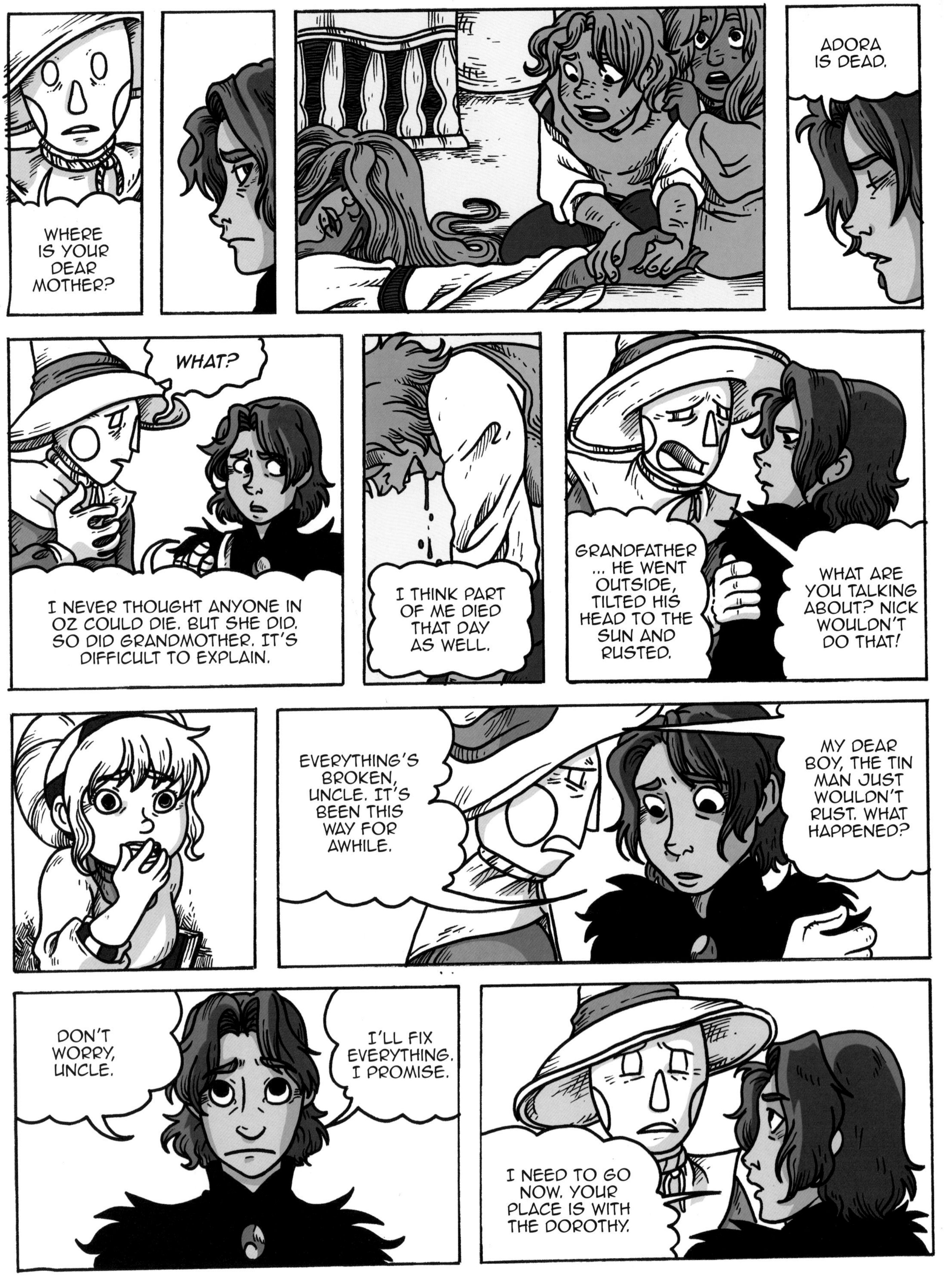
WHERE IS YOUR DEAR MOTHER?
ADORA IS DEAD.
WHAT?
I NEVER THOUGHT ANYONE IN OZ COULD DIE. BUT SHE DID. SO DID GRANDMOTHER. IT'S DIFFICULT TO EXPLAIN.
I THINK PART OF ME DIED THAT DAY AS WELL.
GRANDFATHER ... HE WENT OUTSIDE, TILTED HIS HEAD TO THE SUN AND RUSTED.
WHAT ARE YOU TALKING ABOUT? NICK WOULDN'T DO THAT!
EVERYTHING'S BROKEN, UNCLE. IT'S BEEN THIS WAY FOR AWHILE.
MY DEAR BOY, THE TIN MAN JUST WOULDN'T RUST. WHAT HAPPENED?
DON'T WORRY, UNCLE.
I'LL FIX EVERYTHING. I PROMISE.
I NEED TO GO NOW. YOUR PLACE IS WITH THE DOROTHY.

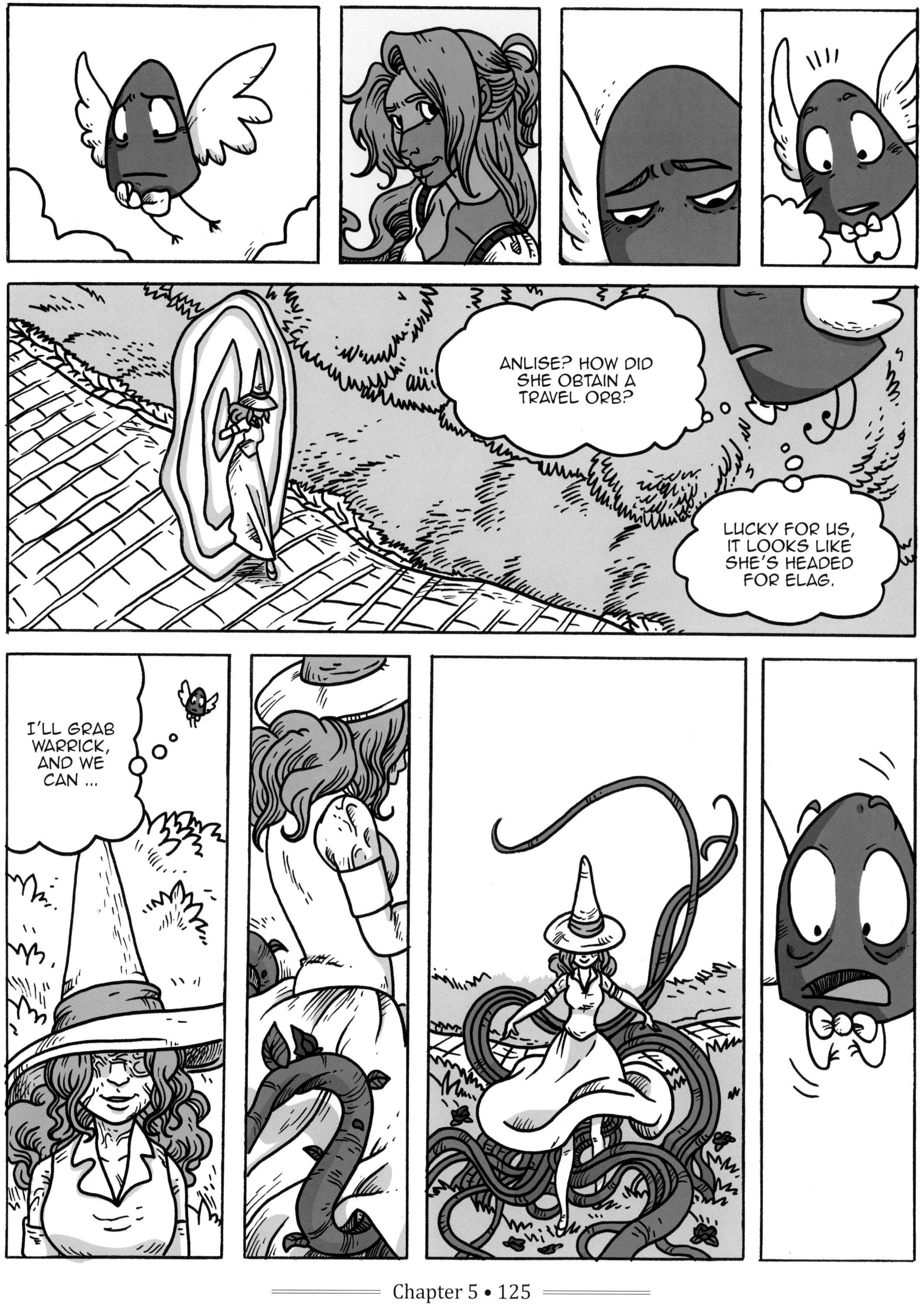
ANLISE? HOW DID SHE OBTAIN A TRAVEL ORB?
LUCKY FOR US, IT LOOKS LIKE SHE'S HEADED FOR ELAG.
I'LL GRAB WARRICK, AND WE CAN ...

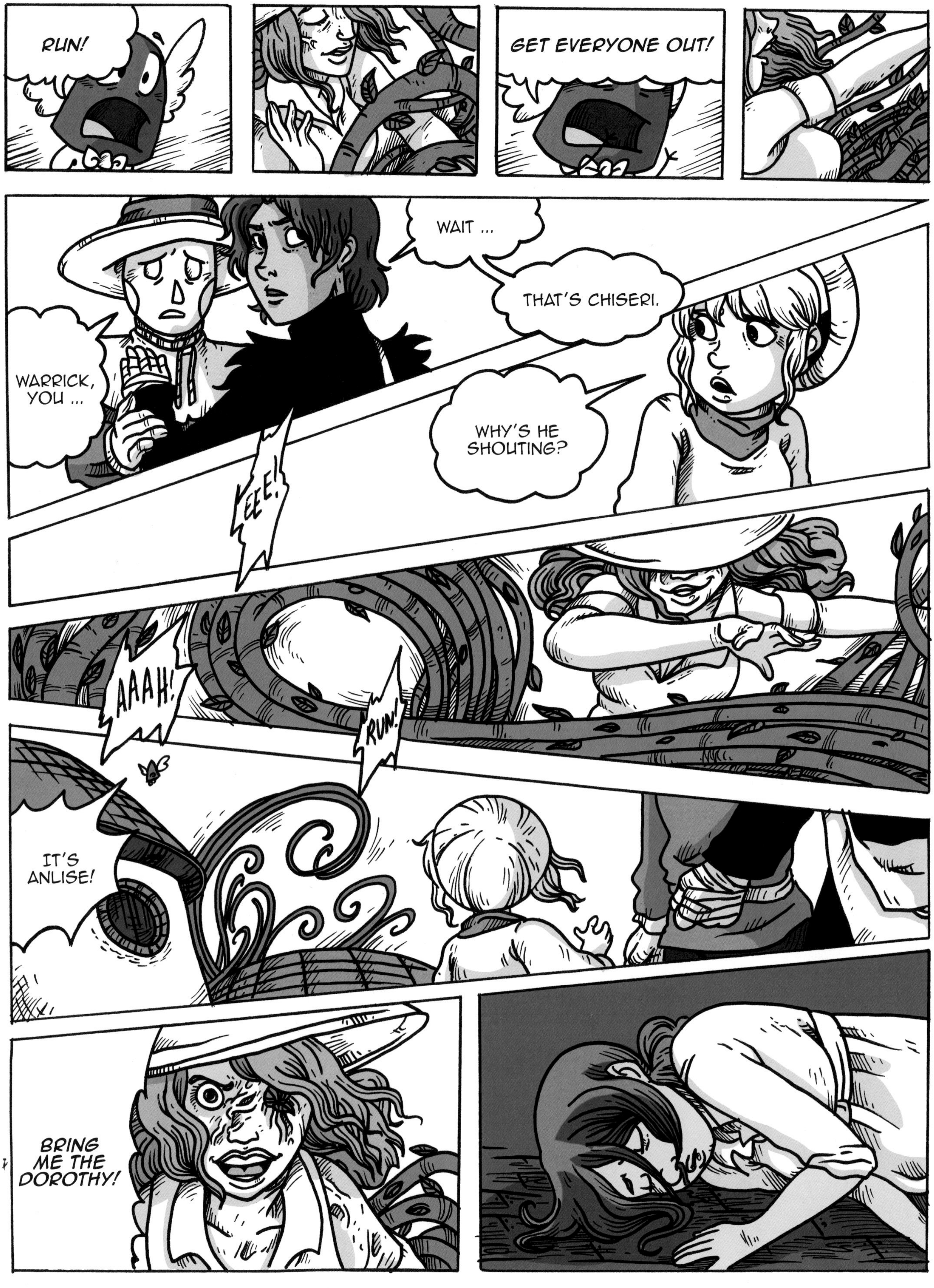

RUN!
GET EVERYONE OUT!
WAIT ...
THAT'S CHISERI.
WARRICK, YOU ...
WHY'S HE SHOUTING?
EEE!
AAAH!
RUN!
IT'S ANLISE!
BRING ME THE DOROTHY!

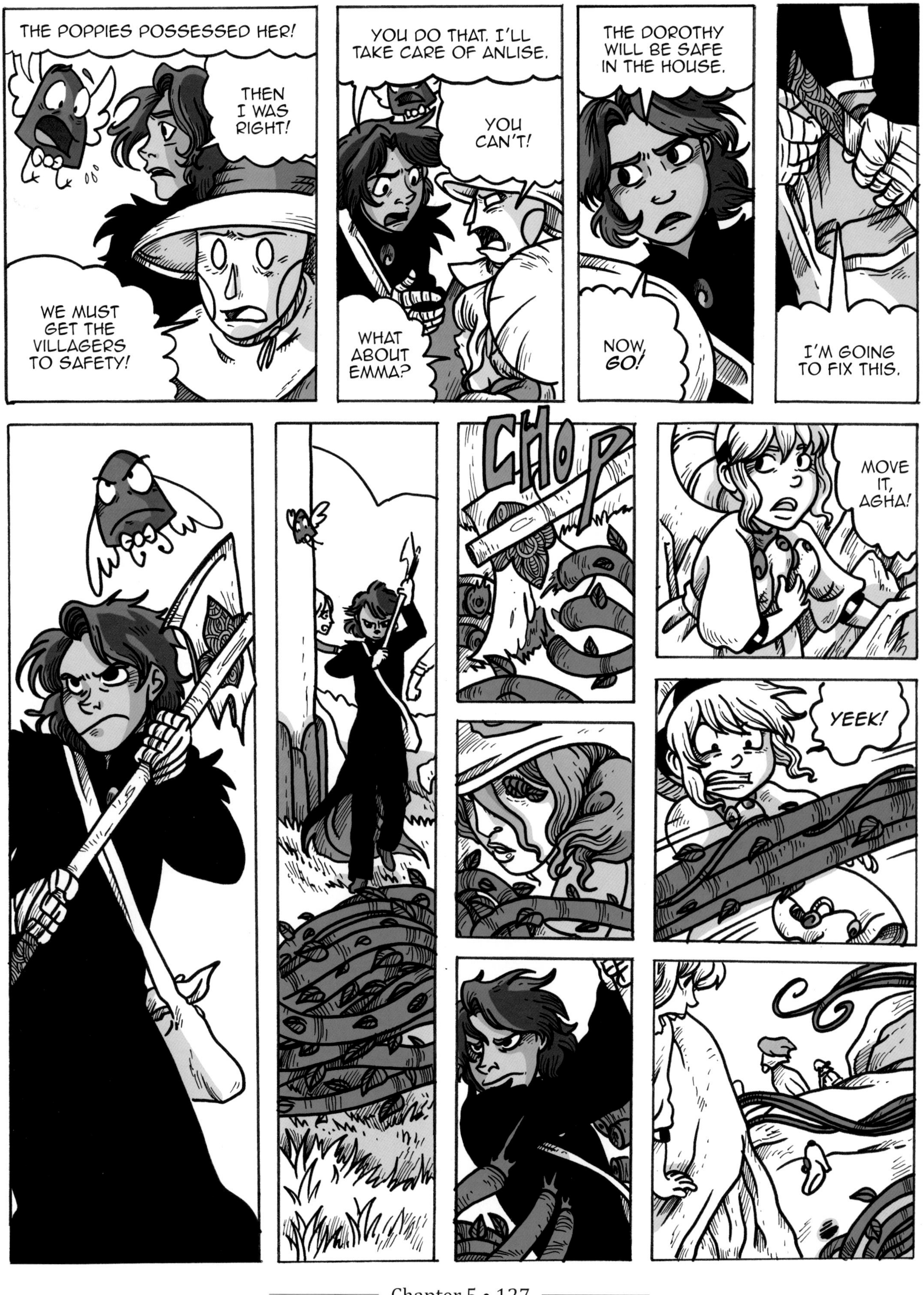
THE POPPIES POSSESSED HER!
THEN I WAS RIGHT!
WE MUST GET THE VILLAGERS TO SAFETY!
YOU DO THAT. I'LL TAKE CARE OF ANLISE.
YOU CAN'T!
WHAT ABOUT EMMA?
THE DOROTHY WILL BE SAFE IN THE HOUSE.
NOW, GO!
I'M GOING TO FIX THIS.
CHOP
MOVE IT, AGHA!
YEEK!

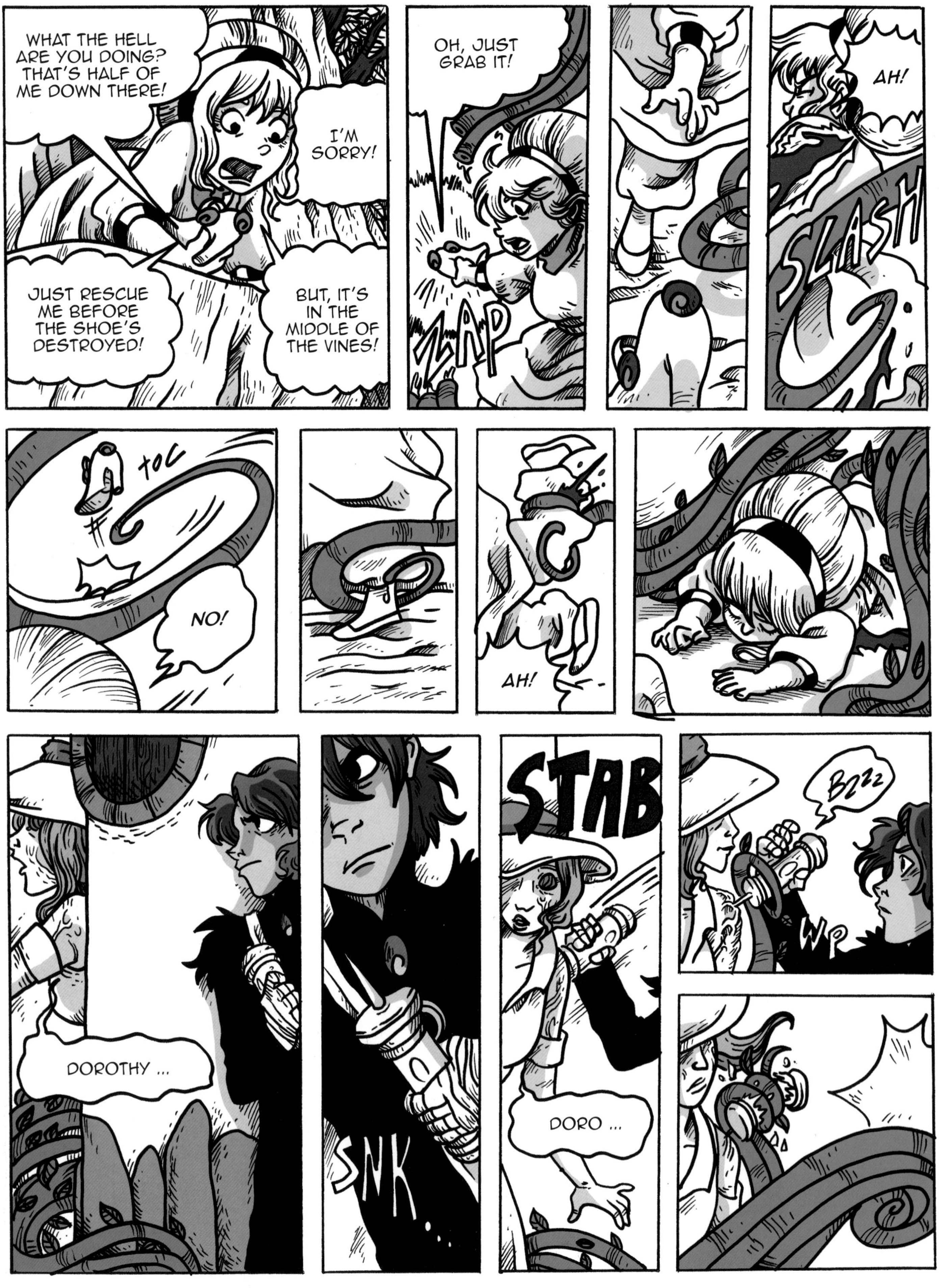
WHAT THE HELL ARE YOU DOING? THAT'S HALF OF ME DOWN THERE!
I'M SORRY!
JUST RESCUE ME BEFORE THE SHOE'S DESTROYED!
BUT, IT'S IN THE MIDDLE OF THE VINES!
OH, JUST GRAB IT!
ZAP
AH!
SLASH
TOC
NO!
AH!
DOROTHY ...
SNK
STAB
DORO ...
BZZZ
WP

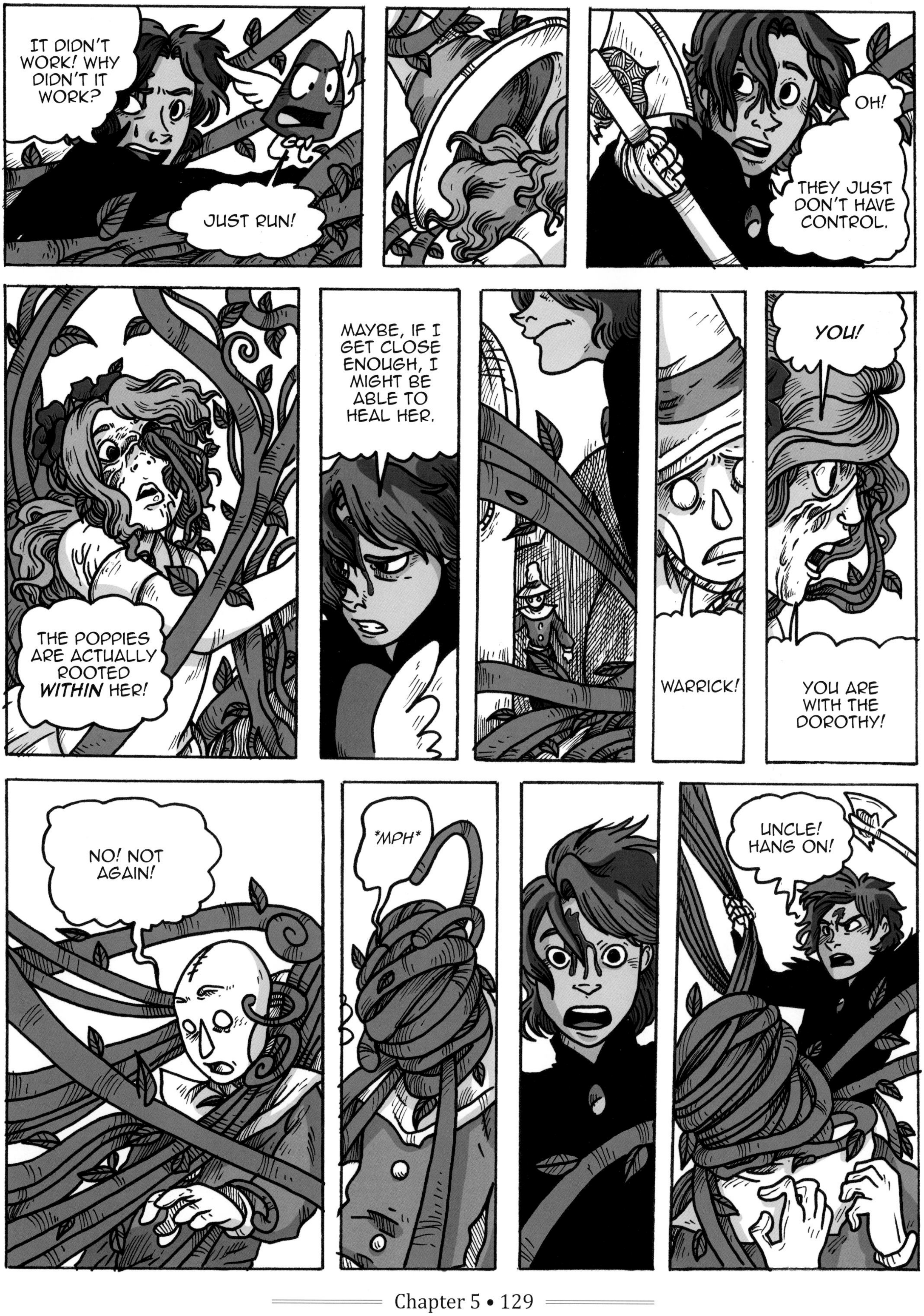
IT DIDN'T WORK! WHY DIDN'T IT WORK?
JUST RUN!
OH!
THEY JUST DON'T HAVE CONTROL.
THE POPPIES ARE ACTUALLY ROOTED *WITHIN* HER!
MAYBE, IF I GET CLOSE ENOUGH, I MIGHT BE ABLE TO HEAL HER.
WARRICK!
YOU!
YOU ARE WITH THE DOROTHY!
NO! NOT AGAIN!
MPH
UNCLE! HANG ON!

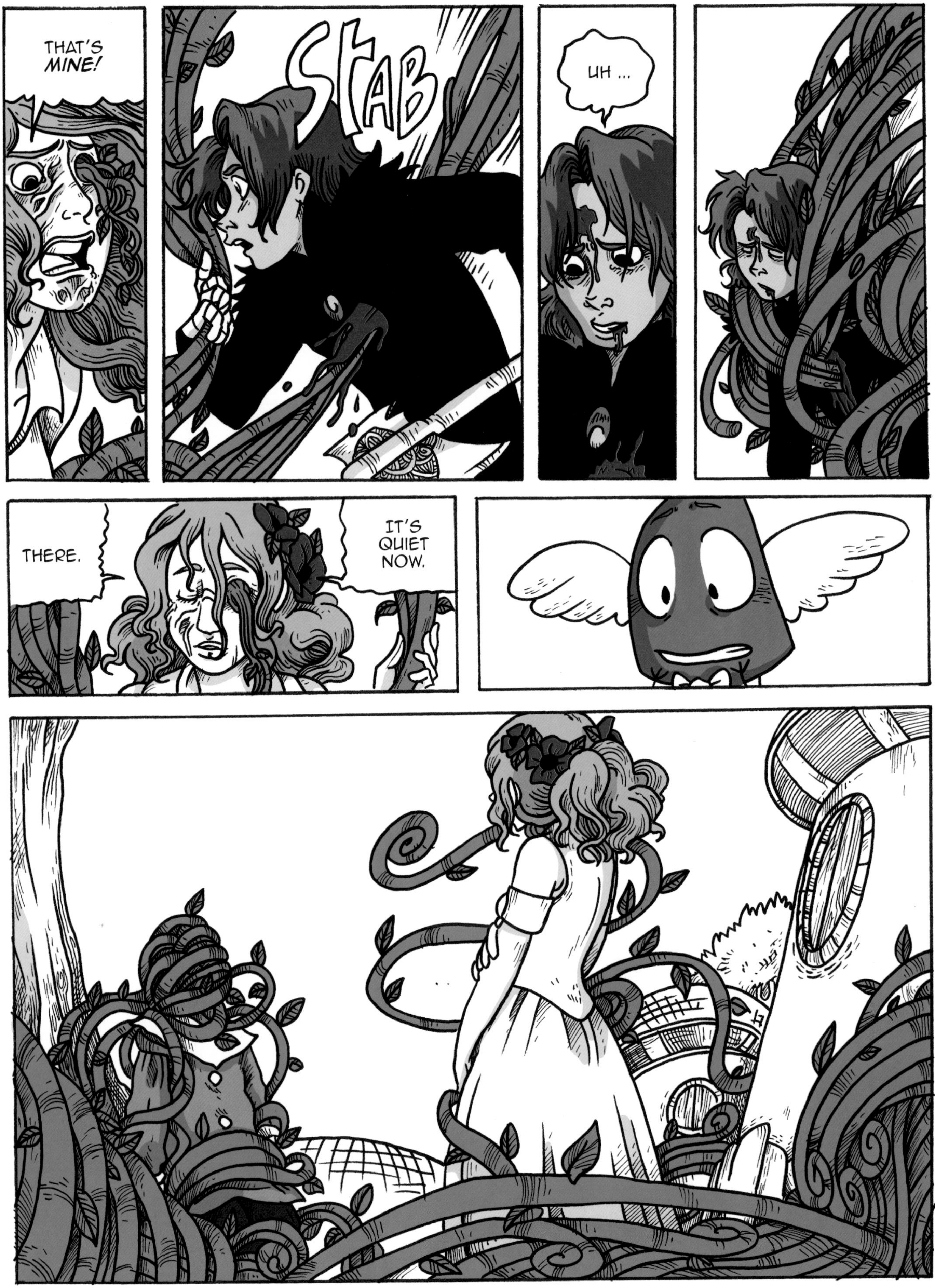
THAT'S *MINE!*
STAB
UH ...
THERE.
IT'S QUIET NOW.

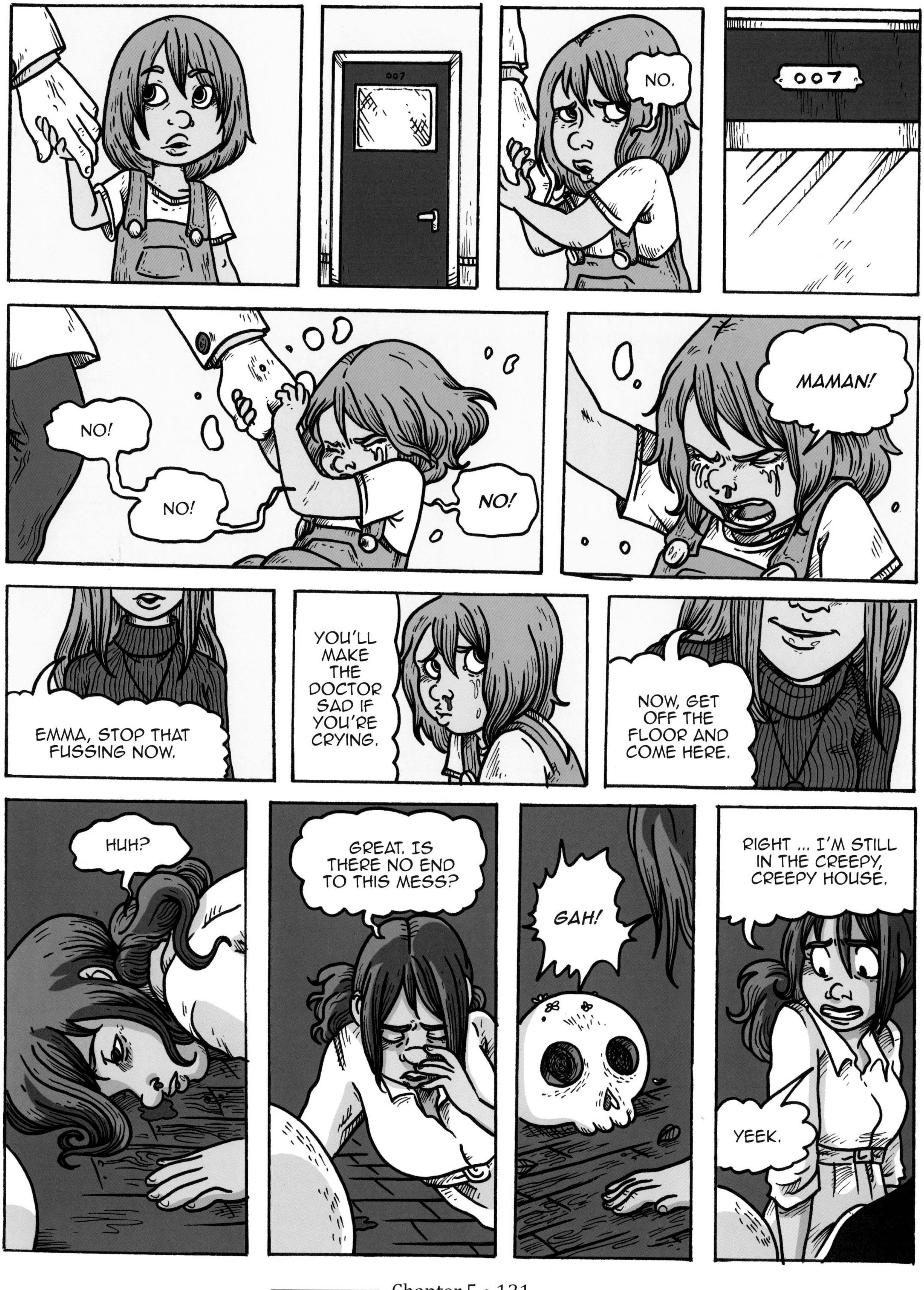
NO.
007
NO!
NO!
NO!
MAMAN!
EMMA, STOP THAT FUSSING NOW.
YOU'LL MAKE THE DOCTOR SAD IF YOU'RE CRYING.
NOW, GET OFF THE FLOOR AND COME HERE.
HUH?
GREAT. IS THERE NO END TO THIS MESS?
GAH!
RIGHT ... I'M STILL IN THE CREEPY, CREEPY HOUSE.
YEEK.

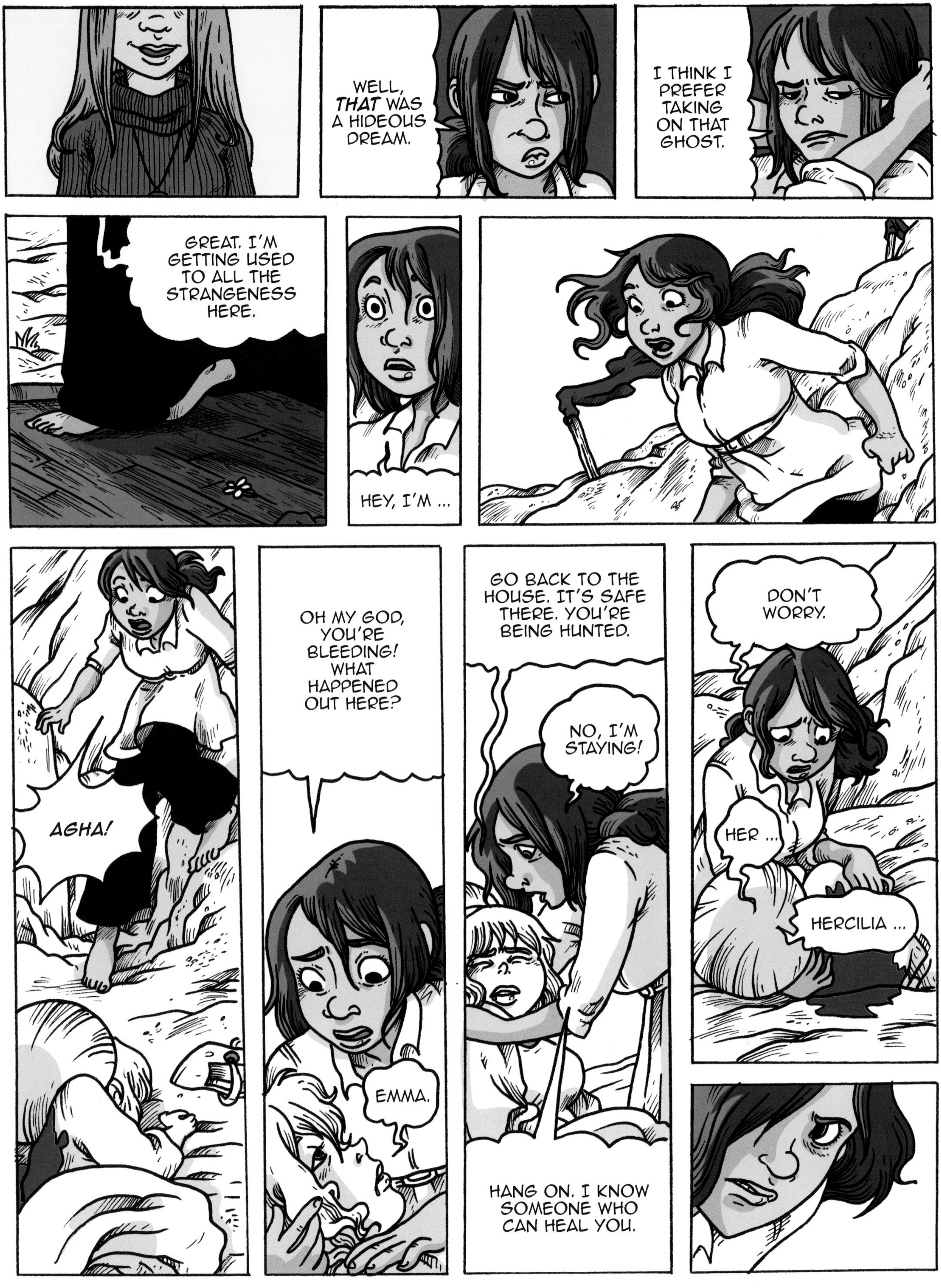
WELL, THAT WAS A HIDEOUS DREAM.
I THINK I PREFER TAKING ON THAT GHOST.
GREAT. I'M GETTING USED TO ALL THE STRANGENESS HERE.
HEY, I'M ...
AGHA!
OH MY GOD, YOU'RE BLEEDING! WHAT HAPPENED OUT HERE?
EMMA.
GO BACK TO THE HOUSE. IT'S SAFE THERE. YOU'RE BEING HUNTED.
NO, I'M STAYING!
HANG ON. I KNOW SOMEONE WHO CAN HEAL YOU.
DON'T WORRY.
HER ...
HERCILIA ...

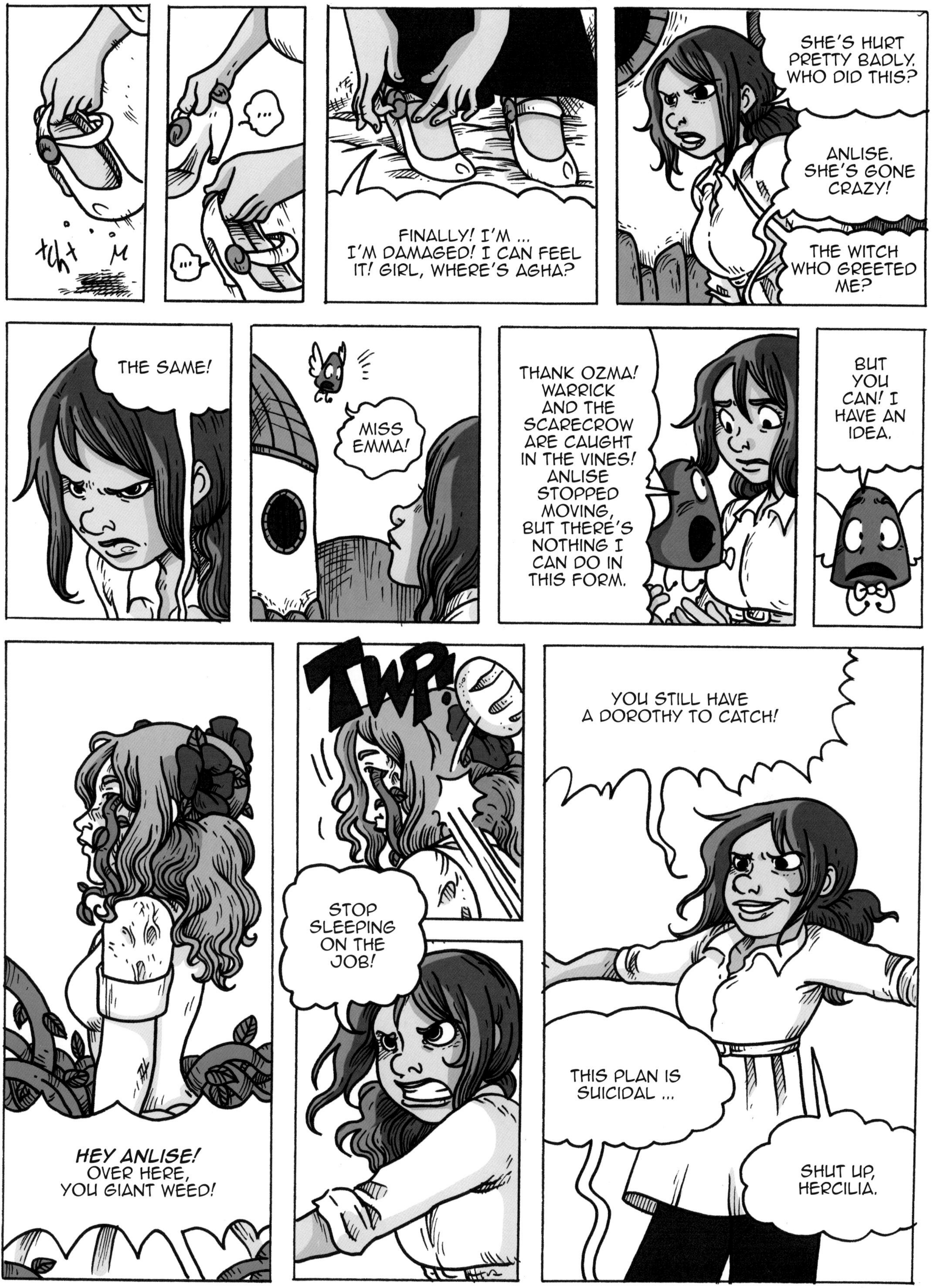
...
...
FINALLY! I'M ... I'M DAMAGED! I CAN FEEL IT! GIRL, WHERE'S AGHA?
SHE'S HURT PRETTY BADLY. WHO DID THIS?
ANLISE. SHE'S GONE CRAZY!
THE WITCH WHO GREETED ME?
THE SAME!
MISS EMMA!
THANK OZMA! WARRICK AND THE SCARECROW ARE CAUGHT IN THE VINES! ANLISE STOPPED MOVING, BUT THERE'S NOTHING I CAN DO IN THIS FORM.
BUT YOU CAN! I HAVE AN IDEA.
HEY ANLISE! OVER HERE, YOU GIANT WEED!
TWP
STOP SLEEPING ON THE JOB!
YOU STILL HAVE A DOROTHY TO CATCH!
THIS PLAN IS SUICIDAL ...
SHUT UP, HERCILIA.

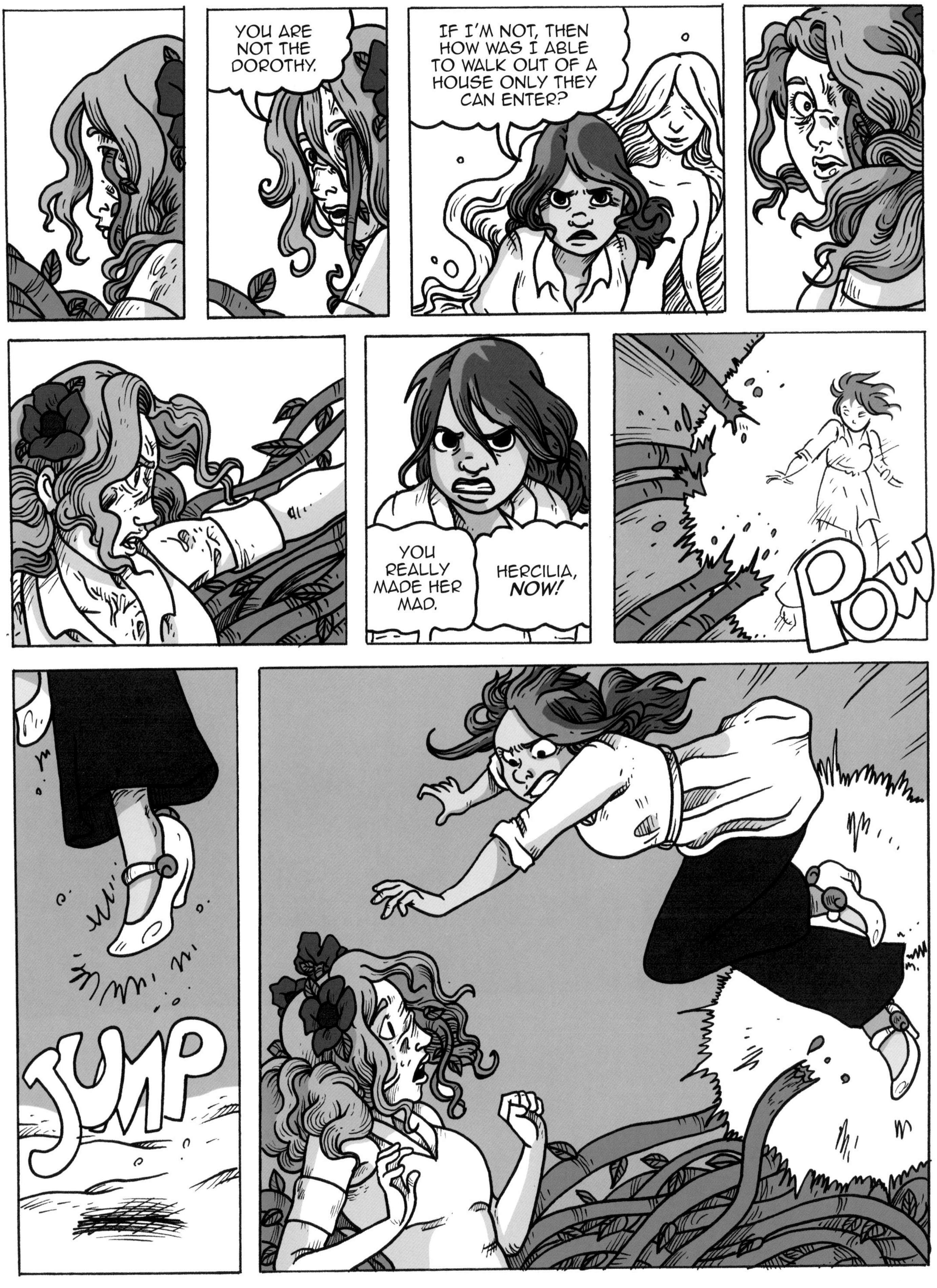
YOU ARE NOT THE DOROTHY.
IF I'M NOT, THEN HOW WAS I ABLE TO WALK OUT OF A HOUSE ONLY THEY CAN ENTER?
YOU REALLY MADE HER MAD.
HERCILIA, **NOW!**
POW
JUMP

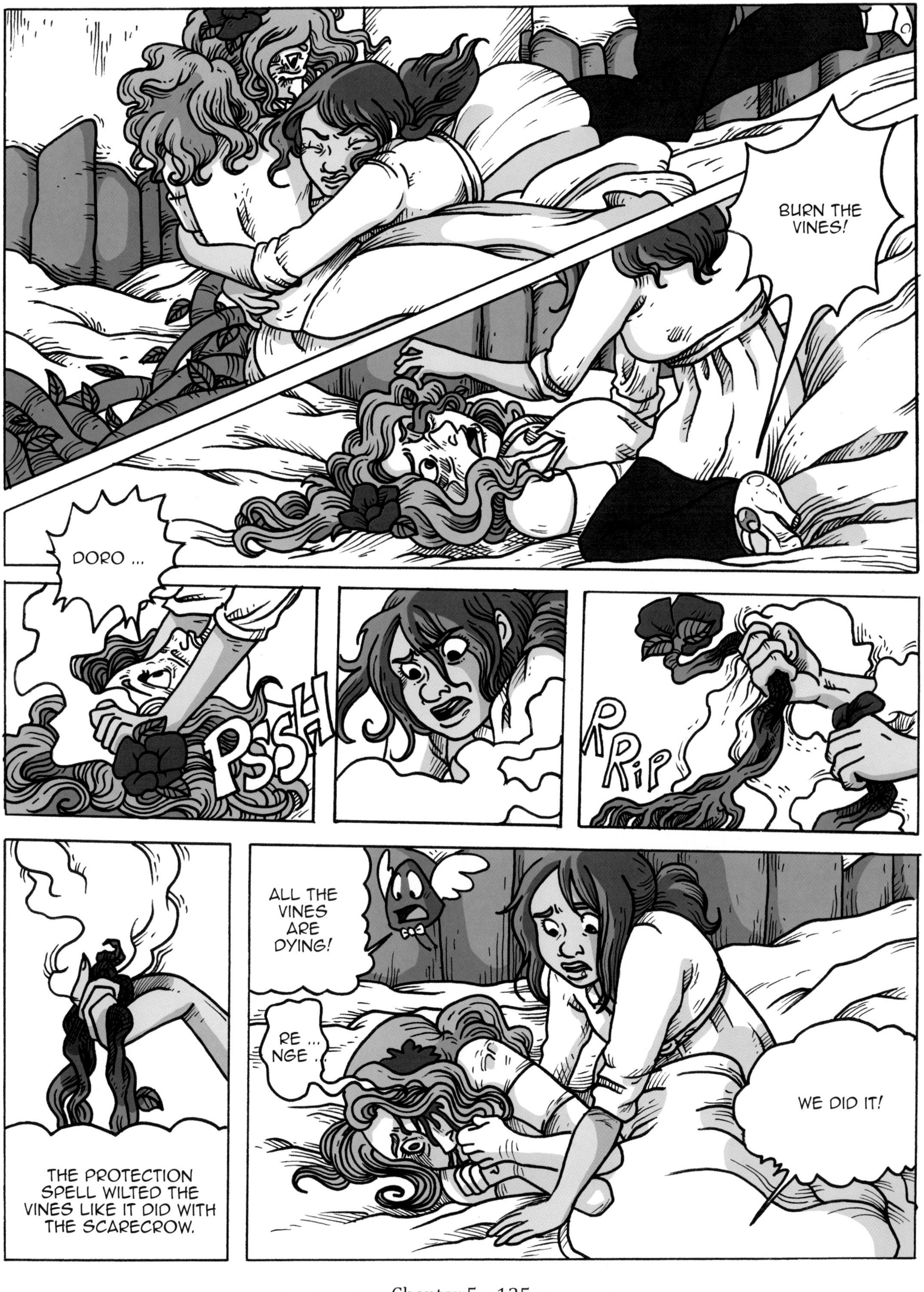
BURN THE VINES!
DORO ...
PSSH
RRRIP
THE PROTECTION SPELL WILTED THE VINES LIKE IT DID WITH THE SCARECROW.
ALL THE VINES ARE DYING!
RE ... NGE ...
WE DID IT!

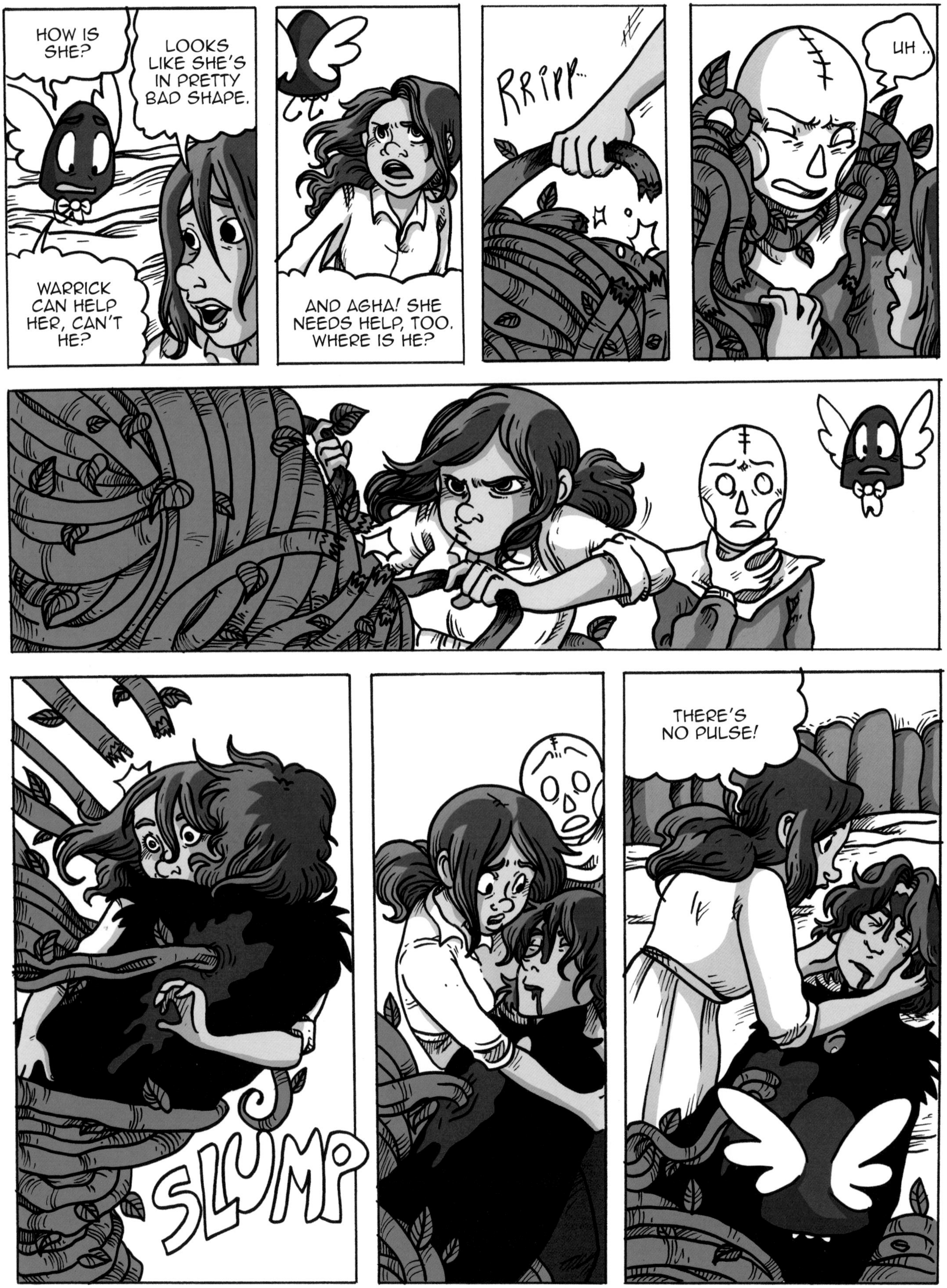
HOW IS SHE?
LOOKS LIKE SHE'S IN PRETTY BAD SHAPE.
WARRICK CAN HELP HER, CAN'T HE?
AND AGHA! SHE NEEDS HELP, TOO. WHERE IS HE?
RRIPP...
UH ..
SLUMP
THERE'S NO PULSE!

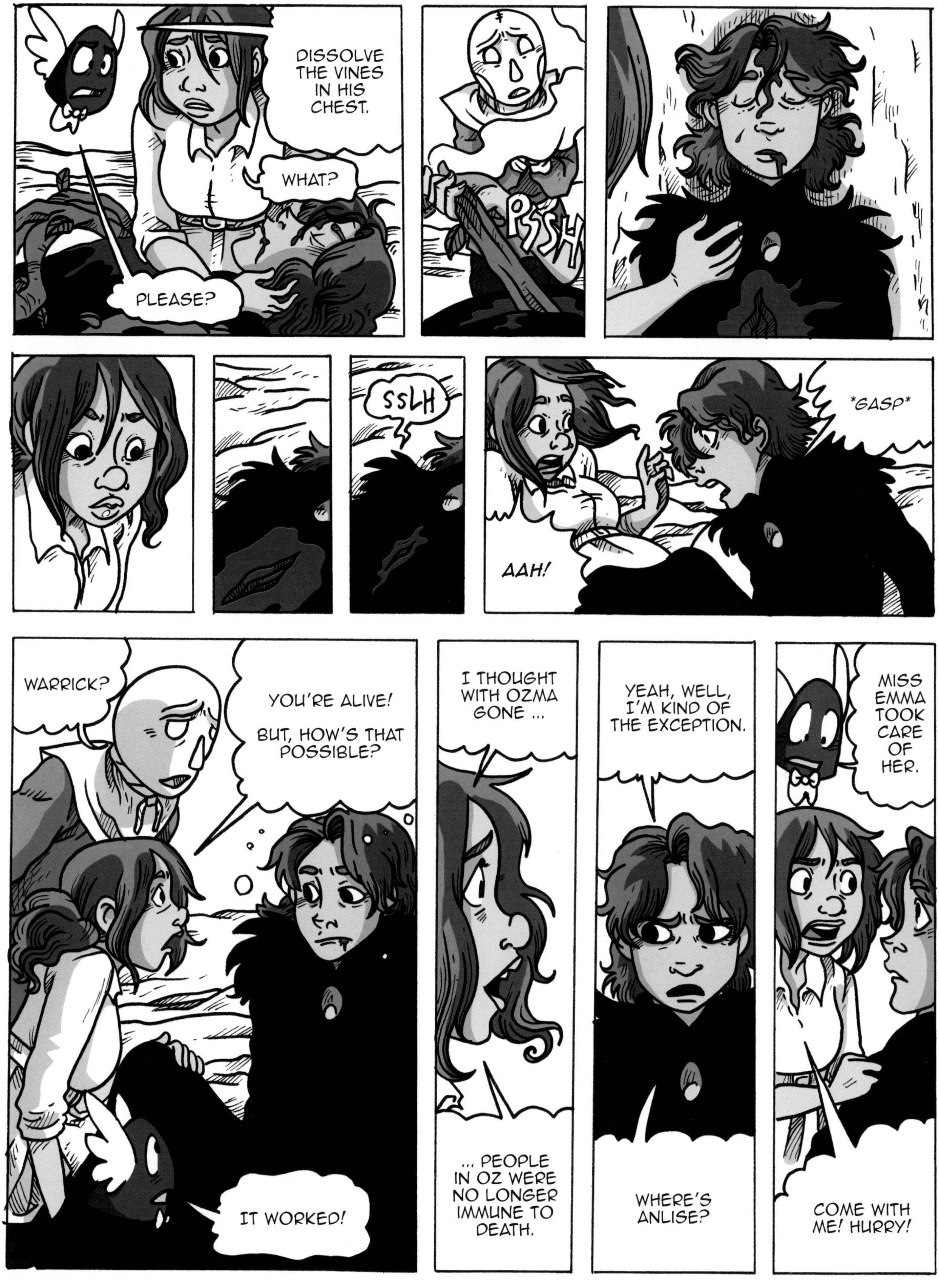
DISSOLVE THE VINES IN HIS CHEST.
WHAT?
PLEASE?
PSSH
SSLH
GASP
AAH!
WARRICK?
YOU'RE ALIVE!
BUT, HOW'S THAT POSSIBLE?
IT WORKED!
I THOUGHT WITH OZMA GONE ...
... PEOPLE IN OZ WERE NO LONGER IMMUNE TO DEATH.
YEAH, WELL, I'M KIND OF THE EXCEPTION.
WHERE'S ANLISE?
MISS EMMA TOOK CARE OF HER.
COME WITH ME! HURRY!

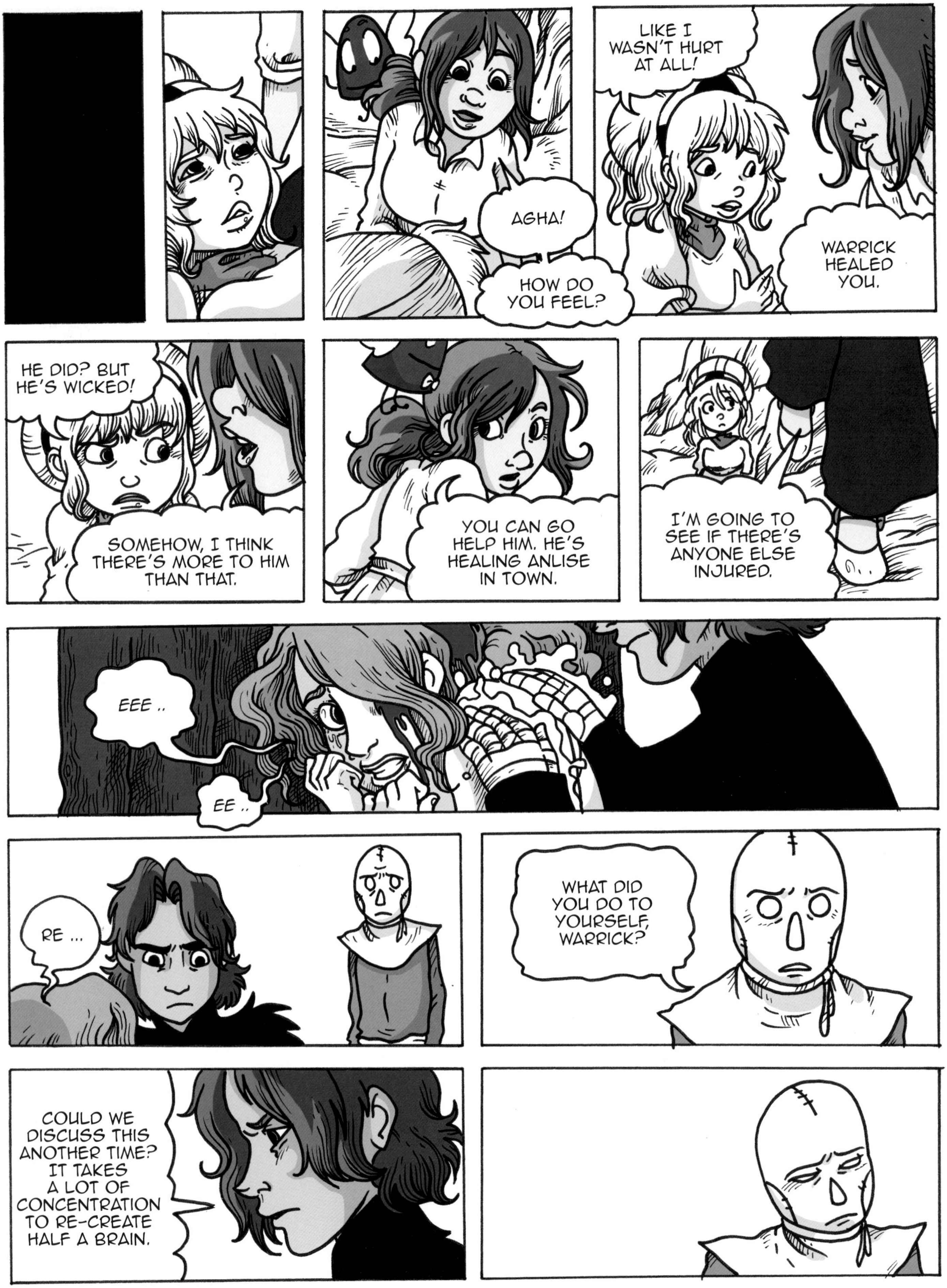
AGHA!
HOW DO YOU FEEL?
LIKE I WASN'T HURT AT ALL!
WARRICK HEALED YOU.
HE DID? BUT HE'S WICKED!
SOMEHOW, I THINK THERE'S MORE TO HIM THAN THAT.
YOU CAN GO HELP HIM. HE'S HEALING ANLISE IN TOWN.
I'M GOING TO SEE IF THERE'S ANYONE ELSE INJURED.
EEE ..
EE ..
RE ...
WHAT DID YOU DO TO YOURSELF, WARRICK?
COULD WE DISCUSS THIS ANOTHER TIME? IT TAKES A LOT OF CONCENTRATION TO RE-CREATE HALF A BRAIN.

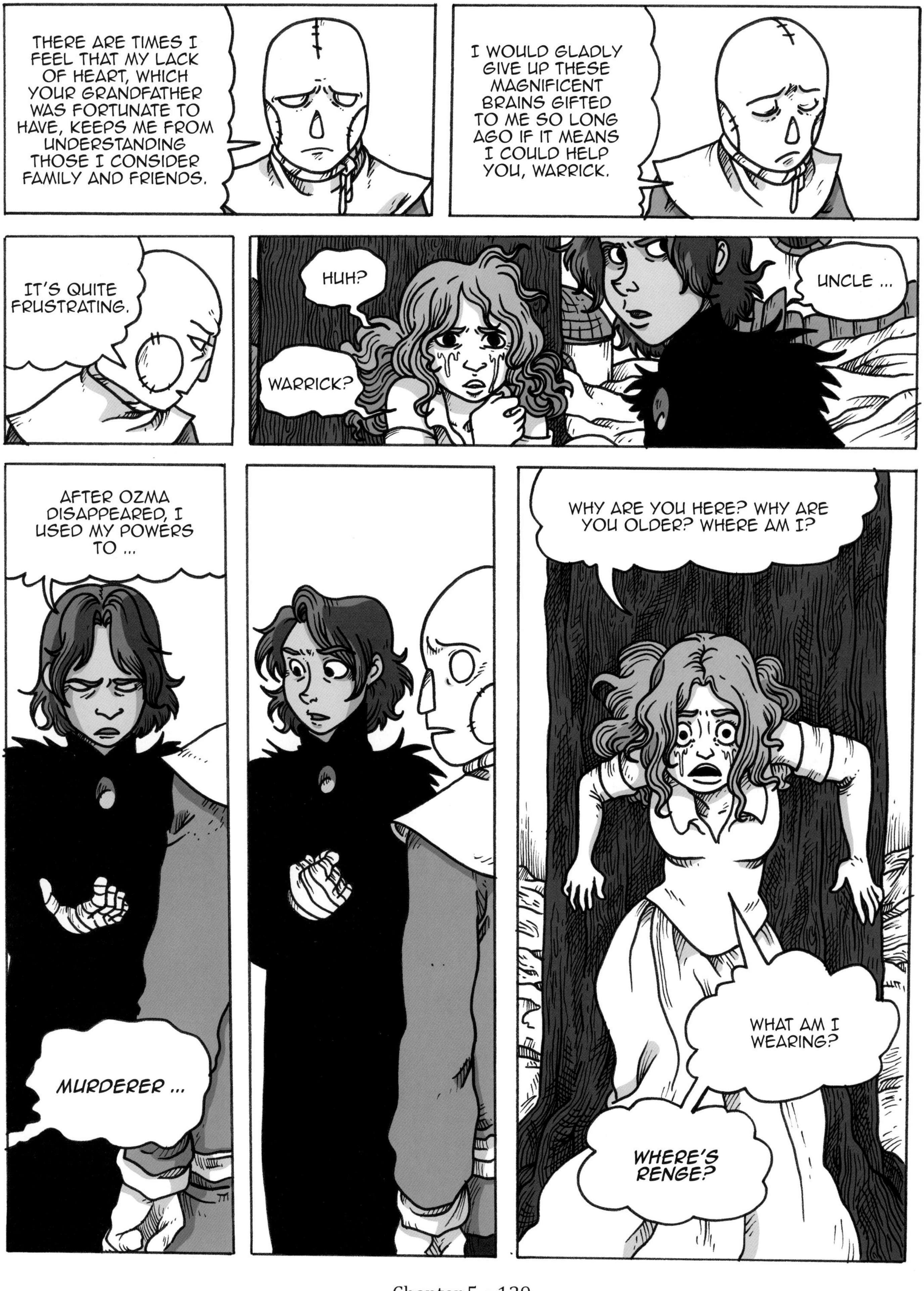
THERE ARE TIMES I FEEL THAT MY LACK OF HEART, WHICH YOUR GRANDFATHER WAS FORTUNATE TO HAVE, KEEPS ME FROM UNDERSTANDING THOSE I CONSIDER FAMILY AND FRIENDS.
I WOULD GLADLY GIVE UP THESE MAGNIFICENT BRAINS GIFTED TO ME SO LONG AGO IF IT MEANS I COULD HELP YOU, WARRICK.
IT'S QUITE FRUSTRATING.
HUH?
WARRICK?
UNCLE ...
AFTER OZMA DISAPPEARED, I USED MY POWERS TO ...
MURDERER ...
WHY ARE YOU HERE? WHY ARE YOU OLDER? WHERE AM I?
WHAT AM I WEARING?
WHERE'S RENGE?

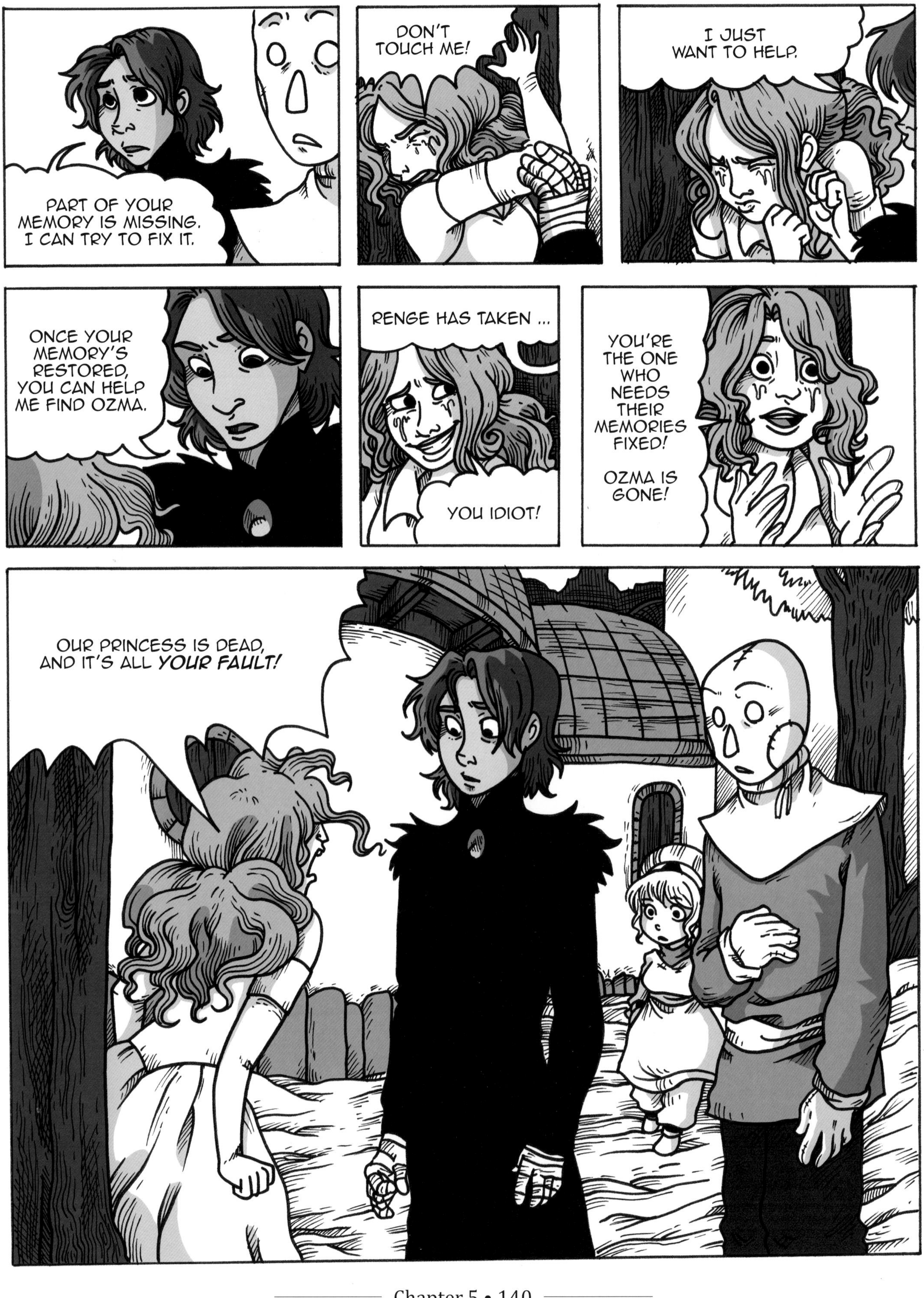
PART OF YOUR MEMORY IS MISSING. I CAN TRY TO FIX IT.
DON'T TOUCH ME!
I JUST WANT TO HELP.
ONCE YOUR MEMORY'S RESTORED, YOU CAN HELP ME FIND OZMA.
RENGE HAS TAKEN ...
YOU IDIOT!
YOU'RE THE ONE WHO NEEDS THEIR MEMORIES FIXED!
OZMA IS GONE!
OUR PRINCESS IS DEAD, AND IT'S ALL *YOUR FAULT!*

Extras

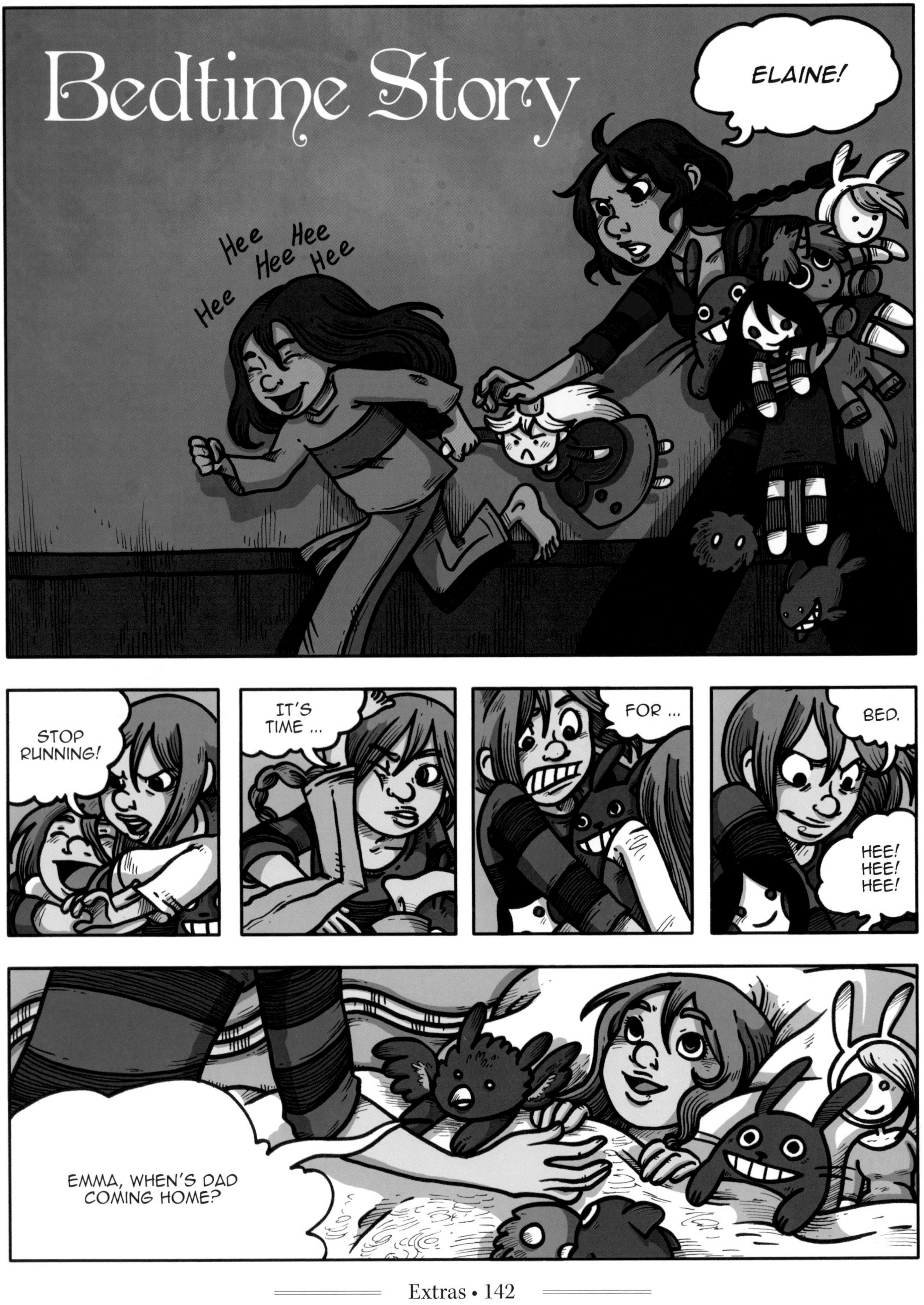
Bedtime Story
ELAINE!
Hee Hee Hee Hee Hee
STOP RUNNING!
IT'S TIME ...
FOR ...
BED.
HEE! HEE! HEE!
EMMA, WHEN'S DAD COMING HOME?

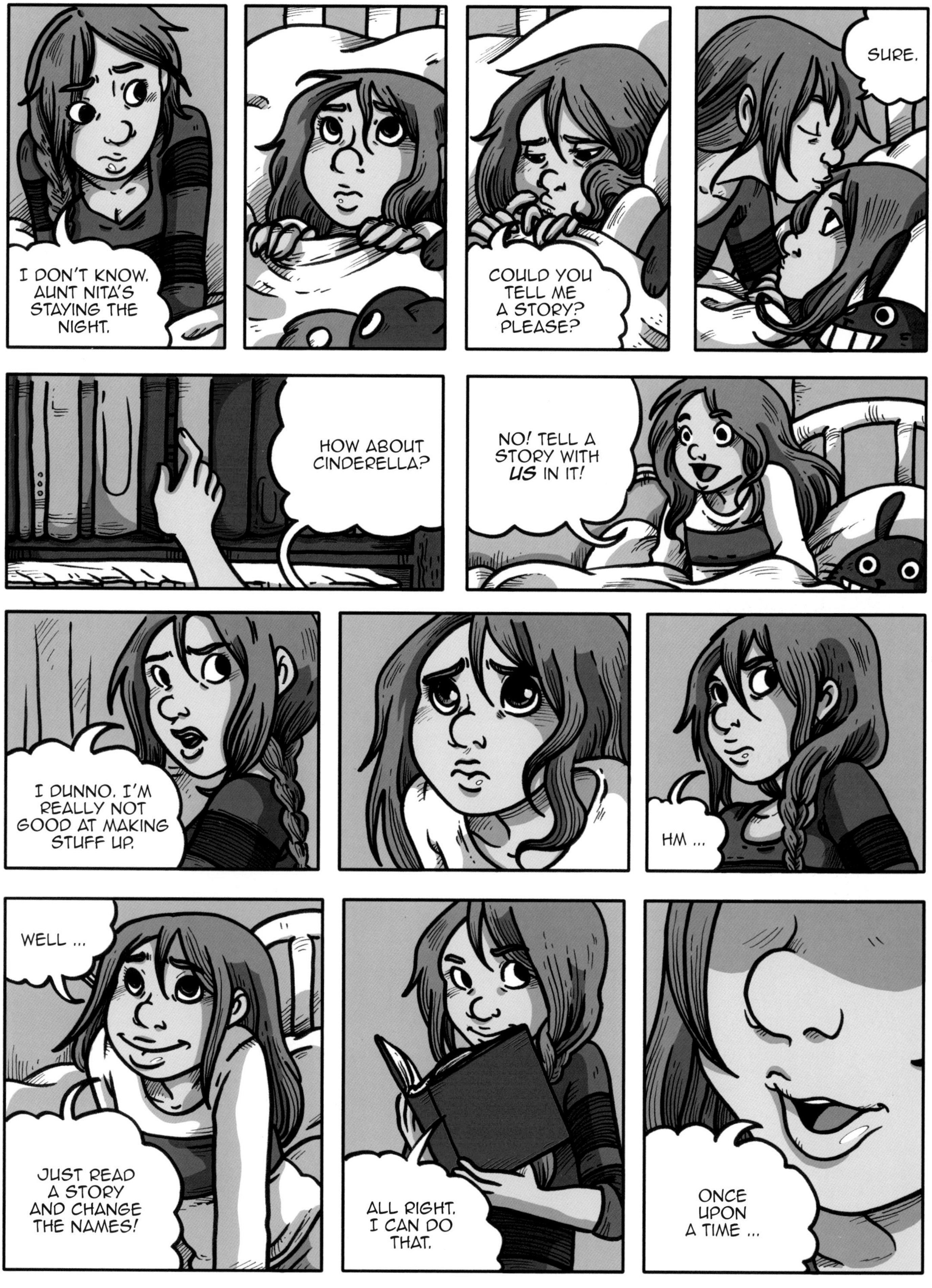
I DON'T KNOW. AUNT NITA'S STAYING THE NIGHT.
COULD YOU TELL ME A STORY? PLEASE?
SURE.
HOW ABOUT CINDERELLA?
NO! TELL A STORY WITH *US* IN IT!
I DUNNO. I'M REALLY NOT GOOD AT MAKING STUFF UP.
HM ...
WELL ...
JUST READ A STORY AND CHANGE THE NAMES!
ALL RIGHT. I CAN DO THAT.
ONCE UPON A TIME ...

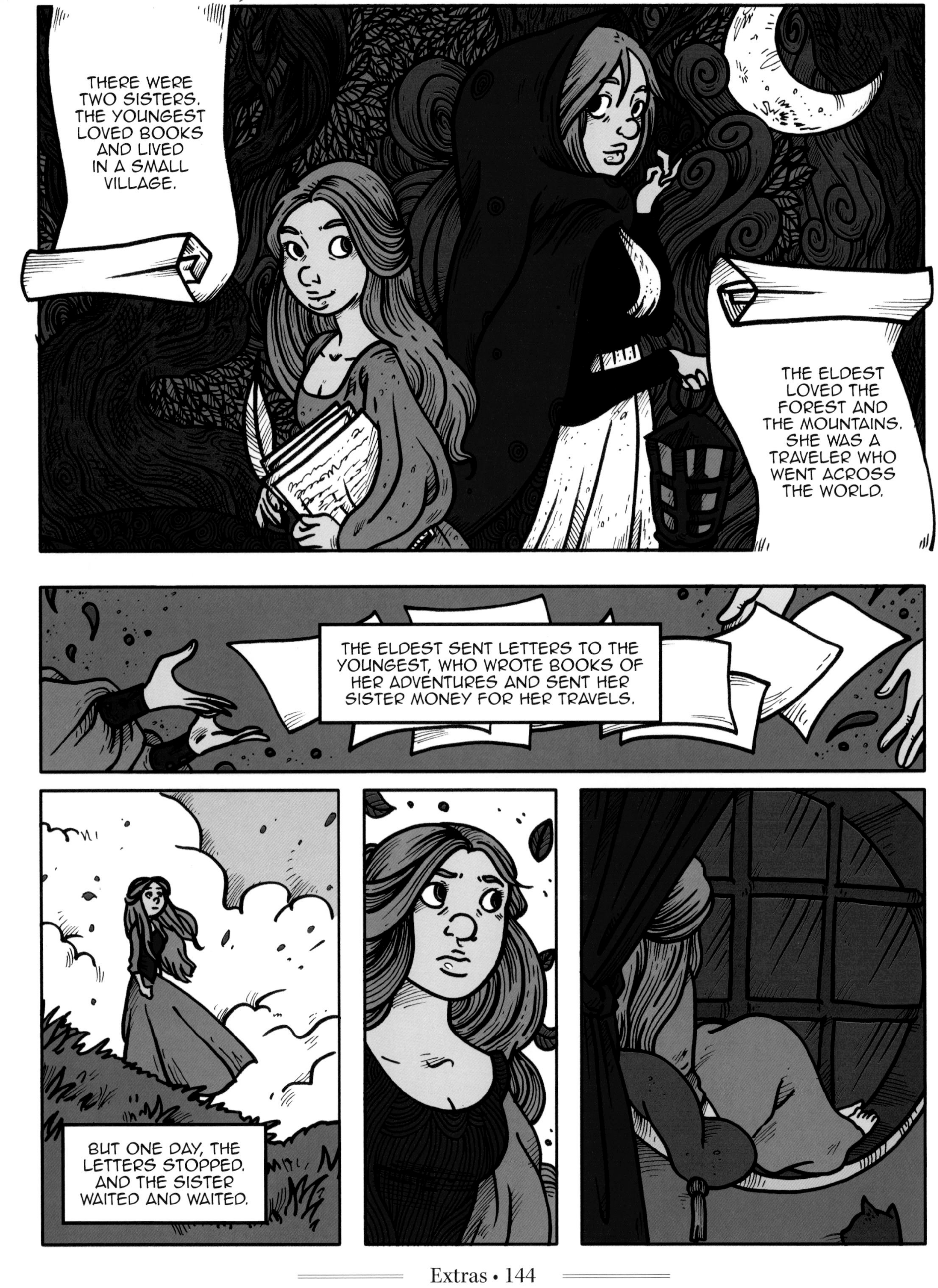
THERE WERE TWO SISTERS. THE YOUNGEST LOVED BOOKS AND LIVED IN A SMALL VILLAGE.
THE ELDEST LOVED THE FOREST AND THE MOUNTAINS. SHE WAS A TRAVELER WHO WENT ACROSS THE WORLD.
THE ELDEST SENT LETTERS TO THE YOUNGEST, WHO WROTE BOOKS OF HER ADVENTURES AND SENT HER SISTER MONEY FOR HER TRAVELS.
BUT ONE DAY, THE LETTERS STOPPED. AND THE SISTER WAITED AND WAITED.

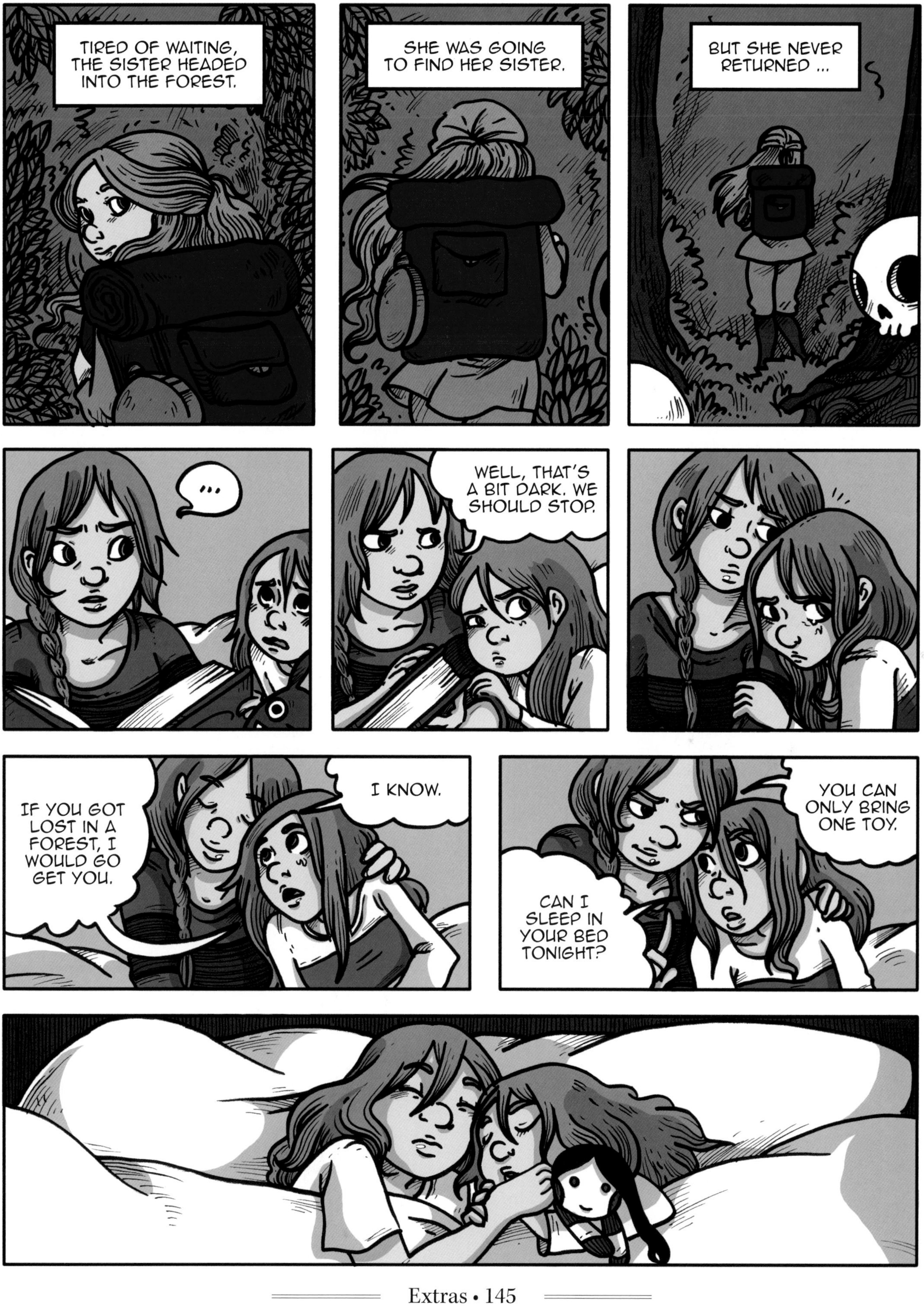
TIRED OF WAITING, THE SISTER HEADED INTO THE FOREST.
SHE WAS GOING TO FIND HER SISTER.
BUT SHE NEVER RETURNED ...
...
WELL, THAT'S A BIT DARK. WE SHOULD STOP.
IF YOU GOT LOST IN A FOREST, I WOULD GO GET YOU.
I KNOW.
CAN I SLEEP IN YOUR BED TONIGHT?
YOU CAN ONLY BRING ONE TOY.

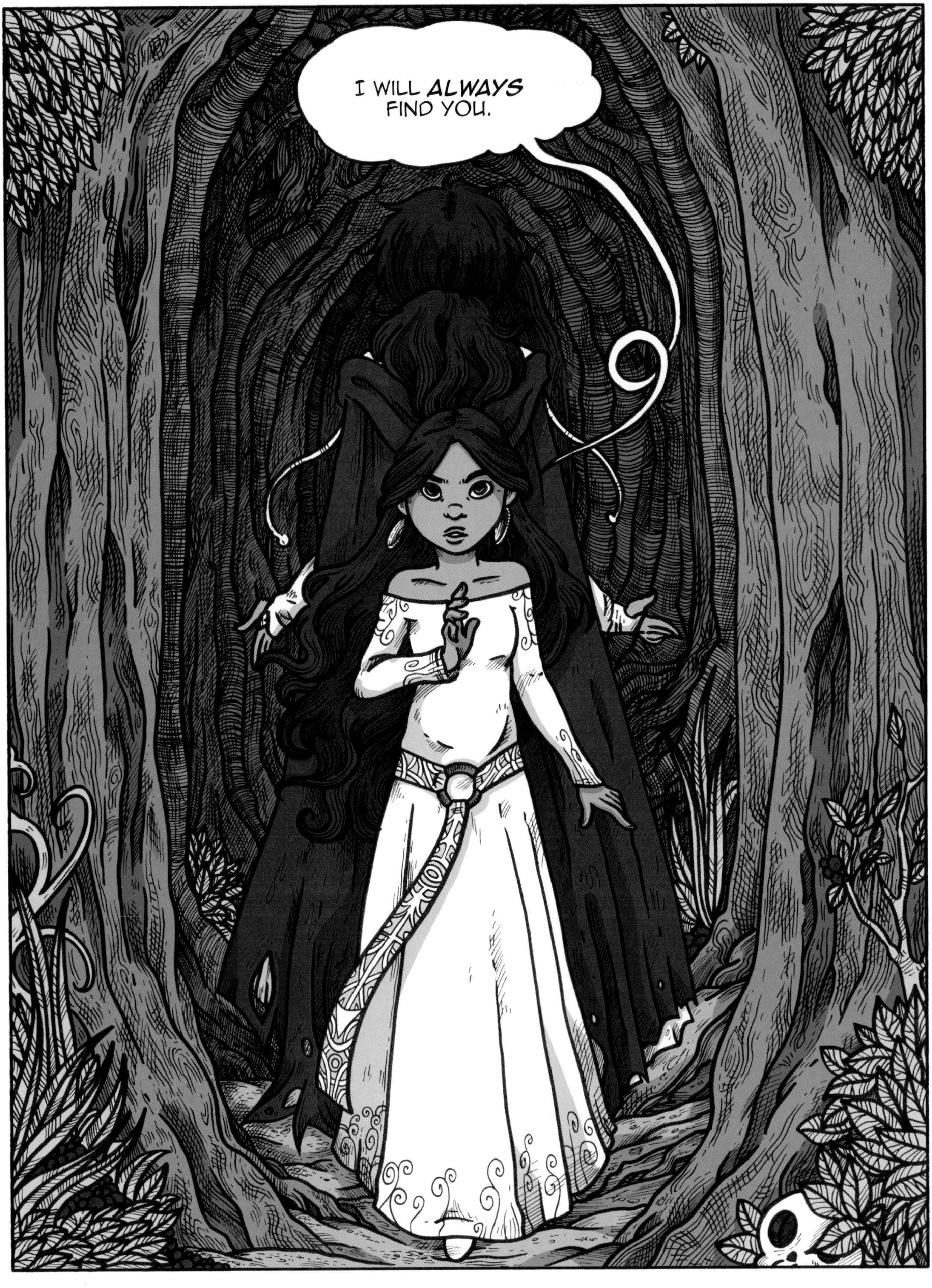
I WILL ALWAYS FIND YOU.